THE CAPITAL
BUDGETING DECISION

THE CAPITAL

HAROLD BIERMAN, JR., PH.

Associate Professor of Accounti
Graduate School of Busin
and Public Administrat
Cornell Univers

BUDGETING DECISION

AND

SEYMOUR SMIDT, PH.D.

Associate Professor of Managerial Economics
Graduate School of Business
and Public Administration
Cornell University

The Macmillan Company
New York

First printing

Library of Congress Catalog Card Number: 60–6844

The Macmillan Company, New York
Brett-Macmillan Ltd., Galt, Ontario

Printed in the United States of America

Preface

Businessmen and economists have been concerned with the problem of how financial resources available to a firm should be allocated to the many possible investment projects. Should a new plant be built? Equipment replaced? Bonds refunded? A new product introduced? These are all to some extent capital budgeting decisions to which there are theoretically sound solutions. The purpose of this book is to express the solution of the economist in the language of the business manager.

Decades ago, economists such as Bohm-Bawerk, Wicksell, and Irving Fisher laid the theoretical foundation for a sound economic approach to capital budgeting. In recent years the technical literature has contained articles (such as those by Dean, Solomon, Lorie, Savage, and Hirshleifer) that have significantly increased our understanding of what is required for sound capital budgeting decisions. However, these works have not been directed towards business managers and, until recently, the work of these men has had no perceptible influence on the way businessmen actually made capital investment decisions. Businessmen have tended to make capital budgeting decisions using their intuition, rules of thumb, or investment criteria with faulty theoretical foundations, thus apt to give incorrect answers in a large percentage of the decisions.

The purpose of this book is to present for an audience, which may be completely unfamiliar with the technical literature on

economic theory or capital budgeting, a clear conception of
how to evaluate investment proposals.

The authors are convinced that the "present-value" method
is superior to other methods of evaluating the economic worth
of investments that have been discussed in the business literature. They recognize that considerations other than that of
economic worth are also important in making investment decisions. The early pages of the book show "cash payback"
and "return on investment" may give incorrect results. The
"yield" or "investor's method" is shown to be inferior to the
present-value method, especially where there are several alternative investments available. The explanation of the reasons
for the inferiority of yield to present value is particularly
timely, since popular business magazines have carried many
articles praising the yield method without mentioning its important drawbacks. In Chapter 4, a positive explanation of the
meaning of present value is presented.

The first four chapters present an over-all picture of the
method of analysis advocated in this book that would be a
suitable introduction for management at any level who need
to be informed about the ideas involved in evaluating capital
investments, but who are not directly involved in preparing investment evaluations. The remainder of the book is concerned
with elaborating on the basic description of the first four chapters and in giving material that will assist a person in actually
preparing the analysis of investments.

The authors would like to thank those who aided in the
preparation of this book: our wives, who patiently suffered the
long working hours and short tempers that accompanied the
writing; the Graduate School of Business and Public Administration of Cornell University which provided stenographic
assistance; the typists headed by Mrs. Sally Comfort who re-

peatedly converted the debris of countless conversations between the authors into readable form; and Messrs. Colin Park and James B. Weaver who reviewed early drafts and offered numerous helpful suggestions.

Harold Bierman, Jr.
Seymour Smidt

Ithaca

Contents

Sirs:

The Indian who sold Manhattan for $24.00 was a sharp salesman. If he had put his $24 away at 6% compounded semiannually, it would now be $9.5 billion and could buy most of the now-improved land back.

S. BRANCH WALKER

Stamford, Conn.

(Life, *Aug. 31, 1959*)

1

The Problem of Capital Budgeting

The controller points to the ancient, gray, six-story structure and says with pride, "This is one reason we can keep our costs down. Our plant is fully depreciated, so we don't have the large depreciation charges our competitors have."

Another company in the same industry sells a relatively new plant because it is not large enough for a three-shift operation. Rather than operate what is considered to be an inefficient production line (the production line had been completely overhauled within the last twelve months), a new plant is being constructed in another state.

❖   ❖   ❖

The investment philosophies of the two companies making the above decisions were vastly different. One was reluctant to invest money in plant and equipment. The other wanted to operate only the latest in plant and equipment. Which of the two companies was right? Maybe each company was following a policy that was correct for it, or perhaps they were both making faulty decisions. We cannot decide here because the necessary facts are not available to us. But the facts should be available to the responsible executives in both these com-

1

panies, and these facts should be arranged in a useful manner and then interpreted correctly.

Investment decisions are strategic. Future success depends on the investment decisions made today. This point does not need to be stressed. That businessmen are generally aware of it is indicated by the requirement that important investment decisions must be approved by the chief operating executive or the board of directors. In spite of this fact, the procedures used to help management make investment decisions are frequently almost unbelievably primitive. Few manufacturing concerns would sign a long-term contract for supplies of an important raw material without carefully investigating the various sources of supply and considering the relative advantages of each in term of price, service, and quality. Yet, frequently, able management groups approve investments without a careful consideration of available alternatives. Even when there is an investigation of alternatives, the information obtained is generally not used in a manner likely to lead to effective final decisions. Why is it that managements do not do a better job of making the crucial investment decisions? Part of the answer is that managements frequently do not know how to organize the relevant information in a way that will effectively help them make better decisions.

Business organizations are continually faced with the problem of deciding whether the commitments of resources—time or money—are worth while in terms of the benefits to be expected. If the expected benefits are likely to accrue reasonably promptly after the expenditure is made, and if both the expenditure and the benefits can be measured in dollars, the solution to such a problem is conceptually simple. If the expected benefits are likely to accrue over several years, then the solution is more complex.

We shall use the term *investment* to refer to commitments of resources, made in the hope of realizing benefits that are expected to occur over a reasonably long future period of time. Capital budgeting is a many-sided activity that includes searching for new and more profitable investment proposals, investigating engineering and marketing considerations to predict the consequences of accepting the investment, and making economic analyses to determine the profit-potential of each investment proposal. The primary purpose of this book is to help business management analyze the profit-potential of investments in plant and equipment, marketing programs, research projects, and the like.

Investments as Cash Flows

In order to focus our attention on the problems of economic analysis, we begin by assuming that we have investment proposals worthy of preliminary consideration and that for each investment proposal the necessary engineering and marketing research has been completed. We assume that these studies will enable us to measure the dollar value of the resources expended and the benefits received from the investment during each future interval of time. In making this assumption, we exclude many investments. Even business organizations, which carry further than most other organizations the attempt to measure all costs and benefits in dollar terms, find that the costs or benefits of many investments cannot be completely described in terms of dollars. Consider an advertising program designed to build up the prestige associated with the name of a corporation. This is an investment, since the expenditures are made in the hope of realizing benefits that will continue long after the advertising expenditures have been made. But it is difficult to estimate in dollar terms the exact value of the benefits that will accrue from the advertising program.

In nonprofit organizations, whether private or public, investments whose costs and benefits cannot be measured reasonably well in dollar terms are made even more frequently than in business. Nevertheless investment proposals for which both the costs and benefits can be measured in dollar terms do arise in all these organizations, and the quantity of resources involved in such investments is considerable. In designing a building, for example, the architect or engineer is frequently faced with alternative means of accomplishing the same objective. The design of the heating or lighting systems are but two examples. Frequently one alternative will have a high initial cost but low maintenance or operating expenses, while another alternative will have low initial costs but high operating or maintenance expenses. A choice between the two alternatives is in essence an investment decision.

Thus, while not all the investment decisions in an organization can be described in terms of the dollar value of the expenditures or benefits, important decisions that can be described in these terms seem to occur in all organizations in modern society. As we increase our ability to forecast the consequences of our decisions, the number of investments that can be described reasonably well in dollar terms will also increase.

Frequently an investment proposal will involve both benefits and expenditures during one or more time periods. When this occurs, it will be convenient to combine the dollar estimates of the benefits and expenditures for each period of time. If, during a specific period of time, the benefits exceed the expenditures, we may speak of the net benefits or cash proceeds; if the expenditures exceed the benefits we may refer to the net expenditures or cash outlays. We shall adopt the convention of referring to cash proceeds or outlays during a given

net spend, net benefits
or cash or cash
outlays proceeds

period of time by using positive or negative dollar amounts, respectively. We shall refer to the entire series of net proceeds and net outlays associated with an investment as the cash flow of the investment.

If some of the proceeds are subject to taxation, we shall assume that the proceeds are measured after taxes. A business corporation is subject to taxes on its income, and this income in turn depends on the amount of depreciation charges that can be used to offset revenues in computing taxable income. The amount of cash proceeds resulting from an investment in any future year will depend upon the regulations established by the Internal Revenue Service and laws passed by Congress. These laws or regulations will determine the kinds of expenditures that can be charged immediately to expense and those that must be capitalized and written off in subsequent years by depreciating the asset. Nonprofit organizations and governments are not subject to income taxes, and therefore the proceeds they receive from an investment do not depend upon their depreciation accounting systems used.

It should be stressed that the definition of net benefits or cash proceeds given above is *not* identical with the income concept used in corporate accounting. The major difference is that in estimating cash proceeds, depreciation charges and other amortization charges of fixed assets are not subtracted from gross revenues because no cash expenditures are required.

We shall define *conventional* investments (or loans) as those having one or more periods of outlays (or proceeds), followed by one or more periods of cash proceeds (or outlays). Borrowing money is a kind of "negative investment" in which one or more periods of cash proceeds are followed by one or more periods in which there are cash outlays. There are also *nonconventional* investments which have one or more periods of outlays (proceeds) interspersed with periods of positive (negative) cash flows. Any decisions involving measurable cash flows over one or more periods may be implemented by using the capital budgeting procedures to be developed in this book.

The Estimate of Cash Proceeds

It is frequently stated that refinements in capital budgeting techniques are a waste of effort because the basic information being used is so unreliable. It is claimed that the estimates of cash proceeds are only guesses and to use anything except the simplest capital budgeting procedures is as futile as using racing forms to pick winners at the track or as using complicated formulas to determine which way the stock market is going to move next.

As may be expected, there is a large element of truth in these objections. Many estimates of cash proceeds are indeed rough estimates or worse. Fortunately there are a large number of investment decisions where the cash proceeds can be predicted with a fair degree of certainty. But even if we admit that the cash proceeds used in the decision-making process are estimates, this is no excuse for not using the best of the various measures of investment worth to make the decision. Frequently even a crude estimate of the cash flows from each of two alternative investment possibilities will indicate which is preferable, provided the available information is used correctly. Even with an accurate estimate of the cash proceeds, the wrong decision is frequently made because crude rules of thumb are used in evaluating this information.

Applications of Capital Budgeting Techniques

It is interesting to note that many decisions may be thought of as investments and hence incorporated into the capital budgeting process. We shall illustrate in this section some of the situations of this nature.

Replacement Decision

A company is currently using three pieces of equipment which cost $10,000 each and are 70 per cent depreciated. They can be replaced with one unit of equipment that would cost $20,000. It is expected that at normal activity the new machine would save $4,000 a year in labor, maintenance, etc., for a period of five years. Should the machine be replaced?

Size of Plant

A company must choose between a small plant which would cost $1,000,000 and a large plant which would cost $1,500,000. The earnings of both plants are computed, and it is found that the small plant would yield a return of 20 per cent and the large plant a return of 17 per cent. Which plant should be chosen?

Lease or Buy

A company can either buy data processing equipment or rent it. The cost of the equipment is $300,000 and the rental fee is $10,000 per month. It is estimated that improvements will make this equipment obsolete within five years. Should XYZ Company lease or buy?

Refunding of Debt

A company currently has $10,000,000 debt outstanding, bearing a coupon rate of 5 per cent. The debt was issued at a discount which is still unamortized to the extent of $500,000. The company can currently issue bonds to yield 4 per cent. The costs of issuing the new bonds would be $200,000, and there would be a call premium on the old bonds of $300,000. The old bonds have 20 years remaining until they become due. Should the bonds be refunded?

Although none of the above examples contains all the facts that would be necessary for a decision, they illustrate well the kind of problem that will be considered. The analytical methods that will be suggested in this book are applicable to all these examples.

Measures of Investment Worth

In the next chapter we shall introduce some methods of evaluating the worth of investments that are in common use or have been frequently recommended as desirable. We shall find that if we take a group of investment proposals and rank them by each of these methods, each measure will frequently give a different ranking to the same set of investment proposals. In fact it can be said that the different measures will only accidentally give identical rankings to a set of investment proposals. Various executives faced with the same set of investment possibilities, but using different measures of investment worth, will tend to make dissimilar investment decisions. Clearly, all the measures that will be described here cannot be equally valid. Our problem will be to determine which of the measures have some legitimate reason for use and to isolate the circumstances under which they will tend to give satisfactory results.

In current business practice, each of the methods selected has its advocates, and frequently one is used in combination with another. Since investment proposals are rarely accepted by top management solely on the basis of such analyses, it may be argued that the choice of method is of little significance because the investment decision is likely to be influenced by many different factors. Insofar as the executives making the final decision are intimately familiar with the proposals, aware of the risks involved, know the possible technical or operating problems that may be encountered, and realize the potential erosion of earnings resulting from competitive action or changing technology, this criticism may very well be correct. However, in large organizations it is impossible for the top management officials, who must finally approve or disapprove investment proposals, to be intimately familiar with the details of each and every proposal presented to them. To the extent that this intimate knowledge is impossible or impractical, these executives must rely upon the evaluation of the recommendations from their subordinates. In order to make reasonable choices in weighing alternative investments, it is increasingly necessary that various proposals be evaluated as nearly as possible on some uniform, comparable basis. In such circumstances, although the measure of economic worth of an investment should never be the sole factor considered in making a final decision, it may play an increasingly important part in the majority of the investments under consideration by the firm.

Accordingly the fact that the various measures in common use today give different rankings to identical sets of investment proposals is a matter of concern. Substantial improvements in efficiency and income may result if a more adequate measure can be discovered and widely adopted. Any such progress requires first a more general agreement about the desirable characteristics to be possessed by a good index of the economic worth of an investment. We therefore turn to consider the various criteria that can be used in evaluating the adequacy of a measure of the economic worth of an investment proposal.

Criteria for Evaluating Measures of Investment Worth

One important reason for the wide disagreement about which measures of economic worth of an investment should be used is that there is no general agreement about what constitutes a good measure. Various criteria have been proposed, but little has been done to reconcile the criteria or to develop a list that would be widely acceptable. Indeed, the entire question of what criteria should be used in determining the value of the proposed measures has been given very little explicit attention. Those criteria that have been proposed can be divided into two broad groups. The first group attempts to get at the question of whether the measure of investment worth properly reflects the potential benefits of the investment proposal and is consistent with the goals of the organization. The second group includes all other desirable attributes of a measure, which usually refer in one way or another to the administrative feasibility of using the proposed measure.

As anyone who has ever attempted the task will recognize,

it is difficult to develop an explicit statement of the goals of an organization. The task becomes even harder if, as in the present instance, the purpose of the statement of goals is not to provide a symbol around which sentiment and loyalty can develop, but rather is a test of the extent to which activities and programs are appropriate for the organization. In the case of business organizations the measures of investment worth that have been proposed and are developed in this book concentrate on the profit-maximization goal and give little attention to equally important conditions such as the risks associated with the investments undertaken and the future structure of assets and liabilities that will be determined in part by the investment decisions currently being made. It is recognized that a complete statement of the organizational goals of a business enterprise would have to embrace a much wider range of considerations, including such things as the prestige, security, freedom, and power of the management group. But directed activity always leads to a hierarchy of goals in which the goals of one activity become the means to achieve further goals. Insofar as the attainment of a reasonable profit position, without unnecessary risks or an unduly awkward financial structure, is a means of accomplishing the other goals mentioned, the assumption that the pecuniary objectives are the proximate goals of a business organization is tenable. The measure of investment worth that best leads to a maximization of profits is a feasible measure to use in making investment decisions.

Capital Budgeting, the Budget Process, and Planning

Frequently we think of the budget of a firm as being part of the cost control apparatus and forget that it is an important tool for planning. The capital budget for the coming period will affect the cash budget and will be affected in turn by sales forecasts; thus the capital budget must be incorporated into the budgetary process.

The timing of cash flows resulting from capital expenditures is extremely important to the corporate officer attempting to plan the cash needs of the firm. Information is needed as to the specific days the bills will have to be paid and when cash will begin to be generated by the investment. Of course it will hardly ever be possible to predict these events with certainty, but it should be possible to make reasonable estimates that will be useful.

Some firms will prepare a five-year capital budget. If an attempt is being made to project other financial data over one or more years, the composition of the capital budget will affect the nature of the other planning budgets. For example, if an automobile company is planning to enter the steel industry, this would be disclosed in the capital budget and would certainly affect all other budgets.

Thus the capital budget should be an integral part of the budget and planning process. The officer in charge of the capital budget must be in effective communication with the budget officer of the firm (if the positions are separate), since the decisions they make will result in a considerable amount of interaction.

2

Illustrating the Measures of Investment Worth

In this chapter we shall describe and illustrate the applications of six different measures of investment worth, which were chosen either because they are used in current business practice or because logical arguments in favor of their use have been advanced. These six measures by no means exhaust the possible investment measures. Others, in many cases variations of those discussed, have been suggested or are known to be used by one or more firms. After studying this chapter, the reader should be able to analyze and evaluate for himself the probable performance of other measures of investment worth with which he may be familiar.

Before proceeding to a discussion of the measures of investment worth, a series of six hypothetical investments will be described. The six hypothetical investments have been designed so that for selected pairs it is possible to decide that one investment is clearly preferable to the other. If a measure of investment worth indicates that one investment is better than a second, when it is obvious that the second investment is actually better, then clearly there is a danger in using that measure. We shall find that of the six measures considered,

13

four can easily be eliminated because in certain situations they give obviously wrong answers while another measure gives the "right" answer.

The Characteristics of the Investments

In Table 1 a series of hypothetical investments are described in terms of the initial cost of each and the net cash proceeds expected during each year of earning life. The salvage value or terminal value of each is assumed to be zero. We shall illustrate the ranking that may be given to these investments by each of the measures of investment worth under consideration.

Table 1. Description of Hypothetical Investments

Investment	Initial cost	Net cash proceeds per year		
		Year 1	Year 2	Year 3
A	$10,000	$10,000		
B	10,000	5,000	$5,000	$ 5,000
C	10,000	2,000	4,000	12,000
D	10,000	10,000	3,000	3,000
E	10,000	6,000	4,000	5,000
F	10,000	8,000	8,000	2,000

Some comments on the interpretation of these hypothetical investments are in order. In the first place, nothing has been said about the risk characteristics of the various investments. An evaluation of the risk or uncertainty associated with an investment is a crucial part of the investment decision process. However, the concepts of risk or uncertainty are complex and need to be clarified before they can be discussed intelligently. It has seemed advisable to take these problems up separately in Chapter 9, but for present purposes the reader may assume either that the hypothetical investments described in Table 1 are completely riskless or that at least they have equal risk; thus there is no basis of choice between them on these grounds.

Secondly, the question of income taxes needs clarification. Investment proposals should be evaluated on an after-tax basis. Since this is commonly recognized, the discussion of income tax adjustments is deferred to Chapter 8. In the present instance, however, the explicit introduction of income taxes would complicate the task of describing the various hypothetical investments and of illustrating the rankings that would result from the use of each of the various measures. Moreover, an explicit consideration of income taxes would not change, in any of their essentials, the conclusions we reach. For this reason we shall assume in the present chapter that corporate income taxes have already been taken into consideration and that the net cash proceeds used in the computations are proceeds after deducting the income tax of the period.

The outlays are made at the beginning of the first year, and proceeds are earned at the end of each year. Each investment is of a conventional nature, i.e., there are one or more periods of outlays followed by one or more periods of positive cash proceeds. If there were nonconventional investments, e.g., more than one period of outlays interspersed with periods of positive cash flows, the yield method would require additional refinements, since in this type of situation a higher yield may indicate a less desirable investment opportunity.

Ranking by Inspection

It is possible in certain limited cases to determine by inspection which of two or more investments is more desirable. The two situations in which this is true are as follows:

1. Two investments have identical cash flows each year through the final year of the short-lived investment, but one continues to earn cash proceeds in subsequent years. The investment with the longer life would be more desirable. Thus investment D is better than investment A, since all things are equal except that D continues to earn proceeds after A has been retired.

2. Two investments have the same initial outlay and the same earning life and earn the same total proceeds. If at the end of every year (during their earning life) the total net proceeds of one investment are at least as great as, and for at least one year are greater than, the total for the other investment, then the first investment will always be more profitable. Thus investment E is more desirable than investment B, since E earns $1,000 in Year 1 which investment B does not earn until Year 2. The earning of $1,000 in the first year leads to the conclusion that investment E is more desirable than investment B. Investments C and F are also similar in all respects except that investment F receives its proceeds in earlier periods than investment C. Thus investment F is more desirable than C.

The Payback Period

The payback period is one of the simplest and apparently one of the most frequently used methods of measuring the economic value of an investment. The payback period is defined as the length of time required for the stream of cash proceeds produced by an investment to equal the original cash outlay required by the investment. If an investment is expected to produce a stream of cash proceeds that is constant from year to year, then the payback period can be determined by dividing the total original cash outlay by the amount of the annual cash proceeds expected. Thus if an investment required an original outlay of $300 and was expected to produce a stream of cash proceeds of $100 a year for five years, the payback period would be 300 divided by 100, or three years. If the stream of expected proceeds is not constant from year to year, then the payback period must be determined by adding up the proceeds expected in successive years until the total is equal to the original outlay.

Ordinarily the administrator would set some maximum payback period and reject all investment proposals for which the payback period is greater than this maximum. Investigators have reported that maximum payback periods of two, three, four, or five years are frequently used by industrial concerns. The relatively short periods mentioned suggest that different maximum payback periods are required because some kinds of investments (construction, for example) can seldom be expected to have a payback period as short as five years.

Table 2. The Payback Period

Investment	Payback period (years)	Ranking
A	1	1
B	2	4
C	2⅓	6
D	1	1
E	2	4
F	1¼	3

The payback period can also be used to rank investment alternatives, those having the shortest payback periods being given the highest ranking. The investments described in Table 1 are ranked by this method in Table 2.

Let us check the reasonableness of the ranking given the investments by the cash payback approach. Investments A and

D are both ranked as 1, since they both have shorter payback periods than any of the other investments, namely, one year. But investment A earns total proceeds of $10,000, and this amount merely equals the cost of the investment. Investment D, which has the same rank as A, will not only earn $10,000 in the first year but also $3,000 in each of the subsequent two years. Obviously investment D is superior to A. A ranking procedure, such as the payback period, that fails to disclose this fact is deficient.

Consider investments B and E. Both are given identical rankings, since both will return their original outlay by the end of the second year. Both earn an equal amount in their third year of existence. The two investments are in fact identical, with the single exception that out of identical total returns, more proceeds are received in the first year and less in the second year from investment E than is the case with B. To the extent that earnings can be increased by having $1,000 available for reinvestment one year earlier, E is superior to investment B, but both are given the same ranking by the payback period measure.

Thus the cash payback period measure has two weaknesses: (1) It fails to give any consideration to cash proceeds earned after the payback date. (2) It fails to take into account the differences in the timing of proceeds earned prior to the payback date. These weaknesses disqualify the cash payback measure as a general method of ranking investments.

Proceeds per Dollar of Outlay

The investments are ranked according to the total proceeds divided by the amount of the investment.

This ranking fails to consider the timing of the proceeds.

A dollar of proceeds in Year 2 receives the same weight as a dollar received in Year 1. This is inconsistent with the generally accepted principle that a dollar today is more valuable than a dollar in the future. Since the rankings obtained from this procedure ignore the fact that the early proceeds are more valuable than the later ones because the early proceeds can be reinvested, it is inferior to the procedures which take into consideration the timing of the proceeds.

Table 3. Proceeds per Dollar of Outlay

Investment	Total proceeds	Investment outlay	Proceeds per dollar of outlay	Ranking
A	$10,000	$10,000	1.0	6
B	15,000	10,000	1.5	4
C	18,000	10,000	1.8	1
D	16,000	10,000	1.6	3
E	15,000	10,000	1.5	4
F	18,000	10,000	1.8	1

The failure of this procedure to rank investments correctly is indicated by the rankings given to investments B and E and investments C and F. Investments B and E are given the same ranking, although E is obviously superior because the only difference in the two investments is that E receives $1,000 of proceeds a period earlier. In like manner, investments C and F are both ranked the same even though F is clearly superior.

Average Annual Proceeds per Dollar of Outlay

This measure is closely related to the method of proceeds per dollar of outlay. Instead, however, of taking the ratio of

the total cash proceeds over the initial outlay, the total proceeds are first divided by the number of years during which
they are received, and this figure (the average proceeds per
year) is then divided by the original outlay required by the
investment.

This procedure is actually an oddity, and its prime weakness
is enough to disqualify it from further consideration. By failing
to take properly into consideration the duration of the proceeds, it has a bias for short-lived investments with high cash
proceeds. The procedure is dangerous, since it *seems* to take
all years into consideration. Only in the special situation where
the lives of the investments being considered are equal does
this procedure give reasonable results, and then only if we
are willing to ignore the qualification of proper timing of the
cash proceeds.

Table 4. Average Annual Proceeds per Dollar of Outlay

Invest-ment	Total proceeds	Average annual proceeds	Original outlay	Average annual proceeds per dollar of outlay	Ranking
A	$10,000	$10,000	$10,000	1.00	1
B	15,000	5,000	10,000	0.50	5
C	18,000	6,000	10,000	0.60	2
D	16,000	5,333	10,000	0.53	4
E	15,000	5,000	10,000	0.50	5
F	18,000	6,000	10,000	0.60	2

The fact that this method seems to take proper account of
the timing of investment is deceptive. Consider investments B
and E. As previously pointed out, E is superior, although this
method gives them an equal rating. Investments C and F are

also incorrectly given equal rating, although F is superior. The method also ranks investment A above investment D, although the latter is clearly superior.

By taking the *average* annual proceeds, actually no weight is being given to the duration of the proceeds. For example, investment A has average proceeds of $10,000 per year, since it earns that amount for one year. An investment that earned $10,000 of proceeds each year for ten years would also have average proceeds of $10,000 per year.

Average Income on the Book Value of the Investment

In attempting to get a measure of efficiency, analysts frequently use the ratio of the firm's income to the book value of its assets. Some companies also use this measure as a means of choosing among various proposed internal investments. When this measure is used, the average income is computed after depreciation. If the denominator in the ratio is the book value of the investment, the value of both the numerator and the denominator will depend upon the depreciation method used. An alternative procedure is to divide the average income by the cost of the investment (the accrued depreciation is not subtracted). The use of both the book value (net of depreciation) and the cost of the investment will be reviewed here.

The income on book value is a common and useful measure of performance, but it is less useful as a device for ranking investments. Table 5 shows that the same rankings are given to investments B and E and to C and F, although B is preferable to E, and F is preferable to C. This procedure fails to rank these investments correctly, since it does not take into consideration the timing of the proceeds.

An alternative procedure is to divide income by the cost of

Table 5. Average Income on Book Value

Invest-ment	Average proceeds	Average depre-ciation *	Average in-come (pro-ceeds less depreci-ation)	Average book † value	Income on book value, %	Ranking
A	$10,000	$10,000	$ 0	$5,000	0	6
B	5,000	3,333	1,667	5,000	33	4
C	6,000	3,333	2,667	5,000	53	1
D	5,333	3,333	2,000	5,000	40	3
E	5,000	3,333	1,667	5,000	33	4
F	6,000	3,333	2,667	5,000	53	1

* Assuming straight line depreciation.
† Investment divided by two.

the investment (accumulated depreciation not being sub-tracted). For purposes of measuring performance and com-puting return on investment, the use of undepreciated cost has certain advantages over the use of book value. These advan-tages are not so important in capital budgeting and are relatively unimportant compared to the failure to take into

Table 6. Average Income on Cost

Investment	Cost	Average income	Average income on cost, %	Ranking
A	$10,000	$ 0	0	6
B	10,000	1,667	16.67	4
C	10,000	2,667	26.67	1
D	10,000	2,000	20.00	3
E	10,000	1,667	16.67	4
F	10,000	2,667	26.67	1

consideration the timing of the cash proceeds. It is this failing that leads to the same incorrect rankings resulting from the use of book value.[1]

Introduction to Discounted Cash Flow Methods of Ranking Investments – *takes into account the timing of cash proceeds, outlays over entire life of invest.*

We have considered four proposed methods for measuring the value of an investment. In the case of each proposed measure, we have been able to find at least one pair of investments where it was obvious that one of the pair was more desirable, and yet the proposed measure of investment worth gave either the same ranking to both investments or a higher ranking to the less desirable of the pair. On the basis of such evidence we have been able to reject all four of the proposed measures of investment worth because of their undesirable characteristics.

One of the flaws that eliminated from consideration each of the measures reviewed has been the inability of the measure to take proper account of the timing of cash proceeds from the investments. The payback period represents one extreme in this regard, since all the proceeds received before the payback period are counted and treated as equals, and all the proceeds received after the payback period are ignored completely. In the other measures analyzed, the proceeds were related by simple averaging techniques to such things as the original cost of the investment, its book value, and the number of years over which the proceeds were received. None of these methods succeeded in bringing the timing of cash proceeds into the analysis.

---

[1] The methods described in this section are commonly referred to as "rate of return analysis" or "return on investment analysis." Terminology is a problem, since both these terms are also used to describe other procedures.

We turn in the following sections to two proposed measures of investment worth that employ different methods for evaluating the timing of future cash proceeds. As a group these could be called the *discounted cash flow measures*. Before proceeding to analyze them, it is necessary to introduce and explain the concept of the present value of a future sum, since in one way or another this concept is utilized in both these measures.

The present value of $100 payable in two years can be defined as that quantity of money necessary to invest today at compound interest in order to have $100 in two years. This will depend upon the rate of interest at which the money will grow and the frequency at which it will be compounded. We shall assume that funds are compounded annually. The manner in which a rate of interest will be chosen will be discussed later in Chapters 10, 11, and 12. For the present let us assume we are given a 3 per cent rate of interest. Let us examine how the present value of a future sum can be computed by using that rate of interest.

Suppose an investment promises to return a total of $100 at the end of two years. Since $1.00 invested today at 3 per cent compounded annually would grow to $1.0609 in two years, we can find the present value at 3 per cent of $100 in two years by dividing $100 by $1.0609. This gives $94.26. Therefore, a sum of $94.26 that earns 3 per cent interest compounded annually will be worth $100 at the end of two years. By repeated applications of this method, we can convert any series of current or future cash payments (or outlays) into an equivalent present value. Since tables are available that give the appropriate conversion factors for various rates of interest, the calculations involved are relatively simple.

We have seen that the measures of investment worth previously considered may give obviously incorrect results because they fail either to consider the entire life of the investment or to give adequate attention to the timing of future cash proceeds. The discounted cash flow concept provides a method of taking into account the timing of cash proceeds and outlays over the entire life of the investment. We now turn to a consideration of two measures of investment worth that incorporate present-value concepts.

The Yield of an Investment Method

This method utilizes present-value concepts but seeks to avoid the arbitrary choice of a rate of interest in evaluating an investment proposal.[2] The procedure is to find a rate of interest that will make the present value of the cash proceeds expected from an investment equal to the present value of the cash outlays required by the investment. Such a rate of interest can be found by trial and error. For example, if we know the cash proceeds expected and the cash outlays required by an investment in each future year, we can start with any rate of interest and find for that rate the present value of the cash proceeds and the present value of the cash outlays. If the present value of the cash proceeds exceeds the present value of the outlays, then ordinarily some higher rate of interest would make them equal. By a process of trial and error, the approximately correct rate of interest can be determined. This rate of interest is referred to as the *yield* of the investment.

The method is commonly used in security markets in evaluating the yields of bonds and other debt instruments. The yield on a bond having a coupon rate of 5 per cent will be equal

[2] Other terms used to define the same concept are interest rate of return, internal rate of return, return on investment, present-value return on investment, discounted cash flow, profitability index, investor's method, and marginal efficiency of capital.

to 5 per cent only if the current price of the bond is 100. If the current price is greater than 100, the yield will be something less than the coupon rate; if the current price is less than 100, the yield will be greater than the coupon rate.

The yield of a conventional investment has an interesting interpretation that may be referred to at this point. It represents the highest rate of interest an investor could afford to pay, without losing money, if all the funds to finance the investment were borrowed and the loan (principal and accrued interest) was repaid by application of the cash proceeds from the investment as they were earned.[3] Because of this interpretation,

Table 7. Yield of an Investment (Rate of Return)

Investment	Yield (%)	Ranking
A	0	6
B	23	5
C	27	3
D	37	2
E	24	4
F	44	1

those who advocate use of the yield measure for ranking investments usually recommend the following procedure: First, rank all the available investment possibilities in descending order according to their yields. Second, accept all those investments for which the yield is as great as or greater than the investor's cost of capital. The concept of cost of capital will be more fully developed in Chapters 10 and 11.

---

[3] It should be remembered that all investments being considered in this chapter are conventional investments, consisting of periods of outlays followed by periods of proceeds. For other patterns of cash flows, the interpretation of yield given above may not apply (see Chapter 3).

In Table 7 we show the yield for each of the investments listed in Table 1 and the ranking of investments that would result if this method were used. The yields are rounded off to the nearest whole percentage.

It will be instructive to examine the rankings given by this method for each of the pairs of investments in this list for which we were earlier able to determine which one of each pair was more desirable.

We previously compared three pairs of investments and decided that investment D was preferred over A, F over C, and E over B. In each case if preference had been determined by using the yield of an investment method, the pairs would be given the correct ranking. This is the first method that we have used which gives the correct rankings of all three pairs.

A,	0%	C,	27%	B,	23%
D,	37%	F,	44%	E,	24%

Net Present Value (*direct application of present-value concept*)

This measure is a direct application of the present-value concept. Its computation requires the following steps: First, choose an appropriate rate of interest. Second, compute the present value of the cash proceeds expected from the investment. Third, compute the present value of the cash outlays required by the investment.[4] The present value of the proceeds minus the present value of the outlays is the net present value of the investment. The recommended accept or reject criterion

---

[4] If all the cash outlays required by the investments are made in the first period, then, of course, the present value of these outlays is equal to the actual amount expended. This is true of all the hypothetical investments described in Table 1, and which are used as examples in this chapter.

is to accept all independent investments whose present value is greater than or equal to zero and to reject all investments whose present value is less than zero.

Since the present value of an investment will depend upon the rate of interest used, there is not one present-value measure but a group of measures, depending upon what rate of interest is chosen. This should not be interpreted as meaning that this approach provides purely arbitrary indications of the worth of an investment. In most cases definite recommendations can be made as to what rate of interest is appropriate.[5]

The present value of an investment, at the cost of capital, may be described as the maximum amount a firm could pay for the opportunity of making the investment without being financially worse off. Since usually no such payment must be made, the expected present value is an unrealized capital gain from the investment, over and above the minimum required return on the company's capital. The capital gain will be realized if the expected cash proceeds materialize. If the cost of capital is 10 per cent, a company could make a maximum immediate outlay of $11,000 in the expectation of receiving $12,100 a year later. If it can receive the $12,100 with an actual outlay of only $10,000, the net present value of the investment would be $1,000. The $1,000 represents the difference between the actual outlay of $10,000 and the $11,000, the most the company would have been willing to spend to receive $12,100 a year later.

It will be instructive to note the rankings that will be given to the hypothetical investments of Table 1 by the present-value method, using two sample rates of interest. In Table 8 we present the results of using the present-value method and a 6 per cent rate of interest.

In discussing the measures of investment worth that do not use the discounted cash flow method, we pointed out that the

[5] See Chapters 10, 11, and 12.

relative ranking of certain pairs of these six investments was obvious. That is, it is obvious from examining the cash flows that investment D is preferable to A, E is preferable to B, and F is preferable to C. The reader may note that in each case the present-value method using a 6 per cent rate of interest ranks these investment pairs in the correct relative order.

outlays – expenditures   *proceeds – benefits*

Table 8. Present Value of the Investment

Rate of Interest: 6 per cent

Investment	Present value of proceeds	Present value of outlay	Net present value	Ranking
A	$ 9,430	$10,000	$− 570	6
B	13,365	10,000	+3,365	5
C	15,526	10,000	+5,526	2
D	14,620	10,000	+4,620	3
E	13,418	10,000	+3,418	4
F	16,344	10,000	+6,344	1

In Table 9 the same investments are ranked by the present-value method, using a 30 per cent rate of interest instead of 6 per cent. The relative rankings of investments C and D change with the change in the rate of interest. Investment C, which was ranked second when a 6 per cent rate of interest was used, is ranked third when the 30 per cent interest rate is used. The ranking of investment D is changed from third to second by the change in the rate of interest. The higher rate of interest results in the proceeds of the later years being worth less relative to the proceeds of the early years. The change in rankings points up the importance of choosing the appropriate rate of interest when using the present-value method.

It is important to note that even with a 30 per cent rate of interest, the relative ranking of each of the three pairs of investments for which an obvious preference can be determined are ranked in the correct order. Thus we still find investment D preferred to A, E preferred to B, and F preferred to C. This result is not an accident resulting from the specific choice of hypothetical investments and interest rates used in our examples. Whenever it is possible to determine obvious prefer-

Table 9. Present Value of the Investment

Rate of Interest: 30 per cent

Investment	Present value of proceeds	Present value of outlay	Net present value	Ranking
A	$ 7,690	$10,000	$—2,310	6
B	9,080	10,000	— 920	5
C	9,366	10,000	— 634	3
D	10,831	10,000	+ 831	2
E	9,257	10,000	— 743	4
F	11,798	10,000	+1,798	1

ences between pairs of investments by the methods described earlier, the present-value method will rank these investments in the correct order, no matter what rate of interest is used to compute the present value.[6] Thus we are justified in concluding that, in the sense that it will not make certain kinds of obvious errors, the present-value method even when used with the "wrong" rate of interest will give better results than measures that do not incorporate the discounted cash flow method.

[6] This conclusion is true only if the same rate of interest is used to determine the present value of both the investments.

Summary of Rankings

The rankings given by each measure of investment worth for each of the hypothetical investments described in Table 1 are summarized in Table 10.

Table 10. Summary of Rankings

Measure of investment worth	Investments					
	A	B	C	D	E	F
Payback period	1°	4°	6	1°	4°	3
Proceeds per dollar of outlay......	6	4°	1°	3	4°	1°
Average annual proceeds per dollar of outlay	1	5°	2°	4	5°	2°
Average income on book value or cost	6	4°	1°	3	4°	1°
Yield of an investment..........	6	5	3	2	4	1
Present value: at 6 per cent.....	6	5	2	3	4	1
at 30 per cent.....	6	5	3	2	4	1

° Indicates tie between two investments.

The most striking conclusion to be drawn from Table 10 is the tendency for each measure of investment worth to give a different ranking to the identical set of investments. This emphasizes the need to give careful consideration to the choice of measures used to evaluate proposed investments. Obviously all these measures cannot be equally valid. By considering specific pairs of investments, we have shown that the measures of investment worth that do not involve the use of the discounted cash flow method can give rankings of investments that are obviously incorrect. For this reason these measures will be excluded from further consideration.

At a 30 per cent rate of interest the ranking given the investments by the present-value measure is identical with that given by the yield of an investment measure. However, that this need not be the case is illustrated by the ranking which results when present values are computed by using a 6 per cent rate of interest. Neither of these rankings can be eliminated as being obviously incorrect; yet, since they are different, they could lead to contradictory conclusions in certain situations. In Chapter 3 we shall continue our investigation in an attempt to determine whether the present value or the yield of an investment measure gives the most satisfactory results.

A NOTE ON THE RELATIONSHIP BETWEEN PAYBACK AND PRESENT VALUE

Under certain circumstances it is possible to construct a theoretically correct payback period. Assuming that an investment with a yield equal to the cost of capital of the firm will earn equal proceeds each year, the *maximum* payback period which should be acceptable is equal to the present value of a dollar per period for n periods (where n is the life of the investment) discounted on the basis of the cost of capital.

$$\text{Proceeds per period} \times A_{\overline{n}|r} = \text{cost of investment}$$

$$\text{Payback period} = \frac{\text{cost of investment}}{\text{proceeds per period}}$$

Substituting and canceling cost of investment:

$$\text{Payback period} = A_{\overline{n}|r}$$

where $A_{\overline{n}|r} = $ present value of a dollar per period for n periods discounted at an r rate of interest.

Because of the limiting assumptions, especially equal annual proceeds, this formula is not useful in making decisions, but it is useful in showing the absurdity of certain payback conventions.

Example: The ABC Company requires a two-year payback period or less before accepting equipment. A piece of equipment is being considered which costs $5,000 and is expected to earn cash proceeds per year of $1,000 for a life of ten years. Should the equipment be purchased, assuming a cost of capital of 10 per cent?

The equipment has a payback of five years; thus it seems to be undesirable. However, if the yield of the equipment were 10 per cent (it is actually higher), it could have a payback of 6.1446 years ($A_{\overline{10}|10} = 6.1446$) and would still be acceptable. Both the yield and present-value procedures would give "accept" decisions in this case. Using a two-year payback for an investment with these characteristics leads to the rejection of investments that should have been accepted.

3

Present Value versus Yield

In the preceding chapter we saw that neither of the discounted cash flow procedures for evaluating an investment could be eliminated as being obviously incorrect. In many situations the yield procedure will lead to the same decision as the net present-value procedure. However, there are also situations where the yield method may lead to different decisions than those obtained by using the present-value procedure. When the two methods lead to different decisions, the present-value method tends to give better decisions.

It is possible to use the yield method in such a way that it gives the same results as the present-value method.[1] In this sense the two methods are identical, and *if* they are used correctly, either one is acceptable. However, *if* is the biggest two-letter word in the English language. It is easy to use the present-value method correctly. It is much more difficult to use the yield method correctly—more difficult to describe what comparisons are appropriate for a given decision, and more

[1] This statement is true as long as the rate of discount at which it is appropriate to discount future cash proceeds is the same for all future years. If the appropriate rate of interest varies from year to year, even if that pattern of variation is known in advance, then the two procedures cannot be used in a way that will give identical answers.

difficult to carry out the required calculations. For both these reasons this book will consistently recommend the use of the present-value method. In the remainder of this chapter we shall explain why we believe the yield method is inferior, and in the process we shall show how that method could be used correctly in arriving at the same answers as the present-value method.

Accept or Reject Decisions

Frequently the investment decision to be made is whether or not to accept or reject a project. We speak of this type of investment as being an independent investment. With the yield procedure the usual recommendation is to accept an independent investment if its yield is greater than the company's cost of capital. If the cash flow corresponding to the investment consists of one or more periods of cash outlays followed only by periods of cash proceeds, then this method will give the same "accept" or "reject" decisions as the present-value method, using the cost of capital as a discount rate. Since most independent investments have cash flow patterns that meet the specifications described above, it is fair to say that in practice the yield and present-value methods would give the same recommendations for independent investments.

It is sometimes suggested that one of the advantages of the yield procedure is that it may be utilized without deciding on the cost of capital, whereas the present-value method requires that the cost of capital be incorporated into the computations. The weakness of this suggestion becomes evident when we consider the accept or reject type of investment decision. The yield of an investment must be compared with the cost of capital. The cost of capital is no less important to yield than to present value, although it enters at an earlier stage in the computations of the present-value method.

Mutually Exclusive Investments

If undertaking any one of a set of investments will decrease the profitability of the other investments, the investments are substitutes. An extreme case of substitution exists if undertaking one of the investments completely eliminates the expected proceeds of the other investments. Such investments are said to be mutually exclusive.

Frequently a company will have two or more investments, any one of which would be acceptable, but because the investments are mutually exclusive, only one can be accepted. For example, assume that a company is trying to decide where to build a new plant. It may be that either of two locations would be profitable. But the company will have to decide which one is likely to be the more profitable, since only one new plant is needed. An oil company may need additional transport facilities for its products. Should it build a pipeline or acquire additional tankers and ship by water? Either of these alternatives may result in a net profit to the firm, but the company will wish to choose the one that is more profitable. Suppose that it has decided to build the pipeline. Should a 6- or 10-inch diameter pipeline be installed? Again the problem is to choose the more profitable of these alternatives. In all the above discussion, the choice is between mutually exclusive investments.

Mutually exclusive investment alternatives are common. The situation frequently occurs in connection with the engineering design of a new installation. In the process of designing such an installation, the engineers are typically faced at a great many points with alternatives that are mutually exclusive. Thus a measure of investment worth that does not lead to correct

Present Value versus Yield

mutually exclusive choices will be seriously deficient. In this light, the fact that the two discounted cash flow measures of investment worth may give different rankings to the same set of mutually exclusive investment proposals becomes of considerable importance.

Incremental Benefits

The yield method gives less correct recommendations for mutually exclusive investments than those that result from the application of the present-value method because it neglects the incremental cash flows. Let us assume that we must choose one of the following investments for a company whose cost of capital is 10 per cent: investment A requires an outlay of $10,000 this year and has cash proceeds of $12,000 next year; investment B requires an outlay of $15,000 this year and has cash proceeds of $17,700 next year. The yield of A is 20 per cent and that of B is 18 per cent. A quick answer would be that A is more desirable, on the hypothesis that the higher the yield, the better the investment. To see why this answer may be wrong, consider that a yield of 1,000 per cent on an investment of a dime is a poor substitute for a yield of 15 per cent on $1,000 if only one of the investments can be undertaken.

Clearly, when only the yield of the entire investment is considered, something important is left out—and that is the size of the investments. The important difference between investment B and investment A is that B requires an additional outlay of $5,000 and provides additional cash proceeds of $5,700. The yield of the incremental investment is 14 per cent, which is clearly worth while for a company that can obtain additional funds from the capital market at 10 per cent.

Two mutually exclusive investments may have different yields, but both may require the same initial outlay. This case seems to be different from the one we have just discussed because there is no incremental investment. *(both require the same outlay)* Actually the difference is superficial. Consider investments Y and Z described in Table 1. Suppose they are mutually exclusive investments for a company whose cost of capital was 5 per cent. The yield of Y is 20 per cent, while that of Z is 25 per cent. However, if we take the present value of each of the investments at 5 per cent, we find that the ranking is in the opposite order. The present value of Z is less than the present value of Y. Neither investment can be said to be obviously superior to the other, and both require the same cash outlay in the first year. Which is preferable for a company with a 5 per cent cost of capital?

Table 1

Invest-ment	Year	Cash flows		Yield, %	Net present value at 5%
		Outlays	Proceeds		
Y	0	$100.00	.....	20	$27.89
	1	.....	$ 20.00		
	2	.....	120.00		
Z	0	100.00	.....	25	23.58
	1	.....	100.00		
	2	.....	31.25		

Suppose we attempt to make an incremental comparison as follows:

Period 0	0	Cash flows identical
1	$80.00	Cash flow of Z exceeds that of Y
2	$88.75	Cash flow of Y exceeds that of Z

We see that the cash flow of Y is $80.00 less in Year 1, and $88.75 more than Z in year 2. As before we can compute the yield) on the incremental cash flow. An outlay of $80.00 that returns $88.75 one year later has a yield of 10.9 per cent. An investment such as this would be desirable for a company whose cost of capital is only 5 per cent. Again we are really dealing with a problem of the scale of the investment, but in this case the opportunity for the additional investment occurs one year later.

The same result can be reached by a somewhat different route if we ask how much cash the company would have on hand at the end of the second year if it accepted investment Y and if it accepted investment Z. Both investments give some cash proceeds at the end of the first year. The value of the investment at the end of the second year will depend upon what is done with the cash proceeds of the first year. Since the cost of capital is 5 per cent, we can assume that the cash proceeds of the first year could be reinvested to yield 5 per cent.[2] Then investment Y would result in a total cash accumulation by the end of the year of $141.00 (105 per cent of $20 plus $120). Investment Z would result in a cash accumulation of only $136.25 (105 per cent of $100 plus $31.25).[3]

---

[2] The term cost of capital as used in the first eleven chapters of this book refers to a rate of interest which measures both the lending rate (the yield of available investments outside the firm) and the cost of borrowing (obtaining capital from sources outside the firm). The *lending rate* is assumed to be equal to the *borrowing rate;* thus funds have a minimum cost to the firm equal to the cost of capital. (The firm can lend the funds and obtain a return equal to that yield.) It would *not* be appropriate to assume that funds have a cost *higher* than the cost of capital, since the firm can always borrow funds to take advantage of such investments. Compare the above discussion with Chapter 12, where we examine the consequences of relaxing the assumption that the lending rate and the borrowing rate are equal.

[3] The yield method implicitly assumes that proceeds are reinvested at the same return as the yield of the investments. The present-value method implicitly assumes that the proceeds are reinvested at the cost of capital. The fact that the latter assumption is more valid (see footnote 2) is one reason why the present-value method is the preferred method.

One of the disadvantages associated with the use of the yield method is the necessity of computing the yield on the incremental cash proceeds in order to determine which of a pair of mutually exclusive investments is preferable. If there are more than two mutually exclusive investments, we shall have to conduct an elimination tournament among the mutually exclusive investments. Taking any pair, we compute the yield on the incremental cash flow and attempt to decide which of the two investments is preferable. The winner of this round would then be compared in the same manner with one of the remaining investments until the grand champion investment was discovered.

Multiple Yields

When the yield method is used, the ability to choose the best of two investments depends on whether a given series of incremental cash flows is like a conventional investment, in which case the higher the yield, the better; or is like a loan, in which case the lower the yield or interest cost, the better. The following example illustrates a case where the choice is not obvious. The cash flows represented by two mutually exclusive investments, R and S, are given in Table 2. The last line, labeled I, shows the incremental cash flows.

Table 2

Investment	Cash flows		
	Period 0	Period 1	Period 2
R	− 90,000	$+190,909	$+ 60,000
S	− 72,727	+ 20,000	+160,000
I	$−162,727	+170,909	−100,000

The cash flows, R and S, are conventional investments because they have outlays *followed by proceeds.* But for investment I, the outlays of Period zero are followed by proceeds in Period 1 and then by further outlays in Period 2. With this kind of cash flow we cannot say, "The higher the yield, the better," or "The lower the yield, the better."

Suppose the mutually exclusive investments R and S are available to a company whose cost of capital is 15 per cent. If the yield of the incremental cash flows I is 10 per cent, should the company accept R or S? If the yield of the incremental cash flows I is 25 per cent, should the company accept R or S? It turns out that the present value of the cash proceeds is equal to the present value of the cash outlays at a 10 per cent rate of discount and at a 25 per cent rate of discount. The yield of I is *both* 10 and 25 per cent.

Interpretation of Multiple Yields

To help illustrate the relationship between the yield of an investment and the present-value measure, and to explain why multiple yields occur and how they should be interpreted, it is helpful to introduce a graph at this point. In Table 3 we describe three series of cash flows, T, U, and I. T can be thought of as a simple 1-year loan at 15 per cent interest, as seen from the point of view of the lender. U is the same loan, as seen from the point of view of the borrower, who first receives funds and later repays them with interest. I is the multiple-yield, incremental cash flow described previously. For T, U, and I in Figure 1, the vertical axis represents the net present value of the corresponding cash flow for various possible rates of interest, which are measured along the horizontal axis. By net present value we mean the algebraic sum of the

present value of the proceeds and the present value of the
outlays.

Table 3

Investment	Cash flows		
	Period 0	Period 1	Period 2
T	− 100	+ 115	
U	+ 100	− 115	
I	−72,727	+170,909	−100,000

[margin note:] I yr loan at 15% int

Since the yield of a cash flow is defined as the rate of interest
that makes the net present value zero, the yield is the point at
which the net present-value line crosses the horizontal axis
(which measures the rate of interest).

[margin note:] multiple yield
incremental cash flow I

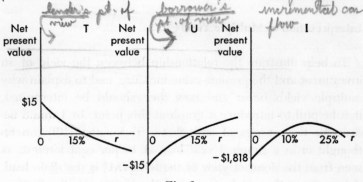

[handwritten labels: lender's pt. of view T   borrower's pt. of view U]

Fig. 1

In Figure T the net present-value line drops as the rate of
interest increases. At interest rates lower than 15 per cent, the
net present value is positive; at interest rates greater than 15
per cent, it is negative. This general configuration typifies
those conventional investments in which a series of cash outlays

is followed by a series of cash proceeds. For such cash flows, the yield represents the highest rate of discount at which the net present value would be positive and the investment desirable.

Figure U is similar to Figure T but inverted. From the point of view of the borrower, the loan is worthwhile only if the rate of interest at which he finds it appropriate to discount future funds (which represents how much these funds are worth to him) is greater than the rate of interest he pays on the loan. Thus, for the borrower, the net present value of the transaction is negative for rates of discount less than 15 per cent and positive for higher rates of discount. For the loan type of cash flows, the yield represents the lowest rate of discount at which the net present value would be positive and the borrowing desirable.

Figure I shows the graph for the multiple-yield cash flow I. The first part of the graph is typical of that of a loan; the second has the downward slope typical of the ordinary investment. This series of cash flows would be worthwhile at rates of discount between 10 and 25 per cent; outside this range it is not advisable. There is a corresponding inverted cash flow that could be obtained by converting the proceeds to outlays and the outlays to proceeds. The resulting cash flows would be desirable only at interest rates that were less than 10 per cent or greater than 25 per cent. Thus we can compare the cash flows that would result from undertaking investment R instead of investment S and obtain a decision of R is more desirable than S at interest rates greater than 10 per cent and less than 25 per cent. Or we can compare the cash flows that result from undertaking S instead of R and obtain a decision that S is more desirable than R at interest rates less than 10 per cent and greater than 25 per cent. These are equivalent ways of saying the same thing.

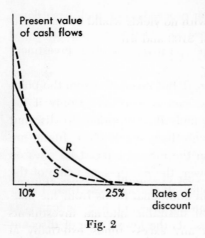

Present value of cash flows

R

S

10%   25%   Rates of
                      discount

Fig. 2

In each case, a simple calculation of the net present value of the investment at the correct rate of discount would have provided the correct answer and would have bypassed the problem of multiple yields and the loan type of investments. Figure 2 shows that R has a higher present value at rates of interest of 10 to 25 per cent.

Significance of Nonconventional Cash Flows

Earlier,[4] we defined conventional investments (or loans) as those in which there were one or more periods of net cash outlays (or net proceeds) followed by one or more periods of net cash proceeds (or net outlays). It is important to determine whether a series of cash flows is conventional because *a conventional investment will have one and only one yield.*

If an investment is not conventional, we consider it to be a nonconventional investment. With a nonconventional investment, any of the following is possible:

1. The investment has *no* yield.
2. The investment has *one* yield.
3. The investment has *more than one* yield.

An example of a nonconventional investment with two yields was given in the preceding section. An example of a

[4] See page 5.

nonconventional investment with no yields would be an investment having cash proceeds of $100 and $150 in Periods 1 and 3, respectively, and cash outlays of $200 in period 2. This "investment" has no yield, but it has a positive present value for all rates of interest.[5]

Summary

If a corporation knows its cost of capital (at least approximately) and can either obtain additional funds from the market at that cost of capital, if desirable internal investments are available, or can invest any excess funds externally at that cost of capital, then either of the two discounted cash flow procedures can be used to make correct investment decisions.

If the present-value method is used, the rules for making correct investment decisions are quite simple in principle. They are: (1) for each investment proposal, compute the net present value of the proposal, using the cost of capital as the discount rate; (2) if the choice is between accepting or rejecting the investment, accept it if its net present value is greater than zero, and reject it if the net present value is less than zero; (3) if a series of investment proposals is available and the present value of each is greater than zero, but only one can be accepted, then accept the one for which the present value is the greatest.[6]

[5] Mathematically, finding a yield for this series of cash flows is equivalent to finding a real number x that would satisfy the folowing equation:

$$0 = 100 - 200x + 150x^2$$

But this equation has no solution in the domain of real numbers.

[6] The problem of time-period comparability complicates this analysis. See Chapter 5 for an explanation of the procedure to be followed when the lives of two mutually exclusive investments are unequal.

Although the yield method can also be used to make correct investment choices, and if properly used will in fact lead to the same choices as the present-value method, the rules that must be followed if the yield method is to be used properly are quite complex. The complexities arise from the following considerations:

1. A single investment may have more than one yield. The present value of the cash proceeds from an investment may equal the present value of the costs at x and at y per cent. This may mean that the investment is profitable only if the cost of capital is between x and y per cent, or it may mean that the investment is profitable only if the cost of capital is either less than x per cent or greater than y per cent.

2. If a group of two or more mutually exclusive investments is available, a direct comparison of their yields will not necessarily lead to the correct choice of the best alternative. It is necessary to analyze the investment proposals two at a time, decide which one of each pair is more desirable, and then compare the more desirable investment with one of the others, to decide which of those two is more desirable, continuing until by a process of elimination the best one can be determined. By contrast the present-value method indicates immediately which one of a group of mutually exclusive proposals is more desirable.

3. In interpreting the yield of a single investment, it is necessary to first determine whether the cash flows correspond to an ordinary investment or to a loan from the point of view of the borrower.

For most of us, the present-value method is simpler, safer, easier, and more direct. The remainder of this book will proceed in terms of this approach. However, the yield method may be useful to dramatize the desirability of an investment.

For example, an investment may have a net present value of $10,000, using the cost of capital of 10 per cent; thus it should be undertaken. The relative desirability of the investment (the desirability of undertaking it compared to not undertaking it) may be judged better if we know that the yield is 60 per cent or if we know that the yield is 10.1 per cent. Theoretically and mathematically all independent investments with a positive present value should be undertaken, but the practical business-man may want some measure of how much "elbow room" he has before he is financially worse off because of having made the investment. The present-value method does not accom-plish this, since the net present value may result from having made cash outlays of $5,000 or $5,000,000.[7] The yield method does accomplish this to some extent.[8]

A NOTE ON CONTINUOUS CASH FLOWS AND CONTINUOUS DISCOUNTING

The assumption is made throughout this book that all cash flows occur instantaneously, usually at the end or beginning of a period, and that interest is compounded annually. Either of or both these assumptions may be varied. Interest may be compounded monthly, weekly, daily, or continuously. Instead of assuming that the cash flows occur at the end of a period,

---

[7] Some authors suggest dividing the present value of the cash proceeds by the present value of the investment type of outlays to obtain an index of present value (proceeds per dollar of outlay, both expressed in terms of present value). This procedure is not recommended by the present authors because of the impossibility of distinguishing between investment type of outlays and expense type of outlays. For example, is advertising a substraction from the cash proceeds or an addition to investment?

[8] For a detailed explanation of why the ranking is only approximate, see Harold Bierman, Jr., and Seymour Smidt, "Capital Budgeting and the Problem of Reinvesting Cash Proceeds," *The Journal of Business*, October 1957, pp. 276–279.

they may also be presumed to occur monthly, weekly, daily, or continuously.

If there is a finite number of compoundings and payments, then the following formula may be used to compute the present value of an annuity.

$$A = R \frac{1 - \left(1 + \dfrac{j}{m}\right)^{-mn}}{p\left[\left(1 + \dfrac{j}{m}\right)\dfrac{m}{p} - 1\right]}$$

where R = annual rate of payment
   j = nominal rate of interest
   m = number of compoundings per year
   n = number of years
   p = number of payments per year
   A = the present value of the annuity

If we allow m and p to increase beyond bound, that is, to approach infinity, then we have the situation where interest is being compounded continuously and cash flows are occurring continuously.

Continuous Interest

To convert a nominal rate of interest j, which is compounded m times annually, to an effective rate of interest r, compounded annually, we make use of the fact that

$$(1 + r)^{-n} = \left(1 + \frac{j}{m}\right)^{-mn}$$

Since the present value of a dollar may be computed by using $(1 + r)^{-n}$, we can substitute the right-hand side of the equation and compute the present value of a dollar by using

$[1 + (j/m)]^{-mn}$. If m is allowed to increase beyond bound (approach infinity), we have:

$$\lim_{m \to \infty} \left(1 + \frac{j}{m}\right)^{-mn} = e^{-jn}$$

e is equal to 2.71828 and is the base of natural or Naperian system of logarithms.

Thus the present value of a dollar for n periods with interest compounded continuously may be computed by using the nominal interest rate.

Example. Let

$$j = 0.02$$

$$n = 1$$

To compute the present value of a dollar, assuming that interest is compounded continuously,

$$e^{-jn} = e^{-0.02}$$

$$e^{-0.02} = (2.71828)^{-0.02}$$

Using logarithms,

$$\log 2.71828 = 0.434295$$

$$-0.02 \log 2.71828 = -0.00868590$$

$$= 9.99131410 - 10.0$$

$$e^{-0.02} = 0.9802$$

The 0.9802 resulting from continuous compounding should be compared with 0.9804, which is the present value of a dollar, using 2 per cent compounded annually.

Continuous Payments

If instead of $1.00 being received at the end of each year, the payments are received in small installments (i.e., continuously) throughout the period, the present value of the annuity for n years will be

$$A = \int_0^n e^{-jt}dt = \frac{1 - e^{-jn}}{j}$$

where j = nominal rate of interest.

Example: Compute the present value of dollar per period, assuming that interest is compounded continuously and the cash flows occur continuously.

$$j = 0.02$$
$$n = 1$$
$$e^{-jn} = e^{-0.02} = 0.9802 \text{ (see preceding example)}$$
$$A = \frac{1 - e^{-jn}}{j} = \frac{1 - 0.9802}{0.02}$$
$$= \frac{0.0198}{0.02} = 0.99$$

The 0.99 should be compared with the 0.9802, obtained in the preceding example with continuous compounding but one instantaneous payment, and the 0.9804 of annual compounding and one payment.

4

The Meaning of Present Value

The preceding chapters have argued that measures of investment worth that do not utilize discounted cash flow concepts can frequently give incorrect rankings of investments. But the fact that a measure of investment worth incorporates discounted cash flow concepts is no guarantee that it will give correct results in all cases.

The thoughtful reader will have noticed that the argument up to this point has been largely a negative one. We have emphasized the shortcomings of the methods in common use. But we have done little more than hint at the reason for preferring the discounted cash flow approach for measuring the value of an investment. In this chapter we shall attempt to present in a systematic and positive way our reasons for recommending the use of the present-value measure. We hope to make clear the advantages as well as the limitations of this method. It is by no means a cure-all for the problem of the businessman harassed by the difficult problems of developing, evaluating, and choosing long-run investments.

We believe that the present-value method can make a definite and important contribution to the solution of the problems of making investment decisions. But it is vitally important that the user understand what it is he is accomplishing

51

by discounting the cash flow of an investment, and what he is not accomplishing. Unfortunately some of those who have advocated use of this procedure have done so for the wrong reasons or have made claims for it that cannot be fulfilled. All of us recognize that the simple screwdriver is a useful tool when properly used. There is no need to revise that opinion because an inexperienced do-it-yourself enthusiast reports disastrous consequences from his attempt to use a screwdriver where a chisel was required.

A Bird in Hand versus Two in the Bush

Most businessmen will agree that a dollar in hand today is more valuable to them than a dollar to be received a year from now. If we pursue the matter, we would very likely find a variety of reasons for this preference. A survey may reveal the following answers to the inquiry, "Why is a dollar in hand today worth more to you than a dollar to be received in one year?"

1. "As a businessman I live in an uncertain world. A dollar in the bank is something I can count on. A promise to pay me a dollar in one year is only a promise until I actually get the money. The promise may be made in perfectly good faith, but any number of things may occur between now and next year to prevent the fulfillment of the promise."

2. "Human nature naturally attaches more weight to present pleasures than to the more distant joys. Offer a young man the choice between a trip to Europe during the coming summer, or a trip five summers from now, and he will nearly always choose the earlier trip. Since future income is meaningful in terms of the pleasant things it makes possible, we would al-

ways prefer to receive a given total amount of income as nearly as possible in the immediate future, unless considerations of tax effects dictate another choice."

3. "A dollar received now is more valuable than a dollar to be received five years from now because of the investment possibilities that are available for today's dollar. By investing the dollar received today, I can have considerably more than a dollar in five years. For that reason, future receipts should always be discounted."

Our three hypothetical respondents have suggested three separate reasons for attaching more weight to dollars on hand than to dollars that may be received in the future. Each of the reasons is a correct one in important respects. But only the last one of them is sufficient justification for using discounted cash flow procedures in evaluating investment proposals. The other two reasons, insofar as they are appropriate in any situation, need to be taken into account in other ways. Let us consider each of the three reasons in turn.

Uncertainty

Our first hypothetical respondent stressed the fact that one can never be certain about the receipt of future cash. For this reason, when comparing today's dollars with future dollars, some allowance must be made for the possibility that the estimated future dollars may never in fact materialize. It is not the need for this allowance that is in question but the suitability of using present-value approaches to make these allowances. In applying to estimates of future cash proceeds the discount factors found in a present-value table, one is implicitly making a very special assumption about the nature of the uncertainty involved in the estimates. This special assumption may be valid in particular instances. The objection is to the application of this special assumption to investment proposals as a matter of course, without determining whether the special assumption is in fact justifiable.

The special assumption involved in using present-value tables to discount for uncertainty is that the probability of a dollar of estimated cash actually materializing will decrease each year by a fixed percentage of the probability in the preceding year. The amount of the percentage decrease each year depends upon the rate of interest chosen. Suppose we consider an investment to build and equip a plant for producing a new product. In some instances the major uncertainty may be related to the cost of constructing the plant, while the demand for the resulting output may be easily predictable in advance with very little uncertainty. This could be the case if the product to be produced were to be sold in advance through a long-term sales contract, whereas the design, construction, and operation of the plant may involve new or unusual engineering problems creating an unpredictable cost. The use of atomic energy to generate electric power is a tangible example of this situation. In such a situation the discounting of future revenues, themselves fairly certain, seems a poor way of allowing for the uncertainty about how much the fixed plant will cost. In another instance the main element of uncertainty may revolve around consumer acceptance of the product. The alternatives may be either a very high or a very low level of consumer acceptance, with a corresponding probability of either a series of years with very high cash proceeds or a series of years of little or no cash proceeds. Again there seems to be no reason to suppose that the use of present-value discount factors will lead to a correct or appropriate allowance for uncertainty in this instance.

Some suggestions for handling data to improve the judgments of the risks involved in investments will be discussed in Chapter 9. However, no completely satisfactory and universally applicable method is known. In particular, the application of present-value discount factors to preliminary estimates of expected cash flows *will not* ordinarily be an acceptable way of adjusting for risk. In the special situations in which this technique is an acceptable means of adjusting for risk, the resultant discounted cash flows should not be referred to as present values but as expected cash flows adjusted for risk. To allow for time differences in the value of money, present-value discount factors would have to be applied to these estimates a second time.

Subjective Time Preference

The second reason suggested above as a justification for discounting future income is the time preference of the individuals involved. Undoubtedly there are individuals who, if given the choice, would prefer an additional $100 of consumption immediately to the opportunity of obtaining an additional $110 of disposable income available a year from now. Such an individual might be acting rationally if he rejected a riskless opportunity to invest $100 today in such a way that it would return $110 in one year. The investment should be rejected if acceptance of the investment requires a corresponding reduction in the investor's immediate consumption.

But acceptance of the investment will not require a reduction in immediate consumption if opportunities to borrow money at less than 10 per cent are also available now. Suppose the individual in question accepts the investment and at the same time borrows $100 at 5 per cent to maintain his immediate consumption. At the end of a year the proceeds from the investment will enable him to pay off the loan plus its accrued interest and still retain an additional $5.00.

In general, the subjective time preferences of the owners of a corporation do not need to be consulted in making investment decisions for that corporation, provided the corporation can obtain additional funds in the capital market and invest its excess funds, if any, on the capital market. It is only the rates at which it can obtain or lend funds that are relevant. Accordingly the purpose of a business enterprise in discounting expected future cash proceeds is not to take account of the subjective time preferences of the investors (unless the investors do not for one reason or another have access to the capital market).

The manager of a business owned by a small group of individuals may, and sometimes should, adjust the investment policy of the company to take into consideration the cash requirements of the owners. But the shareholders of a large corporation are usually a diverse group. They may pay marginal tax rates on dividends of anywhere from zero (for certain individuals and nonprofit institutions) to 90 per cent for wealthy individuals. At any given time, some shareholders will be reinvesting a part of their dividend receipts, while others will be reducing their portfolios. The large corporation cannot adjust its investment policy to the needs of individual shareholders, and luckily, it does not need to do so in order to serve their best interest. A corporation should be expected to make the best use of the funds available to it, which is the purpose of evaluating investment proposals according to their discounted cash flows by using the cost of capital as the rate of discount.

Alternative Uses of Money

The purpose of discounting the cash flows expected from an investment is to determine whether the investment yields more cash than alternative uses of the same amount of money. In the case of an independent investment proposal in a firm not subject to capital rationing,[1] whose current dividend has been determined, the alternatives to rejecting the investment are to borrow more funds or to invest less outside the firm. If the costs of borrowing are the same as the rate that could be earned by investing elsewhere, the alternatives are equivalent. It should be mentioned that the term *borrowing* is used here in a very broad sense to include raising additional equity capital as well as the more conventional forms of debt. The justification of this use of the term will be presented in Chapters 10 and 11 in connection with our discussion of the costs of capital.

Meaning of the Present-value Calculation when the Alternative Is to Borrow Less

To illustrate the meaning of the present-value computation when the investment must be financed by borrowing, we may use Investment B, described in Table 1 of Chapter 2. This investment requires an initial outlay of $10,000 and offers proceeds of $5,000 per year for three years. At a 6 per cent rate of interest, compounded annually, the present value of the proceeds is $13,365, so that the net present value of the investment is $3,365. The value of the proceeds expected from the $10,000 investment is sufficient to pay off the principal and

[1] For a discussion of capital rationing, see Chapter 12.

accrued interest on a loan of $13,365 at 6 per cent payable in three installments of $5,000 each. One way of interpreting the meaning of the present-value calculation is to realize that a firm could borrow a total of $13,365 at 6 per cent, apply $10,000 of the loan proceeds to the investment, and immediately distribute the remaining $3,365 as income to the owners. The proceeds of $5,000 per year from the $10,000 investment would be sufficient to repay the loan and interest by the end of the third year. The calculations in Table 1 illustrate this arrangement.

Table 1. Loan Values Outstanding at the End of Each Period when a Loan Equal to the Present Value of the Proceeds of an Investment Is Made and Proceeds Are Used to Repay Loan

			Investment B		
Period	Loan outstanding at beginning	Accrued interest (6%)	Total amount owed before payment	Investment proceeds applied to loan	Loan outstanding at end
1	$13,365	$802	$14,167	$5,000	$9,167
2	9,167	550	9,717	5,000	4,717
3	4,717	283	5,000	5,000	0

We mentioned earlier that making allowances for the subjective time preferences with respect to receipt of income is not the purpose of the discounting process as long as the income recipient has access to the capital market. In the case of the above example we assumed that the owners of the firm chose to receive the profit resulting from the investment in the year it was made. Actually any pattern of income receipts, such that their present value was equal to $3,365, could have been selected. If some of or all the income withdrawals were deferred past the year in which the investment was made, the actual withdrawals that could be made would exceed $3,365. Suppose the owners elected to borrow $10,000, the amount required to undertake the investment, and to withdraw their proceeds only after the initial loan had been repaid. Under these circumstances the owners would be enabled to withdraw $4,008 at the end of the third year, since this amount has a present value of $3,365 with an interest rate of 6 per cent. Table 2 illustrates the loan balances outstanding at various times under this arrangement.

Table 2. Loan Balances Outstanding at the End of Each Period when a Loan Equal to the Initial Investment Outlay Is Made and Proceeds Are Used to Repay Loan before Any Withdrawals

	Investment B				
Period	Loan outstanding at beginning	Accrued interest (6%)	Total amount owed before payment	Investment proceeds applied to loan	Loan outstanding at end
1	$10,000	$600	$10,600	$5,000	$5,600
2	5,600	336	5,936	5,000	936
3	936	56	992	992	0

Proceeds available for distribution to owners = $4,008

If the owners preferred to withdraw the same amount each year over the life of the investment, then annual payments of $1,259 could be withdrawn. The reader may wish to test his understanding of the meaning of present-value calculations by working out an example to prove to himself that annual payments of this amount could be made to the owners, the remainder of the cash proceeds applied to repayment of the loan, and the loan completely paid off by the end of the third year.

Meaning of Present-value Calculations when the Alternative Is to Lend Money outside the Firm

So far we have considered the case where the investment within the firm was to be financed by obtaining additional capital from outside the firm. This may seem to be an artificial comparison to a company whose past operations are generating enough cash to undertake all the worthwhile investments that seem to be available within the company. This situation is not uncommon. However, it is a mistake to assume that such funds are "free," since there is the possibility of investing funds outside the firm. For example, if after adjusting for the risk involved, the possibility of earning 6 per cent from investments outside the firm is available, then proposed internal*investments ought to be compared with these external profit opportunities; otherwise, the company may undertake internal investments that are not so pr~fitable as those obtainable outside.

Consider investment B as an example. In the earlier situation, where the funds to finance the investment were obtained from outside the firm, we said that we could interpret the fact that investment B had a present value of $3,365 as meaning that a loan equal to the amount required to finance investment B plus $3,365 could be negotiated, the excess over immediate needs ($3,365) withdrawn, and the proceeds from the investment then would be sufficient to repay the entire loan.

Assume that the firm has funds available from internal sources. The owner has estimated that by applying $10,000 of those funds to internal investment B, the company could generate cash proceeds of $5,000 per year for three years. We could ask how much money would the firm have to invest outside at 6 per cent per year in order to generate cash proceeds of $5,000 per year for three years. Since the present value of $5,000 per year for three years at 6 per cent is $13,365, it would require an external investment of that amount to generate the same cash proceeds that investment B would generate internally from an investment of only $10,000. This is illustrated in Table 3. The reader will note that the figures used in Table 3 are precisely the same for each period as those in Table 1. The only difference is that a different set of labels for the column headings is appropriate in this instance.

Table 3. External Investment Earning 6 Per Cent Required to Produce Cash Proceeds Identical to Those Produced by an Internal Investment

	Investment B				
Period	Initial external investment	Accrued earnings (6%)	Total external investment before withdrawal	Equivalent proceeds withdrawn	Remaining external investment
1	$13,365	$802	$14,167	$5,000	$9,167
2	9,167	550	9,717	5,000	4,717
3	4,717	283	5,000	5,000	0

In the case where funds are available from internal sources, and external investment opportunities to earn 6 per cent per year are available, the fact that an internal investment with a present value of $3,365 is available means that $13,365 would have to be invested externally to generate the same cash proceeds as the internal investment of $10,000.

As in the previous case, the subjective time preferences of the owners should not affect the choice between the internal or external investment. The reader may verify for himself by working out examples that any pattern of cash generated by investing $13,365 externally could also be generated with a commitment of $10,000 in investment B and an appropriate decision in regard to the application of the proceeds.

One further interpretation of the net present value of $3,365 of investment B is possible. The $3,365 is like an unrealized capital gain. For an expenditure of $10,000 we obtain proceeds whose present value totals $13,365 and whose net present value is $3,365. Before investing, we have $10,000 in cash; after investing, we have prospects of cash proceeds whose present value is $13,365. Thus our asset position can be improved in terms of present values (by $3,365) by making the investment.

5

Classifying Investments

In Chapter 1 an investment was defined as a "commitment of resources, made in the hope of realizing benefits that are expected to occur over a reasonably long, future period of time." According to this definition, neither the resources nor the benefits need be in the form of explicit cash flows. A decision to have an accounting executive spend a month studying the capabilities of various types of electronic data processing equipment would be an investment in the sense of this definition. The executive's time is a scarce resource, since he could have spent the month in other activities that are valuable to the firm. In the first instance, at least, the expected benefits will be increased knowledge by management of a relatively new technology. Thus there is no explicit cash outlay or cash inflow, but there is an investment.

Any useful scheme of controlling investments must be based on a classification of types of investments. Different kinds of investments raise different problems, are of different relative importance to the firm, and different persons will be competent to evaluate their significance. By classifying types of investments, each investment proposal will receive attention from persons qualified to analyze it.

Investments may be classified in many ways. Some of these are described below.

1. According to the kinds of scarce resources used by the investment. For example, does the investment require important amounts of cash, of floor space, of the time of key personnel (and personnel may be also classified: sales, production, research, top management, legal staff, etc.)?

2. According to the amount of each of the resources that are required. For example, with respect to the amount of immediate cash outlays required, we could classify investments as requiring less than $500, between $500 and $5,000, and over $5,000.

3. According to the way benefits from the investment are affected by other possible investments. Some investments stand on their own feet. Others will be improved if supplementary investments are made; still others will be useless if competing investments are accepted. For example, the worth of another fork-lift truck may depend on whether or not the plan for adding an automatic conveyor system is accepted.

4. According to the form in which the benefits are received; thus investments may generate greater cash flows, reduce the risks associated with poor business conditions, reduce the accident rate, improve employee morale, or eliminate a community nuisance such as excessive smoke or noise.

5. According to whether the incremental benefits are the result of lower cost or increased sales, or whether they merely prevent a decline in sales or market share.

6. According to the business activity to which they are most closely related. Thus an oil company may classify investments according to which one of the following activities they support: exploration, production, transportation, refining, or marketing.

Many other methods of classification could be suggested.[1] Clearly no single scheme of classification will be equally valid for all uses or for all companies. The essential task is to develop a classification system for investments that is appropriate to the activity of the business and the organizational structure of the particular company.

In this book we are first concerned with investments for which both the resources used and the benefits to be received can be measured to an important degree in terms of cash flows. Secondly, the analytical methods developed in this book will be most useful for investments that are important enough to the firm to warrant a relatively careful study of their potential profitability. In the remainder of this chapter we shall consider the classification of investments that is based on the way the benefits from a given investment are affected by other possible investments.

DEPENDENT AND INDEPENDENT INVESTMENTS

In evaluating the investment proposals presented to management, it is important to be aware of the possible interrelationships between pairs of investment proposals. A given investment proposal may be independent of, or dependent on, another investment proposal. The first investment proposal will be said to be independent of the second if the cash flows (or more generally the benefits) expected from accepting the first investment would be the same regardless of whether the second investment is accepted or rejected. If the benefits to be expected from the first investment are affected by the de-

---

[1] An interesting discussion of possible methods of classifying investments can be found in Joel Dean, *Capital Budgeting,* Columbia University Press, New York, 1951, pp. 82–88.

cision to accept or reject the second investment, then the first investment is said to be dependent on the second. It should be clear that when one investment is dependent on another, some attention must be given to the question of whether decisions about the first investment can or should be made separately from decisions about the second.

Independent Investments

1. Technically possible to undertake investment A whether or not investment B is accepted.

2. Net benefits to be expected from the first investment must not be affected by the acceptance or rejection of the second.

In order for investment A to be independent of investment B, two conditions must be satisfied. First, it must be technically possible to undertake investment A whether or not investment B is accepted. Thus it is *not* possible to build a school and shopping center on the same site, and therefore the proposal to build the one is not independent of a proposal to build the other. Secondly, the net benefits to be expected from the first investment must not be affected by the acceptance or rejection of the second. If the estimates of the cash outlays and the cash inflows for investment A are not the same when B is either accepted or rejected, then the two investments are not independent. Thus it is technically possible to build a toll bridge and operate a ferry across adjacent points on a river, but the two investments are not independent because the proceeds from one will be affected by the existence of the other. The two investments would not be independent in the sense in which we are using the term, even if the traffic across the river at this point were sufficient so that both the bridge and the ferry could be operated profitably.

Sometimes it will happen that two investments cannot both be accepted because the firm does not have enough cash to finance both. This situation could occur if the amount of cash available for investments were strictly limited, by management rather than by the capital market, or if increments of funds obtained from the capital market cost more than previous increments. In such a situation the acceptance of one investment may cause the rejection of the other. But we shall not then say that the two investments are dependent. To do so would make all investments for such a firm dependent, and this is not a useful definition for our purposes.

Dependent Investments

The dependency relationship can be further classified. If a decision to undertake the second investment will increase the benefits expected from the first (or decrease the costs of undertaking the first without changing the benefits), then the second investment is said to be a *complement* of the first. If the decision to undertake the second investment will decrease the benefits expected from the first (or increase the costs of undertaking the first without changing the benefits), then the second is said to be a *substitute* for the first. In the extreme case where the potential benefits to be derived from the first investment will completely disappear if the second investment is accepted, or where it is technically impossible to undertake the first when the second has been accepted, then the two investments are said to be *mutually exclusive*. It is also possible to define an extreme case for investments that are complements. Suppose that the second investment is impossible (technologically) or would result in no benefits whatsoever if the first investment were not accepted. Then the first investment can be said to be a *prerequisite* of the second.

It may be helpful to think of the possible relationships between investments as being arrayed along a line segment. At the extreme left we have the situation where investment A is a prerequisite to investment B. In the center of the line we have a situation where investment A is independent of investment B. At the extreme right-hand end of the line we have the situation where investment A is mutually exclusive with respect to investment B. As we move to the right from the left-hand half of the line, we have varying degrees of complementariness, decreasing as we proceed to the right. Similarly, on the right-hand side of the line, we represent varying degrees of substitutability, increasing as we proceed outward to the the right. A graphic representation is presented below.

			Mutually
Prerequisite		Independent	exclusive
↓ Strong complement	Weak complement ↓	Weak substitute Strong substitute	↓

One additional complication in connection with complementary investments should be mentioned here. The complementary relationship need not be symmetrical. Suppose that we consider the building of a new factory as one investment and the purchase of an air conditioning unit for the factory as the second investment. The two investments are clearly complementary. But the relationship need not be symmetrical, since the new factory may be profitable without air conditioning. With air conditioning, worker efficiency may go up, so that the factory is even more profitable. The additional efficiency resulting from the addition of air conditioning may properly be called the return or benefits resulting from the expenditure on air-conditioning equipment. But the air-conditioning equipment by itself is useless unless there is a factory in which it can be used. The factory is a prerequisite to the investment for the air-conditioning equipment, but the air conditioning is not a prerequisite to the investment in the factory building.

Administrative Implications

The number of possible relationships that may exist between pairs of complementary investments is very large. In dealing with investments that are complementarily related, the most effective technique is to combine sets of investments proposals in such a way that the new proposal is either an independent proposal or one of a set of mutually exclusive proposals. In the preceding example, instead of considering two complementary investment proposals, a factory and the air-conditioning equipment for the factory, we can reformulate the problem as one involving a choice between mutually exclusive investment alternatives, namely, a factory with air conditioning or a factory without air conditioning.

In most large organizations, operating procedures require that proposals for capital investment which exceed specified limits must be submitted by the sponsor to higher executive levels for review and approval before actual expenditures can be authorized. Except in unusual circumstances such proposals should consist of independent investment proposals for which an accept or reject decision is appropriate; or they should comprise a set of mutually exclusive proposals, such that either the whole set must be rejected or only one of the mutually exclusive alternatives can be accepted. No system of controlling capital expenditures can operate effectively if management finds that after having approved a seemingly highly profitable investment, additional investments that do not generate any profits on their own account are presented as being absolutely necessary to implement the profit potential of the initial investment proposals.

Example: The research and development section of a large chemical manufacturing firm submitted technical data on a new product to one of the firm's operating divisions. After investigation of the product by the engineering, production, and sales staffs, the operating division management decided that the product should be added to their line. Since existing facilities were not adequate for the production of the new product, a capital appropriation request for the new plant and equipment was submitted for review and approval to the firm's executive committee. On review by the executive committee the following deficiencies were uncovered: (1) The appropriation request did not include an estimate of the working capital requirements that would be required to operate the new plant and market the resulting product; (2) one of the raw materials required in the new process would be purchased from another operating division of the company, and the increased output of that division would have required additional plant and equipment expenditures by the supplier division; (3) the new product was partially competitive with one of the company's existing products, and the decline in the profit potential from this existing product had not been taken into consideration; (4) distribution of the new product would require acquisition of additional storage facilities, since demand for the product was seasonal, but efficient production would require a steady rate of production. The proposal was returned to the operating division for further study. After additional investigation it was determined that the company could most effectively utilize the new product by licensing other manufacturers to produce and market it.

In developing an investment proposal to be submitted to higher levels for review and approval, the sponsor and his staff should normally include as a part of the single package whatever complementary investments seem necessary or desirable. Similarly, if the proposed investment will serve as a partial substitute for any investments to which the firm is already committed or which are under consideration, this fact should be noted in submitting the proposal.

If some of the choices involved in planning the investment are considered sufficiently important that the final decision must be made by top management, the investment proposal should be submitted in the form of a set of mutually exclusive alternatives. Examples would be the decision on the location of a new plant or the possibility of including an important piece of auxiliary equipment. This procedure has the advantage of enabling top management to examine in an orderly fashion the major alternatives involved. It also enables management to make decisions at a stage in the planning of the expenditure when the special knowledge, experience, and insight of the senior executives can be effectively brought to bear on the proposal. Too often such choices are not presented to management until previous commitments have largely foreclosed the opportunity to exercise choice, and management is presented in effect with a *fait accompli*.

Ordinarily the cost figures contained in an investment proposal submitted to top management will be based on a careful but necessarily preliminary estimate of the final cost of the proposed project. On major projects, the expensive step of preparing detailed specifications and working drawings should be deferred until the project has actually been approved. Once approval has been obtained, management will proceed with the detailed planning of the project. At this stage a great many decisions will have to be made on such questions as the type of materials to be used in construction, the choice of equipment, and even the location of a plant if no definite decision on this point was made in the preliminary plans. Given the general approval for the project as a whole, these choices are mainly among different ways of accomplishing the same objective, that is, the alternatives are mutually exclusive. Although the most important of these choices, such as plant location, may be submitted to higher management levels, many of the less important decisions will necessarily be made by lower levels of management or by staff personnel.

In order to ensure coordination when decision making is

decentralized, it is necessary to set up means of communicating information about policies and objectives of the organization so that decisions made independently in various parts of the organization will contribute to the goals of the organization. When the decentralized decision-making powers grant authority to make investment-type decisions, the procedures recommended in this book can provide an important means of assuring that uniform standards of choice consistent with over-all organizational goals are available to the many separate decision-making centers.

As could be expected, these problems occur not only in business organizations but also in nonprofit organizations, both public and private. The following example is based on a situation that occurred in a university.

Example: The head of the buildings and grounds department of a large university obtained approval to replace and modernize the lighting system in one of the university gymnasiums. The old lighting system had been installed 30 years earlier when the building was built. It was expensive to maintain, and the quality of the lighting was definitely low by modern standards. The detailed job of designing the new lighting system was turned over to a lighting engineer in the Office of the University Architect. Three types of lighting equipment were initially considered. Of these, one was eliminated on the basis of having excessive glare for this application. The two remaining possibilities were both capable of producing satisfactory light conditions, and therefore an attempt was made to choose between the two on the basis of cost. The cost analysis disclosed that system A would require a high initial outlay but would have low maintenance and operating costs. System B would require lower initial outlays but higher maintenance and operating costs than system A. As a result, the lighting engineer felt that no clear choice could be made on the basis of cost; therefore the final decision was made on the basis of admittedly unimportant differences in the quality of the light produced by the two systems. If the engineer had applied the discounted cash flow approach, taking into account the fact that the university was able to earn a 4.5 per cent return on its funds, it would have been clear that system A had a very decided cost advantage.

Comparability

The problem of comparability arises if the profitability of future investment proposals will be affected by decisions made currently. A group of investments will be said to be comparable (and mutually exclusive) if the profitability of subsequent investment possibilities will be the same, regardless of which investment is accepted or if all are rejected. Investment alternatives should be combined into groups that are both mutually exclusive and comparable before a final decision is made.

For example, a new plant could be heated by using forced hot air or steam. These are mutually exclusive alternatives. However, they are not comparable if it seems likely that the installation of an air-conditioning system will become necessary at some time in the future. The air-conditioning system would cost less to install in a building already equipped with air vents, and the present value of this difference in expected costs should be taken into account when choosing the heating system.

This simple example brings out two points. First, it is frequently not possible to make a group of mutually exclusive investment alternatives exactly comparable. In designing a new plant, the number of possible changes that may be desirable at some future date (such as remodeling, installation of new machinery, and additions or extensions) is very large, and the cost of each such possible change will depend upon the basic plant design originally adopted. In such circumstances, to make an analysis of truly comparable investments would require consideration of an unduly large number of alternatives.

Secondly, the importance of having mutually exclusive investments comparable is a matter of degree. In choosing a heating system for a new plant, the importance of the fact that future installation of air conditioning would be more expensive with steam will depend on the likelihood that air conditioning will eventually be required, the lapse of time until it may be required, the extent of the extra installation costs, etc. In deciding whether a group of mutually exclusive alternatives is sufficiently comparable for practical purposes, one must apply a reasonable approach.

Serial Dependence

In practice, the question frequently arises, "Must mutually exclusive investment alternatives have the same lives in order to be comparable?" The answer is "no." In some instances, investment alternatives with different lives will be comparable; in other instances equal future time periods are necessary to achieve comparability. Although the principles involved are the same as for other kinds of dependence, serial dependence is sufficiently important to deserve separate comment.

An example of comparable mutually exclusive alternatives not having the same life occurs in connection with deciding how to exploit a new patented product. One alternative is to sell the patent rights to another firm. This results in a single, lump sum payment. The patent may also be exploited by manufacturing and selling the product.

In this example the two choices are comparable, although the expected cash proceeds from one would extend only one year, and from the second, for a longer period of time.

Replacement Chains

In the preceding example, we considered comparable investments with unequal lives. More commonly we find it is appropriate to compare equal-lived investments. Suppose a real estate company is considering whether to remodel a motel and to continue operating it for an additional ten years, or to raze the old motel and build a new one that would have an economic life of twenty years. On what basis can these two alternatives be compared?

If the alternatives were comparable, we would compare the present value of expected cash outlays and proceeds from the two unequal-lived streams. However, in this instance the two investments are not comparable. If the company chooses to remodel the existing motel now and scrap it after ten years, it will then have the options of selling the land, building a new motel, or using the land in some other way. These possibilities must be taken into account in making the present decision.

One possibility is to convert the two investments into equivalent average annual cash flows. Suppose the company has a cost of capital of 10 per cent and that remodeling the old motel would yield a net present value at 10 per cent of $100,-000 during the next ten years. To convert this into equivalent annual cash flows, we would find the annual amount for ten years which has a present value of $100,000. Similarly, if the expected net present value from building a new motel were $125,000, we would find the 20-year annuity which has a present value of $125,000. At 10 per cent the equivalent annual payments are $16,274 and $14,682. With this system the alternative having the largest average annual cash flow is the most favorable. Note that by using net present value, building a new motel is favored; by using equivalent annual returns, remodeling the present motel is better. Using net present value, we ignore the profits that could result from using the land during years 11 through 20, when the present motel will be torn down if it is remodeled now. This creates a bias toward the alternative of building a new motel now. On the other hand, by converting to equivalent annual returns, we assume that an investment as profitable as remodeling the current motel will reappear ten years from now. Another mechanical assumption would be that ten years from now it will be possible to build a new motel that would be as profitable and long-lived as the new motel to be built now. Although it may turn out upon investigation in a particular case that this assumption is reasonable, we cannot assume that this will be the case.

If we considered ourselves sufficiently clairvoyant, we might attempt to estimate the cost of building a new motel ten years from now and also the cash proceeds that would be generated by operating this new motel. Even this would be of little avail if it turned out that this new motel would last for more than an additional ten years, since the two alternatives would not then be comparable.

Sometimes a practical solution is found by putting an upper or lower limit on the value of potential future opportunities. For example, in the motel problem one can safely estimate that if the motel is remodeled now, in ten years there will be a potential cash flow at least equal to the value of the land at that time. It may turn out that even an optimistic estimate of the value of the land will not be sufficient to make the alternative of remodeling the old motel more attractive than the prospect of constructing a new motel.

Although techniques such as those we are recommending force one to make difficult estimates in the face of imperfect and incomplete information, they have the advantage of focusing attention on the important unknowns. Apparently simpler techniques achieve their simplicity by using general assumptions about the nature of future opportunities rather than conjectures tailor-made to a particular situation. They save time and effort at the expense of a less precise analysis of the decision-making situation.

$$6.1446$$
$$100,000$$
$$614460,000$$

6

Timing of Replacements

In 1950 many people were faced with an investment decision. Should they replace their 12-inch television set with the new 21-inch sets then being sold? Or would it be better to wait until color television had been perfected? Another complication was the feeling that television sets were bound to be less expensive in a few years, just as the price of radio sets had decreased in the years immediately after the introduction of radio. This situation illustrates the type of problem being reviewed in this chapter. There was little question that the 21-inch sets were better than the 12-inch sets and well worth the amount of money they cost. The question was whether it was better to wait another year or two and buy the color sets, thus bypassing the expense of buying another black-and-white set that might be obsolete in a short period of time. This same type of problem carries over to business decisions. Do you replace machine A with a clearly superior machine B if you suspect that a machine C of improved design is coming out in another year or two?

There are essentially two basic procedures used to incorporate into the capital-budgeting analysis the complication described above. One procedure makes general assumptions about the rate of technological change. This procedure is used by both Alchain and Terborgh, although their methods differ considerably.[1] The second procedure makes use of specific information about the future and the likely technological improvements. This second procedure is considered to be more useful for decision making than the application of past rates of technological change to present decisions.

An Assumed Rate of Progress

If technological progress during the past five years has made a machine obsolete, is it safe to predict that the same rate of change will occur in the future? Do all machines and capital equipment have the same rate of technological improvement? The proponents of the procedures that implicitly assume positive answers to these questions would argue that these are reasonable approximations and that when the uncertainties of the future prevent more accurate forecasts, the approximations are better than assuming no technological change. On the other hand, technological advance frequently moves by fits and starts, and often an advance knowledge of future developments is available. The assumption that a certain average rate of technological progress will continue should not be used if more specific information is available. If nothing is known of the future, then the decision maker has the option of ignoring the timing problem or of assuming a single constant rate of technological change, or of preparing a range of estimates reflecting the impacts of different degrees of obsolescence.

[1] See A. Alchain, *Economic Replacement Policy*, The RAND Corporation, Santa Monica, California, 1952; and G. Terborgh, *Business Investment Policy*, Machinery and Allied Products Institute, Washington, 1958.

Timing Replacement

It is possible to compare two machines and conclude that the new machine is more desirable than the old machine but to decide not to replace because there is reason to believe that a better machine will be introduced in a near future period. This section will attempt to illustrate a procedure for incorporating this type of information into the replacement analysis. The example presented will show the net cash flows made possible by following different investment decisions. The cash flows may be different for the different decisions because of changes in revenues, changes in costs, or some combination of the two.

The method of solution will be to find which investment plan will maximize the present value of the cash flows. This requires consideration not only of the decision to, or not to, replace this year but also of the possibility of deferring the investment for one or more years.

Let us assume that a type of pump has a maximum physical life of four years and has no expected salvage value at the time of retirement or replacement. All cash flow estimates are on an after-tax basis. The cost of capital is 10 per cent. The pump currently in use is one year old. The cash proceeds resulting from running the pump currently in use, the proceeds connected with the pump being considered this year, and the proceeds of the pump that is expected to be developed in the next year are as follows:

Pump	Initial outlay	Expected annual net cash proceeds
Currently in use	...	$ 20
Currently being considered......	$236	100
Expected at the end of one year..	200	100

Let us compare the cash flows resulting from three possible courses of action:

Plan A. Do not replace until three years from now.
Plan B. Replace now, keep the pump for four years, and then replace again.
Plan C. Defer the replacement for one year.

There are other alternatives, such as replacing at the end of the second year or replacing now and again at the end of one year, but these possibilities will be ignored, since to include them in the computations would complicate the analysis, and we can intuitively reject them.

The table that follows shows the cash flows resulting from each of the three investment plans being considered. The investment that has the largest present value, using a discount rate of 10 per cent (the cost of capital) may be accepted as the optimum investment plan. This procedure is essentially experimental in nature. It tests all possibilities and chooses the plan that maximizes the cash flows.

Invest-ment plan	\multicolumn{9}{c}{Cash flows at end of year}
	0	1	2	3	4	5	6	7	8
A ...		$ 20	$ 20	$ 20 [$200]	$100	$100	$100	$100 [$200]	$100
B [236]		100	100	100	100 [200]	100	100	100	100 [200]
C ...		20 [200]	100	100	100	100 [200]	100	100	100

Note: Outlays to purchase pumps are bracketed.

The above table stops with eight periods, but we should imagine that the table continues past the eight years and

Computation

Plan A	Present value of cash flows		Explanations
20 (2.4869)	=	$ 50	$20 a period for three periods
$100 \times 10 \times (1.10)^{-3}$	=	751	A perpetuity of $100 discounted for three periods
$63.09 \times 10 \times (1.10)^{-3}$	=	(474)	The annual equivalent outlay for perpetuity discounted for three periods
		$ 327	Net present value for Plan A

Plan B			
236.00	=	$ (236)	An immediate outlay
100×10	=	1,000	Cash flows of $100 for perpetuity
$63.09 \times 10 \times (1.10)^{-4}$	=	(431)	The annual equivalent outlay for perpetuity discounted for four periods
		$ 333	Net present value for Plan B

Plan C			
$20 (1.10)^{-1}$	=	$ 18	$20 discounted for one period
$100 \times 10 \times (1.10)^{-1}$	=	909	A perpetuity of $100 discounted for one period
$63.09 \times 10 \times (1.10)^{-1}$	=	(574)	The annual equivalent outlay for perpetuity discounted for one period
		$ 353	Net present value for Plan C

extends to perpetuity. Note that for each alternative, there is a pattern of cash flows that repeats itself.

Plan A has an outlay of $200 in period 3 and additional outlay of $200 every fourth year. The cash proceeds are $20 a year for three years and then $100 for perpetuity.

Plan B has cash proceeds of $100 in all periods. It has $236 of investment-type outlay in period 1 and $200 in period 4 and in every fourth year thereafter.

Plan C makes repetitive investment outlays every four years, starting in period 1. It has cash proceeds of $20 in period 1 and $100 in every period thereafter.

By using the present value of cash flows the best of the three investment plans can be chosen.

The computations indicate that investment plan C is the most desirable. The assumptions made should be noted. We have assumed knowledge of the investments available now (period 0) and at the end of period 1. We have assumed that the investments available at the end of period 1 will not be improved upon in future periods. If there is reason to suspect that further improvements will be made in a future period (for example, period 2), then this fact may be incorpo-

---

Notes for computations on page 82:

1. The $63.09 per period is equivalent to $200 every four periods.

2. The factor 10 appearing in each computation is the present value of a dollar per period for an infinite number of periods, assuming a rate of discount of 10 per cent.

3. The present values are being computed as of the end of period 0 or the beginning of period 1. The investment and cash flows of each period are assumed to take place at the end of the indicated period.

4. Instead of converting the $200 outlay every four years to an annual equivalent of $63.09, it is also possible to convert the annual interest of 10 per cent to an equivalent interest of 46.4 per cent over a four-year period, and compute the present value of a perpetuity of $200 per period (each period, four years) using the 46.4 per cent.

rated into the analysis by considering additional investment plans:

Plan D. Do not replace until period 2.
Plan E. Replace in period 0 and period 2.
Plan F. Replace in period 1 and period 2.
Plan G. Replace in periods 0, 1, and 2.

The computations may become more complex, but solutions are possible if we consider the cash flows from all possible investment alternatives that may be encountered.

If we remove the restriction of the four-year physical life, then the number of alternative investment plans is greatly increased. Obviously, for an investment of small dollar value, it would not be desirable to spend a large amount of time analyzing this type of problem. Where the investment is large (such as a firm renting or owning a large number of automobiles), the decision is important, and a large amount of effort could be expended determining the optimum time to replace equipment.

Replacing Equipment with Infinite Physical Lives

A piece of equipment may be considered to have an infinite physical life if the replacement of parts as they fail are considered to be maintenance costs. When should equipment of this nature be replaced rather than repaired? An example of this type of equipment is an automobile that may be kept running indefinitely by replacing each individual part as it breaks down.

Assuming that we have the repair cost figures for each year of life, and constant technology, the solution is not difficult. Our goal is to *minimize* the present value of the costs of running automobiles. We can compute the present value of the costs, assuming replacement at the end of one year, two years, etc. It is important that investment streams be made comparable, i.e., that the use of automobiles be considered for an equal number of years for each alternative.

Example: The cost of a new car is $1,000; the cost of capital is 10 per cent. Compute the optimum moment of replacement for automobiles, assuming the following fictitious cost information:

Age of car	Repairs for year	Salvage value at end of year
1	$ 500	$800
2	1,000	640
3	1,000	512

Assume that repairs are made at the end of each year if the car is to be retained but that they are not necessary if the car is to be sold for its salvage value.

To illustrate the basic computations, let us first decide whether it would be better to replace at the end of year 1 or year 2. We assume that a one-year-old car is now owned by the company. The cash flows of following the two alternatives are as follows:

Replacement period	Cash flows for year		
	0	1	2
1 year	($1,000)	$800 (1,000)	$800
2 years	(1,000)	(500)	640

An inspection of the cash flows of the two alternatives reveals that the automobiles should be replaced at the end of each year. The outlays required at the end of period 1 are less ($200 compared with $500), and the salvage received at the end of period 2 is greater ($800 compared with $640).

At any positive rate of discount the decision to replace annually will be preferable.

It should be noted that the above analysis carried out both alternatives to a common period of two years. If we had included the possibility of a life of three years, it would have been necessary either to carry the analysis to six years (the lowest common multiple of years, which is done below), compute the equivalent cost per year for each proposal, or find the cost for a perpetuity.

Replacement period	Cash flows for year						
	0	1	2	3	4	5	6
1 year	($1,000)	($200)	($200)	($200)	($200)	($200)	$800
2 years ...	(1,000)	(500)	640 (1,000)	(500)	640 (1,000)	(500)	640
3 years	(1,000)	(500)	(1,000)	(1,000) 512	(500)	(1,000)	512

Making use of present-value tables, we find the present value of the costs of the three alternatives to be:

Replacement period	Present value of costs for six years
1 year	$1,307
2 years	2,323
3 years	3,321

Using this analysis, the conclusion reached is that it is desirable to replace the automobile annually. The most undesirable of the three choices is to replace at the end of three years.

It is interesting to note that frequently a decision such as the one being illustrated will result in the old equipment being retained indefinitely. In such cases a replacement verdict may result, not because of cost considerations but because management does not consider the equipment being used to be as attractive in appearance or as safe as more modern equipment.

CONCLUSIONS

As we move from a static analysis of considering only the investments presently available, to a dynamic analysis of considering future investments as well, we introduce a considerable amount of complexity into the computations. Where the forecast of the future is well founded, including future investment possibilities, this adds to our ability to arrive at a reasonable answer to the question as to when to replace a piece of equipment presently being used. A similar problem arises when a decision must be made about the timing and frequency of introducing new models. All these decisions must be solved by taking into consideration all alternatives and by choosing those alternatives that maximize the present value of the cash flows.[2] The decisions that maximize the present value of the cash flows, taking into consideration the changes in the future, will tend to lead to a maximization of profit through time.

While there is no question that characteristics of equipment available in the future are relevant to investment decisions made today, especially when the decision under consideration can be deferred, there still remains the question as to the extent to which we should incorporate into our present analysis our guesses (or estimates) about the future. This is a matter of judgment and intuition and is also dependent to a great extent on the quality of the information we have about future changes in the technology.

[2] The objective should be to maximize the positive cash flows or minimize the negative flows (which are actually cost streams). Rather than maximizing an absolute amount without reference to the sign (positive or negative), the goal is to maximize the algebraic sum of the present values.

7

The Use of Cash Flows in Evaluating Investments

We have argued that investments ought to be evaluated in terms of the present value of the cash flows expected from them, in preference to any other measures of investment worth that have been suggested. However, we have not given a complete or careful definition of the term *cash flows*. In the present chapter we shall attempt to do this and also to explain some of the difficulties that arise in applying a cash flow analysis to investment proposals. In the next chapter the influence of income taxes on the timing of cash flows will be discussed, and in Chapter 13 a suggested framework for systematically recording estimates of cash flows will be presented.

Cash Flows and Profits

Cash flows are not identical with profits or income. Changes in income can occur without any corresponding changes in cash flows. During a period of investment in plant and inventories, a corporation can even experience a decrease in cash at the same time that income is increasing.

The popular conception of an investment is typified by a one-period outlay of funds, followed by a series of periods in which incomes are earned. The incomes are then related to the investment, and some type of return on investment is computed. One of the main advantages of the cash flow procedure is that it avoids difficult problems underlying the measurement of corporate income which necessarily accompanies the accrual method of accounting. These problems include the following:

1. In what time period should revenue be recognized?

2. What expenses should be treated as investments and therefore capitalized and depreciated over several time periods?

3. What method of depreciation should be used in measuring income as reported to management and stockholders (as distinct from income measurement for tax purposes)?

4. Should LIFO (last in, first out), FIFO (first in, first out), or some other method be used to measure inventory flow?

5. What costs are inventoriable? Should fixed, variable, direct, indirect, out-of-pocket, unavoidable, administrative, or selling costs be included in evaluating inventory?

There are disagreements as to the answers to each of these questions. Different approaches may lead to different measures of income. If income is used to evaluate investment worth, investments may look good or bad, depending on how income is measured. The cash flow procedure minimizes many of these complications.

Absolute and Relative Cash Flows

Every investment analysis involves a comparison of alternatives. If there are not at least two possibilities, then there is no problem of choice. Usually the number of alternatives is large. The question may be whether the company is better off with investment A or without it, or whether investment A is better than investment B, or whether both A and B should be accepted or both should be rejected. In any case, since the investment analysis involves a comparison of two or more alternatives, it is not surprising to find that any estimate of cash flows must also be on a comparative basis.

Suppose the question is whether to start a new business. After a careful analysis we arrive at an estimate of the net cash flows that we expect to occur in each future period after we start the business. Our estimate will tell us how much money we would have to invest during each period as the business got started and how much money would be available after necessary expenses and additional investments in each period after it began to operate successfully. Perhaps we would plan to sell the business after five years if it were successful, and we would include as a cash flow the amount we would expect to receive for the business five years hence. The present value of the net cash flows might then be calculated using a rate of discount of 10 per cent. What comparisons are we making in analyzing the investment? What comparisons are we making in estimating the net cash flows?

If we say that the cash outlay in the first year is $100,000 (since that amount of money would have to be expended during that period, over and above any cash receipts), then we are implicitly comparing the cash flows from operating the business with a cash flow of zero. When cash flows are being compared with zero cash flows, we shall speak of *absolute* cash flows. In evaluating the present value of these cash flows, using a 10 per cent rate of interest, we are implicitly comparing this investment with an investment that would return 10 per cent per year indefinitely for each net outlay.

Suppose now that the question is whether to start one kind of business or another; for example, a retail store or a whole-sale distributorship. One possible analysis would be to esti-mate the absolute cash flows from each business and compute the present value of the corresponding cash flows. Again, in this case, we are comparing each business separately against a hypothetical investment that could earn 10 per cent. Since the hypothetical standard of comparison is the same for both businesses, the two can be readily compared with each other by noticing which business would probably give a higher present value of cash flows. In practice, the final decision would depend on many other factors as well, such as the degree of risk involved in each business, the degree of confidence we feel in our estimates, and so on. See Chapter 9 for a further discussion of some of these factors.

An alternative analysis would be to compare directly one business with the other. In looking at the cash flow estimates, for example, we could subtract (algebraically) the cash flows of the retail store from the cash flows in corresponding periods of the wholesale distributorship. If the difference was positive in a particular period, it would tell us how much better the cash flows from the wholesale business are than those from the retail business during that period. The cash flows, in this case, can be called *relative* cash flows; the wholesale business is being measured relative to the retail business. Again we could compute the present value of this series of relative cash flows. It can be shown that the present value of this series of relative cash flows would be the same as the present value of the absolute cash flows from the wholesale distributorship minus the present value of the absolute cash flows from the retail business. Thus the present-value method will lead to the same conclusion, whichever approach is used.

There is an important difference between the two series of cash flows, however. With the series of absolute cash flows, if the corresponding investment (the retail or wholesale businesses) were accepted and actually began to operate, we could compare, period by period, the actual cash flows with our previous forecasts. There is not, however, any similarly identifiable series of cash flows that could be compared with the relative cash flow estimates. If we decided to operate the wholesale business on the basis of a comparison of relative cash flows, and wished after a few periods to compare our actual results with those we had forecast earlier, we should need to know what assumptions had been made about the retail business in order to make this comparison.

Frequently, when we are considering investments to be made in a going business, it is not possible to define the absolute cash flows that would result from the investment. A relative cash flow concept must then be used. Suppose, for example, that an automobile manufacturer is trying to decide whether to invest in the tools and dies necessary to make a particular modification in the body style of his product. He will need to compare what sales would be if he made the investment and what they would be if he did not make the investment. This, of course, is a very difficult question to answer, since all sorts of other changes are taking place at the same time, both in his product and marketing strategy, and in those of his competitors.

Importance of Considering All Alternatives

Apart from those difficulties in making estimates of relative cash flows that are a by-product of the difficulties of estimating the incremental effects of various actions of the firm, there is an important conceptual danger that must be avoided in estimating relative cash flows. As previously explained, an estimate of relative cash flows always involves an explicit comparison of two alternatives. The size of the estimated relative cash flows from making a particular investment will depend upon the alternative that is used as a basis of comparison. *This means that almost any investment can be made to seem worth while if it is compared with a sufficiently bad alternative.* Consider a problem that was faced by many railroads in the not too distant past. Should the old coal-burning locomotive used on a particular passenger run be replaced with a modern and more efficient diesel? Assuming that the change would not affect passenger revenues, the natural basis of comparison would appear to be to take the present value of the extra outlays required to purchase the new engine (minus the scrap value of the old coal burner) and the cash savings resulting from the difference between the operating costs of the old and the new engines. On this basis it may seem that the investment in a new diesel engine would be quite profitable. But suppose, using the old coal burner, the revenues from the passenger run are insufficient to cover the incremental out-of-pocket costs of operating the train. In such circumstances the purchase of a diesel may serve to decrease the loss, but it may not convert the passenger run into a profitable operation. If there is no possibility of eliminating the passenger run, the decision to purchase the diesel may be wise. But if the passenger train could be eliminated, purchase of the diesel would not be justified. This situation could be handled by examining the absolute cash flows generated by the diesel, i.e., by comparing the cash flows resulting from the passenger train with a diesel locomotive and the cash flows resulting from no train at all. When using relative cash flows, we must remember to consider all alternatives, including the alternative of continuing as we are now or abandoning the operation entirely, if these are possible.

In general an investment should not be accepted unless the relative cash flows generated by it are positive when compared with the next best alternative. Frequently the analyst will be faced with a situation in which there are quite a number of possible alternatives whose relative advantages are not yet known. In such cases any one of the investments can be used as the standard of comparison, and the relative advantage of each estimate can be compared to this standard. If all the other alternatives have a negative present value when compared with the standard, then the standard is the most advantageous, so far as explicit cost and revenue considerations are the determinants. In the railroad locomotive example given above, if continuance of operating the coal-burning locomotive were taken as the standard, it could turn out that discontinuing the passenger train altogether would give a higher present value than buying a diesel, although the latter is better than continuing to operate the coal-burning locomotive. As long as all the feasible alternatives are considered, it makes no difference which one of the alternatives is tentatively accepted as the standard of comparison. The final answer will be the same in any case. The choice of a standard of comparison may lead to mistaken conclusions only if some advantageous alternatives (such as ceasing production entirely) are excluded from the analysis.

Opportunity Costs

Usually the cash outlays included in the computation of net cash flows are the outlays incurred because of the investment that would not be incurred otherwise. Outlays that would be incurred by the firm whether or not the investment is accepted should not be charged to a particular investment project. Thus the practice of allocating a share of general overhead to a new project on the basis of some arbitrary measure, such as direct labor hours or a fraction of net sales, is not recommended *unless* it is expected that general overhead will actually increase if the project is accepted.

On the other hand, in some instances an investment project may require the use of some scarce resource available to the firm, although the explicit cash outlays associated with using that resource may be nonexistent or may not adequately reflect the value of the resource to the firm. Examples are projects that require a heavy drain on the time of key executive personnel or that use valuable floor space in a plant or store already owned by the business. The costs of using such resources are called *opportunity costs,* and they are measured by estimating how much the resource (the executives' time or the floor space) would earn for the company if the investments under consideration were rejected.

It may appear that the practice of charging opportunity costs against an investment project when no corresponding cash outlay can be identified is a violation of, or exception to, the procedure of evaluating investments in terms of actual cash flows. Actually, including opportunity costs is not so much an exception to the cash flow procedure as an extension of it. The opportunity cost charged should measure net cash flows that could have been earned if the project under discussion had been rejected. Suppose one floor of a factory building owned by a business could either be rented out at $1,000 per month or used to produce a new product. After an initial outlay for equipment, the new product could produce an absolute net cash inflow of $2,000 per month after taxes but before an allowance has been made for use of the factory space. The figure of $2,000 per month overstates the benefits to be derived from the new product, since the space required could otherwise be used to earn $1,000 per month. By charging a rental opportunity cost of $1,000 per month against the new product, a more meaningful measure of its actual value to the company is obtained. An alternative procedure would be to estimate the relative cash flow from the new product compared with that produced by renting the extra space and not producing the new product.

In some instances it will be extremely difficult to estimate opportunity costs. The temptation then is to use some other more easily identifiable basis of charging for the use of such things as floor space or the time of key executives. This temptation must be viewed with some skepticism. The pro rata share of the costs of owning a building may be much higher or much lower than the true opportunity costs of using that space. When there is really no basis for estimating the opportunity costs associated with the use of a factor, such as the time of certain key executives, it may be preferable to note merely that the proposed project is likely to require considerably more or considerably less than the usual amount of attention from such key executives.

Acquiring Assets without Cash Disbursements

The term *cash outlay* is also applied to a transaction where an asset is acquired by incurring a long-term debt or by issuing stock. Even though there may be no explicit borrowing of cash, receipt of cash, and disbursement of cash, these transactions are assumed to occur when an asset is acquired via a promise to pay in some distant time period, and the transaction is treated as if there has been a cash outlay as well as a source of new capital.

Where an asset is acquired by the incurrence of a noninterest-bearing, current liability, the convention is adopted in this book that it is the timing of the actual cash disbursement which is important. Thus, if the investment results in an increase in inventories of $100 and the source of capital is an increase in current liabilities of $100, the net cash outlay that is required in the period of inventory acquisition is zero. If the $100 increase in inventories required cash outlays of $20 and current liabilities increased by $80, then the net cash outlay in the period of inventory acquisition is $20.

Excluding Interest Payments

There is a temptation to include outlays for interest payments when computing the cash flows of a period. Cash disbursed for interest should not affect the cash flow computation. The interest factor is taken into consideration by the use of the present-value procedure. To also include the cash disbursement would result in double counting. The effect of interest payments on income taxes is also excluded from the cash flow computation. This is brought into the analysis when computing the effective rate of interest of debt sources of capital, which is used in the determination of the cost of capital. A similar treatment is also accorded preferred stock dividends.

Salvage and Removal Costs

The salvage and removal costs introduce no real problem if we keep in mind that we are interested in the periods when cash outlays are made or when cash flows into the firm. In the following descriptive material, the term *salvage* refers to net salvage; removal costs have been subtracted.

Let us first consider the salvage value of the new investment. Any funds obtained from selling the new investment when it is retired will increase the flow of cash in the last period. Thus salvage value of the new investment will increase the cash flow of the last period of use.

When the investment is being made to replace an item of equipment currently being used, there are two additional salvage values to be considered. One is the salvage value now of the old equipment, and the other is the salvage value at the end of its physical or useful life (whichever comes first). If the asset is replaced now, the present salvage will have the effect of increasing the cash flow of this period (or decreasing the required cash outlay). However, if the old equipment is being retired now, the salvage that would have been obtained at the end of its life will not be obtained. Thus there is a decrease in the relative cash flows of that last period, for the salvage which will not be obtained at that time. To summarize:

Salvage value of the new equipment: Increase the cash flow of the last year of use.

Present salvage value of the old equipment: Increase the cash flow for this year (decrease the cash outlay).

Salvage value of the old equipment at time of normal retirement: Decrease the cash flow of that year (since the salvage value would be obtained if the replacement did not take place and will not be obtained if the replacement does take place).

The cash flows arising from salvage of the old equipment would be treated in a somewhat different manner if the present values of the alternatives were computed individually. It would only increase the cash flows at the time of retirement.

The analysis of the cash flows arising from salvage is complicated by the fact that the cash flow analysis may be made in terms of relative or absolute cash flows. The preceding description assumes that the cash flows are relative, i.e., the cash flows from buying the new equipment minus the cash flows which would occur if the old equipment were retained. It is frequently reasonable to analyze the absolute cash flows of the several alternatives. Thus the cash flows of retaining the old would be computed, as would the cash flows of purchasing the new equipment. The present salvage value of the old equipment and the future salvage of the new equipment would affect the cash flow of the alternative of purchasing the new equipment. The salvage of retirement of the old would affect the cash flow of retaining the old equipment.

Illustration: Assume the present equipment has a salvage value now of $1,000 and an expected salvage value in five years of $400 (at which time the equipment would be physically unusable). The new equipment will have a salvage value at the time of its expected retirement of $650. All figures are on an after-tax basis. The cash flows arising from the salvage values would be:

	Year		
	0	5	10
Absolute flows of:			
Retaining the old		$400	
Purchasing the new	$1,000	...	$650
Relative flows of:			
Replacing now	$1,000	$(400)	$650

Terminal Value

Salvage value is one form of terminal value. Another form of terminal value is the release of cash necessary to operate the investment. Other examples of items that may result in released cash at cessation of operations are collections of accounts receivable and reduction in required inventories. All these items gave rise to outlays of cash when they were purchased but now lag in their generation of cash. When the outlays of cash cease, since the production is being phased out, then the coming periods will have increases in cash flows resulting from the conversion of these noncash current assets into cash; similarly, reductions of current liabilities reduce cash.

Income Taxes and Cash Flows

The question of income taxes and cash flows is reviewed in detail in Chapter 8. It should be remembered that *the term cash flows in this chapter refers to flows after the deduction of income taxes.* The income taxes are computed by applying the expected tax rate for each period to the taxable income (excluding interest charges) of that period. The taxable income will not be equal to the cash flow of the period, and frequently the taxable income will not equal the income computed in accordance with generally accepted accounting principles. Thus no matter what method is being used to accept or reject investments, often it will be necessary to compute the income for tax purposes as a separate computation.

Cash Flows and Uncertainty

It should be recognized that each computation of cash flows makes certain assumptions about the level of business activity, actions of competitors, future availability of improved models of machines, costs of factors of production, future sales, and the like. Since there is a large amount of uncertainty connected with each of these factors, it should be appreciated that computations using the present-value method are indications rather than numbers with 100 per cent certainty and accuracy. A more detailed discussion of the consequences of uncertain estimates and some suggestions for making analyses when basic assumptions are subject to great uncertainty are presented in Chapter 9. It should be stressed that any decision about investments must in the last analysis be based on as complete a consideration of all the relevant factors as it is possible to provide, and that the probable present value of an investment proposal is only one factor, although a very significant one, that must be considered in arriving at a final decision.

8

Income Taxes and
Investment Decisions

Accounting theory suggests three basically different methods of recording a cash outlay for an asset or cost factor; these in turn affect the measurement of income. The outlay may be considered to be an expense of the period in which it is incurred, to represent the acquisition of a wasting asset that will be charged to expense over a number of future periods, or to represent the acquisition of a nonwasting asset, in which case it is never charged to expense. The first is typified by outlays for salesmen's salaries, the second by outlays for plant and equipment, and the third by outlays for land. For some outlays a reasonable case can be made for one or another accounting treatment. Thus outlays for research, certain types of advertising, and some kinds of maintenance may be treated as current expenses or capitalized and depreciated over a longer period; outlays for land may be treated as wasting assets if the important characteristics of the land are its possession of certain minerals or soil fertility, or as partially nonwasting if its site value is considered.

The accounting treatment accorded a particular outlay will influence the amount and timing of income measurement. But in the absence of income taxes, the choice of investments should not be influenced by the method of accounting for a particular outlay. It is the amount and timing of the cash outlays and the amount and timing of future cash proceeds that are relevant to the choice of investments.

In the case of corporations subject to income taxes, the accounting treatment adopted for income tax purposes must be considered in evaluating a potential investment, since it will affect the amount and timing of the income tax payments. Since income taxes do not affect all investments in the same manner, it is necessary to place cash flows associated with each investment on an after-tax basis before evaluating the investments. In this chapter we shall be concerned with the mechanics of computing the after-tax cash flows associated with investments. We shall consider separately the problems associated with depreciable assets, nondepreciable assets, and outlays chargeable to current expense.

Measuring the Effects of Depreciation Charges on Cash Flows

Suppose we are considering the purchase of a new piece of equipment that is expected to have no salvage value on retirement. If there were no income taxes, then the cash proceeds resulting from the use of the equipment could be estimated by subtracting the additional cash outlays required to operate the equipment from the additional revenues that result from acquiring it. That is,

$$\text{Before-tax cash proceeds} = \text{revenues} - \text{cash outlays} \qquad (1)$$

The term *cash proceeds* is used here to refer to the proceeds generated by operating the investment. It assumes that all revenues are accompanied by an immediate generation of cash equal to the revenues. It also assumes that all cash outlays except the initial investment are charged to expense, i.e., none is charged to inventory, and that inventory is not reduced. Thus cash outlays are equal to the expenses (excluding depreciation) in this simple example.

For a nonprofit hospital or government bureau, this is the only calculation that would be necessary. For a business it is necessary to subtract the additional tax liability that occurs because of the investment.

$$\text{After-tax proceeds} = \text{revenues} - \text{cash outlays} - \text{income tax} \quad (2)$$

or

$$\text{After-tax proceeds} = \text{revenues} - \text{expenses other than depreciation} - \text{income tax} \quad (3)$$

The income tax liability is computed by applying the income tax rate to the additional taxable income. One of the allowable deductions for tax purposes is the depreciation of the investment. It is possible to express the determination of the income tax in the following ways:

$$\text{Income tax} = (\text{tax rate}) \times (\text{taxable income}) \quad (4)$$

and

$$\text{Income tax} = (\text{tax rate}) \times (\text{revenues} - \text{expenses other than depreciation} - \text{depreciation}) \quad (5)$$

From Equation 5 it can be seen that the higher the depreciation taken for income tax purposes, the lower the income tax will be and the greater the after-tax cash proceeds. Substituting Equation 5 in Equation 3 and simplifying give Equations 6 and 7.

After-tax proceeds = $(1 - $ tax rate$) \times ($revenues
$\qquad - $ expenses other than depreciation $-$ depreciation$)$
$$+ \text{depreciation} \quad (6)$$

or

After-tax proceeds = $(1 - $ tax rate$) \times$
$\qquad ($revenues $-$ expenses other than depreciation$)$
$$+ (\text{tax rate}) \times (\text{depreciation}) \quad (7)$$

Equations 6 and 7 are mathematically identical, and therefore give identical answers, although one or the other formula may be easier to use in a particular instance. Equation 7 is particularly useful, since it highlights the fact that the cash proceeds of the period are increased by the allowable depreciation times the tax rate. Thus we can compute the present value of the "tax savings" by multiplying the depreciation by the expected tax rate of each period and discounting that amount back to the present.

Illustration: A piece of new equipment costs $10,000. It can be depreciated for tax purposes in four years, and it has been decided to use the sum-of-the-years'-digits method. It is expected to have no salvage value on retirement. The company uses straight-line depreciation for book purposes. The equipment is expected to result in an increase in revenues (sales are all for cash) of $8,000 and additional costs requiring cash outlays of $4,000 (not including depreciation of the equipment). The income tax rate is 52 per cent. The cost of capital is 10 per cent.

The first step is to compute the taxable income and income tax of each year. This is accomplished in Table 1.

It should be noted that the use of a tax rate of 52 per cent for all years carries an assumption that the tax rate will not be changed. If a change is expected, the tax rates of the future years should be used.

Table 1. Computation of Income Tax

Year	Revenues	Other costs	Depreciation for tax purposes	Taxable income	Tax rate (%)	Income tax
1	$8,000	$4,000	$4,000	$ 0	52	$ 0
2	8,000	4,000	3,000	1,000	52	520
3	8,000	4,000	2,000	2,000	52	1,040
4	8,000	4,000	1,000	3,000	52	1,560

The second step is to compute the cash proceeds of each year. It is important to note that the book depreciation does not enter into this computation at all, but the depreciation for tax purposes influences the income tax and thus does indirectly affect the proceeds.

Table 2. Computation of Cash Proceeds

Year	Revenue	Other costs	Income tax	Cash proceeds
1	$8,000	$4,000	$ 0	$4,000
2	8,000	4,000	520	3,480
3	8,000	4,000	1,040	2,960
4	8,000	4,000	1,560	2,440

The next step is to compute the present value of the cash flows, using the cost of capital of 10 per cent as the rate of discount (see Table 3).

The present value of the proceeds, $10,403, is greater than the cash outflows of $10,000; thus the investment is apparently desirable.

In the above example the "other costs" allowed for tax purposes were equal to the "other costs" for which cash outlays were made. It is possible for these two amounts to differ. For example, costs may be incurred that are not allowable for tax purposes because the cost factors are in inventory. The cash outlays are required, but they do not give rise to decreases in the income tax of the period.

Table 3. Computation of the Present Value of Proceeds

Year	Cash proceeds	Discount factor (using 10 per cent as cost of capital)	Present value of the proceeds
1	$4,000	0.9091	$ 3,636
2	3,480	0.8264	2,876
3	2,960	0.7513	2,224
4	2,440	0.6830	1,667
			$10,403

A different schedule of depreciation deductions for tax purposes is obtained if the twice straight-line declining balance method is used.

Table 4. Computation of Depreciation
Twice Straight Line

Year	Decreasing balance	Rate (%)	Depreciation of the period	Accumulated depreciation
1	$10,000	50	$5,000	$ 5,000
2	5,000	50	2,500	7,500
3	2,500	50	1,250	8,750
4	1,250	100 *	1,250	10,000

* Assuming the asset is to be retired at end of the fourth year.

The company using the twice straight-line declining balance procedure for tax purposes has the option to switch to the straight-line procedure. When the depreciation charge following twice straight line becomes less than it would be following straight line, the company should switch to the latter procedure. This will result in $1,250 of depreciation for year 4. The next step would be to compute the taxable income, income tax, and cash proceeds for each year of the life of the investment so that present value of the cash flows may be computed, just as was done when using the sum-of-the-years'-digits depreciation.

Choosing the Most Advantageous Depreciation Procedure

Under the Internal Revenue Code of 1954, a company has a choice (among other methods) of depreciating a new asset by using straight-line depreciation, sum-of-the-years' digits, or twice straight line on the declining balance. In the often discussed problem of what depreciation method to use, it has frequently been noted that the choice of depreciation method will affect the profitability of the investment. It has not usually been realized that the best depreciation method for a company may depend upon its cost of capital as well as upon the life of the investment and its expected salvage value. The present-value method can be put to use in making this decision. For this purpose Equation 7 for computing the after-tax cash proceeds is most advantageous, since it divides the after-tax cash proceeds into two parts: The first part is independent of the depreciation method, and the second part depends only on the depreciation method. The depreciation method giving the highest present value should be chosen.

Table 5. Present Value of After-tax Cash Proceeds
Excluding Depreciation

Year	(1) *Revenues less current expenses*	(2) *After-tax equivalent (Col. 1 × 0.48)*	(3) *Discount factor*	(4) *Present value (Col. 2 × Col. 3)*
1	$ 4,000	$1,920	0.9091	$1,745
2	4,000	1,920	0.8264	1,587
3	4,000	1,920	0.7513	1,443
4	4,000	1,920	0.6830	1,311
Total	$16,000	$7,680	3.1698	$6,086

As is indicated in Table 5, the present value of the after-tax equivalent of $4,000 a year for four years is $6,086 when the tax rate is 52 per cent and the discount rate is 10 per cent. This part of the calculation is independent of the depreciation method used.

To determine the best depreciation method, we need to compute the present value of the tax saving resulting from the use of each possible depreciation method. These computations are shown in Table 6, assuming a 52 per cent tax rate and a 10 per cent rate of discount. It is clear from this table that the investment would be most advantageous if it could be used with the twice straight-line method of depreciation, since in that case the present value of the cash proceeds would be $10,457 ($6,086 + $4,371). The present value of the proceeds, when the sum-of-the-years'-digits method of depreciation is used, would be $6,086 plus $4,317, or $10,403, which is less than the $10,457 obtained above.

In this example the present value of the savings from the most advantageous method of depreciation as compared with the next best method amounts to about one-half of 1 per cent

Table 6. Present Value of Tax Savings from Different Methods of Depreciation, Assuming a 10 Per Cent Rate of Discount

Year	Depreciation method											
	Straight line			Twice straight line			Sum-of-the-years' digits		
	Allowable expense	Saving (52%)	Present value	Allowable expense	Saving (52%)	Present value	Allowable expense	Saving (52%)	Present value
1	$ 2,500	$1,300	$1,182	$ 5,000	$2,600	$2,364	$ 4,000	$2,080	$1,891
2	2,500	1,300	1,074	2,500	1,300	1,074	3,000	1,560	1,289
3	2,500	1,300	977	1,250	650	488	2,000	1,040	781
4	2,500	1,300	888	1,250	650	445	1,000	520	356
Total	$10,000	$5,200	$4,121	$10,000	$5,200	$4,371	$10,000	$5,200	$4,317

of the initial outlay of $10,000, or $54. In the case of a similar investment whose initial cost was $10 million, the present value of the difference between the two depreciation methods would be $54,000.

Use of Tables to Choose Optimum Depreciation Method

Tables in the Appendix to this book have been prepared to assist in the choice of method of depreciation and in the computation of the tax saving that will result from making the investment. Two tables have been prepared. One shows the present value, following the sum-of-the-years'-digits method, using different discount rates (cost of capital), and assuming assets of different lives. The other table shows comparable data for the declining balance method of depreciation (twice straight line). If an asset has a nonzero salvage value, the tables cannot be used to determine the present value of the depreciation charges for the declining balance method.

To use the tables, it is first necessary to enter the sum-of-the-years'-digits table, using the column that represents the cost of capital and going down it until the life of the asset is found. The amount obtained is the present value of the depreciation per dollar of depreciable base. This amount should be multiplied by the depreciable base (cost less salvage of the investment). The next step is to enter the proper table for the declining balance method (assuming zero expected salvage). The column that represents the cost of capital should be entered, and the number opposite the proper life of the asset should be determined. This number represents the present value per dollar of cost of the depreciation of the investment and must be multiplied by the cost of the investment to obtain the present value of the depreciation.

The choice of the method of depreciation will be dependent on which of the two present values is the greater. The present value of the tax savings can be found by multiplying the present value of the depreciation times the tax rate.

Where a positive salvage value is expected, the present value of the depreciation deductions using the declining balance method must be computed by following the same detailed procedures which were given earlier in this chapter. If the removal costs are expected to exceed the salvage (the salvage value is negative), the tables may be used. For the purposes of computing income taxes, the salvage is zero.

Additional Complications Affecting Choice of Depreciation Methods

The examples presented in the preceding section are intended primarily to illustrate the type of analysis that can be undertaken when it is considered worth the effort to determine the most advantageous method of depreciating a wasting asset. The examples chosen were deliberately oversimplified to bring out the point that the present-value approach can be used to determine the most advantageous method of depreciating an asset. A full treatment of the complications arising in determining a proper and acceptable method of depreciation under the Internal Revenue Code would require a book in itself and is beyond the scope of this chapter. However, some of the more important complications that may arise in practice will be mentioned briefly.

In the examples presented, it was assumed that the assets to be depreciated would have no salvage value at the end of their expected useful life. If a salvage value is expected at the end of the asset's useful life, the amount of depreciation expense will be affected. The salvage value will affect the depreciation of each year using the sum-of-the-years' digits, but by using the twice straight-line, declining balance procedure, it will affect only the change-over point (point at which a shift is made to straight line from twice straight line) and the depreciation after the change-over.

Another complication is that many companies use the group method of depreciation instead of the unit method. Under the group method the rate of depreciation is based on the average life of many units of like items (for example, telegraph poles). This rate of depreciation is then applied to the balance of unretired units. As the units are retired, no loss or gain is recognized at the time of retirement. The depreciation of successive periods is based on the estimate of average life (which is computed by using mortality experience for this type of asset), and the number of units that are retired in each period. Thus the use of the group procedure of depreciation requires a forecast of the number of units in use in each period in order to compute the depreciation of each period as well as a rate of depreciation.

In the examples given in this book, it is assumed that the asset is purchased in year zero and that depreciation expense is not charged until the end of the year. In practice, two other alternatives are also available. Depreciation may be taken on a monthly basis, beginning in the month the asset is acquired. If the cost of the asset is not too large, and especially when straight-line depreciation is not being used, the extra expense involved in computing monthly depreciation charges for each asset may be greater than the possible saving. Another alternative is to adopt what is called the "half-year convention," in which one-half of a year's depreciation is charged in the year the asset is acquired, regardless of when during the year the asset is acquired. When straight-line depreciation is used, the amount to be charged each year under this system is obvious. With the twice straight-line declining balance method, one-half of the usual rate is applied in the first year, and the usual rate is applied to the remaining book value in subsequent years.

A final complication is the timing of tax payments and of tax savings resulting from depreciation. In past years tax payments have lagged the earning of corporate income, but at present they have been advanced to such an extent that assuming the tax payment (or the tax saving) occurs at the end of the period in which income is earned will generally do no great harm (but see page 119 for an example where timing is relevant).

Working Capital and Salvage Value

In focusing attention on outlays for plant and equipment, it is possible to lose sight of the fact that the working capital needed to operate the investment project should also be included in computing the investment outlays. Since residual working capital is recoverable at the termination of operations, this leads to the investment having a net terminal value that should be taken into consideration. The term *working capital* is used here in a net sense, and applicable current liabilities are subtracted from the increase in current assets to compute the use of cash. The additional current liabilities are assumed not to change the proportion of current liabilities to other sources of capital.

An investment in plant assets will invariably lead to funds being tied up in working capital. This will include the cash necessary to meet payroll and other bills, funds invested in the raw material, work-in-process and finished goods inventory, and receivables from customers. The size of these items will depend on the exact nature of the capital investment, but all the above-mentioned fund requirements will usually accompany an investment in long-lived assets. The one possible exception would be an investment that would decrease the need for working capital by increasing efficiency. Examples of this nature are accounting machines that expedite the billing to customers, or storage facilities and inventory control devices that reduce the amount of inventory which must be kept on hand.

A working capital increase has the effect of increasing the investment outflow today. Ignoring this factor will lead toward the acceptance of investments which should be rejected. If the investment has a limited life and the working capital is expected to be recovered at the end of the life of the investment, then the recovery of the working capital in the last period should be considered as cash proceeds and treated in the same manner as the other cash flows are treated. It should not be thought that ignoring the working capital investment and the recovery of working capital will balance each other out. The factor that must be considered is the required return on the working capital during the period of use.

Salvage Value and Taxes

If taxes are introduced into the analysis of working capital, strange things happen to the conclusions of the investment analysis. The presence of taxes in some situations can actually make salvage value undesirable.

High costs of capital, high tax rates, and long-lived assets, combined with accelerated depreciation for tax purposes, can result in the presence of terminal value adversely affecting the desirability of an investment.

Illustration: Assume a cost of capital of 10 per cent, a 50 per cent tax rate, a life of 20 years for the asset, and a tax depreciation scheme that allows a company to write off a depreciable asset in five years (essentially the same as a certificate of necessity). In this case $100 of depreciable assets may be worth more than $100 of terminal value.

Solution: The present value of $100 of terminal value, and the present value of a dollar due in 20 years, assuming a rate of interest of 10 per cent, is

$$(1.10)^{-20} = 0.104$$

$100 \times 0.104 = \$10.40$ (present value of salvage)

The present value of the tax reductions (assuming no salvage value) of the $100 of additional depreciable assets will reduce taxes a total of $50, or $10 per year. The present value of an annuity of $1.00 per period for five periods, with an interest rate of 10 per cent, is $3.791.

$10 \times 3.791 = \$37.91$ (present value of the tax deductions)

With the facts as given, tax deduction is worth substantially more than the terminal value. Note that the facts of this situation are reasonable and close to reality: The corporate tax rate in recent years has been 52 per cent, depreciable assets do frequently have lives of 20 years, 10 per cent is not excessively high for a cost of capital, and assets have frequently been written off for tax purposes over a period of 60 months.

The ideal situation from the point of view of the investor would be to write off the investment for tax purposes as if it had no salvage, and then wait and see if any salvage will develop. Obviously the taxpayer is going to be better off with a conservative estimate of salvage. This is even more important if the gain on disposition of the investment can qualify as a capital gain, thus receiving special tax consideration.

The above analysis leads to several interesting conclusions. In the presence of income taxes situations can develop where, all other things being equal, it may be more desirable to accept an investment that has no terminal value than one which has terminal value. This conclusion must be tested by existing facts; it cannot be assumed. The factors that tend to make it valid are high tax rates, high cost of capital, long-lived investments, and the privilege of writing off an investment for tax purposes at a faster rate than its actual service potential warrants. Not all these factors have to be present, but the presence of all leads to the conclusion that a depreciable asset deductible for tax purposes is more desirable than an asset which is not depreciable for tax purposes. Secondly, other things being equal, an expenditure that can be expensed immediately for tax purposes is more desirable than an expenditure that must be written off for tax purposes over a period of years. Thus, under the present tax code, increasing net revenues via research may be more desirable than increasing net revenues by the same amount through increasing plant and equipment.

Changes in Inventories and Income Taxes

The computation of cash flows makes use of the cash expenditures for factors of production in the period of outlay when computing the amount of outlays. Some of these factors of production may be lodged in inventory at the end of the accounting period and thus not charged against the revenues of the period. This would affect the cash flows of the period, since the items would not be expensed for purposes of computing income taxes. The income taxes of this period will be higher than they would be if all cash expenditures were expenses for tax purposes. In some future accounting period, these items will be expensed and will result in taxes for that period being reduced, thus in effect increasing the cash flows (by decreasing taxes) in a period long after the cash expendi-

ture was made. Thus build-ups of inventory required by an
investment will adversely affect the desirability of the investment by requiring an immediate cash outlay, while the cash
flows, both by reducing income taxes and by generating revenues upon sale of the item, are delayed for one or more
periods. The inventories must generate enough cash flows,
not only to recover the initial outlay of funds but also to pay
the interest costs of the differences in time of outlay and recovery of cash.

The Timing of Tax Payments

The timing of income tax payments is relevant to the investment analysis if the payment of the tax occurs in a time
period significantly later than the earning of the proceeds.
There are two possible methods of incorporating the delayed
income tax payments into the analysis.

One possibility is to consider the cash outlay to occur when
the actual cash disbursement occurs, not when the obligation
to pay is created. The second possibility is to consider the incurrence of the obligation to pay income taxes to consist of two
simultaneous transactions. The government acts as a source of
capital and supplier of assets, the assets are then expended to
"pay" for the income tax expense. This second possibility then
leads to the inclusion of "Income Taxes Payable" as a noninterest-bearing source of capital in computing the cost of
capital. To be consistent with other recommendations made in
this book, the first procedure is recommended.

Example: Assume a firm has an opportunity to invest $20,000
today in promoting a sport contest. The promised return to
be received one year from today is $24,000. The income tax of
$2,080 (assuming a 52 per cent tax rate) is to be paid two

years from today. The cost of capital is 10 per cent. The schedule of cash flows would be as follows:

Year	Cash flows	Present value factor	Present value of cash flows
0	($20,000)	1.0000	($20,000)
1	24,000	0.9091	21,818
2	(2,080)	0.8264	(1,719)
			$ 99

The net present value is positive and therefore the investment should be undertaken.

If the income taxes are assumed to affect the cash flows of period 1, the cash flows of that period would be $21,920, and the net present value of the cash flows, using a 10 per cent rate of discount, would be a negative $83. This would indicate that the investment should not be undertaken.

9

Uncertainty and the Investment Decision

(question asked on p. 125)

Up to this point we have assumed that the basic goal of the business corporation is to maximize profits and that this goal had to be consistent with maximizing the economic well-being of the stockholders. A further complication is recognized in this chapter: uncertainty, with the resulting possibility of losses.[1]

The Element of Uncertainty

If the investment being considered has uncertainty characteristics similar to those arising from the flipping of a coin, then definite statements may be made as to the possibility of realizing profits. On any one toss there is a fifty-fifty chance of success in obtaining a selected side of the coin; thus there is a large chance that we shall be completely correct if we pick heads and an equally large chance that we shall be completely

[1] The term uncertainty is used here to describe all situations in which the decision maker feels that he does not know all relevant consequences of the alternatives under consideration. No attempt is made in this book to distinguish between risk and uncertainty.

wrong. If, however, there are going to be 100,000 tosses of the coin, we can predict that heads will appear approximately half of the time, and we have a fair degree of confidence that we have chosen correctly. There is obviously a higher degree of uncertainty connected with the percentage of heads with one toss than with 100,000 tosses of the coin. The presence of different degrees of uncertainty may also be true in the area of business.

Let us compare the profit potential of an oil company with the chance of success in tossing coins. If a group of investors organize for the purpose of drilling *one* oil well, they can hire statisticians, geologists, and other experts to compute the odds of finding oil and of finding oil in sufficient quantities to make a profit. In fact it would be possible to make a probability curve of the different possible profits and losses. But how relevant is this information in making the investment decision? All we know is the probability distribution. The actual oil well may result in the maximum possible profits, the maximum possible loss, or something in between. There is a great deal of uncertainty as to the outcome of the operation.

Let us next look at a large oil company with a large number of oil wells. This is analogous to tossing a coin 100,000 times. The probability of a success for a single well is the same, but the expected profit per dollar invested of the operation can be predicted with much more certainty.

Of how much help is the above analysis in making investment decisions? In some cases it may be the deciding factor. Let us assume that the investor is interested in a low chance of loss but still wishes to invest in the oil industry. It is obvious that he should steer clear of the small oil company.

In some cases the element of uncertainty will affect only one of the factors, i.e., profit or loss, but not both. For example, consider two bonds that promise to yield 5 and 3 per cent.

The former is an industrial bond and the latter a government bond. There is no uncertainty as to the maximum profit to be obtained. If only the maximum profit or even the most probable outcome were considered, there would be no question but that the higher yielding industrial bond would be chosen. But let us also examine the maximum possible loss. If held to maturity, the government bond will be paid. There is little or no uncertainty about this possibility. There is some possibility of doubt about the industrial bond being paid. The past history of industrial securities indicates that a certain percentage of industrial bonds are not paid at maturity. There is some uncertainty about the maximum possible loss actually being suffered. Both types of securities may find willing investors. The person desiring certainty of possible profits and no possible losses will choose government securities. The person desiring possibility of profits, but who is willing to accept (or to ignore) some uncertainty of possible losses, will invest in industrial bonds.

The Range of Profits

Now, having recognized the element of uncertainty, we must analyze how this affects the internal investment decisions of a firm. The firm may be motivated by many of the same factors that motivate the individual investor. It may be satisfied with a small expected return from an investment if the uncertainty connected with the investment is also small. On the other hand, it may be attracted to the high-yielding investment and ignore the uncertainty connected with the income and the possibility of losses.

There are actually two elements of uncertainty to be considered in making the internal investment decision:

1. What is the likelihood that the estimate of the proceeds is correct?

2. What happens to the profit prediction if the actual events do differ from the predicted events?

Unless we are dealing with promises to pay, backed up by a financially strong governmental unit, there is some possibility that the expected cash proceeds will not be realized. This can occur for many reasons: General business activity may be different than predicted; the company's share of the market may change; the estimated useful life of the investment may be wrong; or the forecasts of price or of costs may be wrong. To what extent is the investment vulnerable to faulty estimates?

The second question follows from the first. If the original estimates are incorrect, how will this affect the desirability of the investment? What is the maximum possible loss that may be incurred if the investment is undertaken? How rapidly, for example, do the proceeds fall with a decrease in business activity?

Obviously these factors must be considered if a reasonable investment decision is to be made. Just looking at profitability for one given set of assumptions, with no statement as to the uncertainty connected with the assumptions or the possibility of lesser profits or losses occurring if the assumptions are not realized, is not a sound method of decision making.

Investors and Management

It was stated in the preceding section that the firm and the individual investor are similarly motivated. However, there are also differences that must be considered. The individual investor may have definite ideas concerning the amount of risk he is willing to assume; thus he can weigh the maximum amount of profit against the maximum amount of loss. The member of management making the investment decision may know his own valuation of gains and losses, but he may not be able to judge those of other members of management or those of the stockholders.

As compared with an individual, how can we estimate for a corporation the pleasure to be gained from making profits and

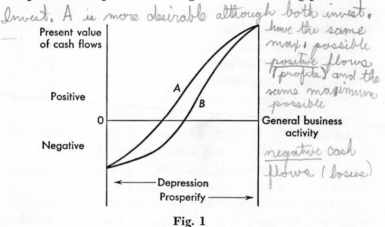

Invest. A is more desirable although both invest. have the same may, possible positive flows (profits) and the same maximum possible

Present value
of cash flows

Positive

A

B

0   General business
                                            activity

Negative

negative cash flows (losses)

◄———— Depression
Prosperify ————►

Fig. 1

the disappointment of suffering losses? Rather than facing up to this decision, perhaps a reasonable alternative would be to place probabilities on the more likely eventualities and to examine the desirability of the investment, taking into consideration more than one set of assumptions. This procedure would not satisfy the theoreticians who would suggest that we should measure the satisfactions possible from attaining the maximum profits, the dissatisfactions from incurring the maximum loss, and also incorporate the reactions from other profit possibilities. This type of analysis is desirable, but we do not know how to implement it for large corporations. On the other hand, studying only one set of data is not desirable. For example, consider investments A and B. The possible net cash flows of the two investments, given different assumptions as to general business activity, are given in Figure 1. Note that both investments have the same maximum possible positive flows and the same maximum possible loss (maximum possible negative cash flows). Yet the diagram indicates that investment A is more desirable. At all points the present value of cash flow of investment A is equal to or greater than that of investment B.

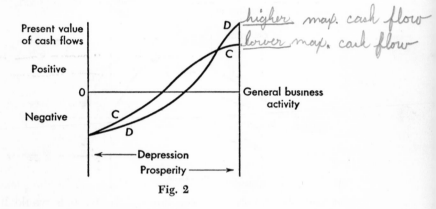

higher map. cash flow
lower map. cash flow

Fig. 2

Consider the mutually exclusive investments C and D as shown in Figure 2. Investment C has a lower maximum cash flow than investment D (the maximum profits are lower). Which of the two would be the better investment? The answer to this question is more complicated. One possible answer is that the investment with the largest area under the curve is the better investment (the negative cash proceeds and the resulting area should be subtracted). The answer would be valid if each possible present value had an equal probability of occurrence. Assuming unequal probabilities, another set of curves must be drawn (see Figure 3).

However, when using Figure 3, it is not clear which of the two investments is more desirable. Both investments have the

Is profit map. related to present value in positive proportion?

same maximum possible loss (V_1), but the maximum possible gains differ. Investment D has a larger maximum gain (V_5) than investment C (V_4). If we consider only the gain associated with the most likely outcome, we note that the most likely outcome of D (V_3) is greater than the most likely outcome for investment C, which is (V_2). One solution would be to multiply each possible gain or loss by the probability that it will occur (the losses being subtracted from the gains).

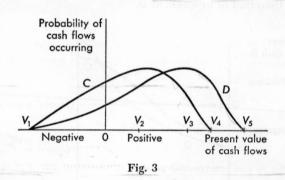

Fig. 3

It should be noted that once we take account of the pleasures and disappointments, i.e., how the individuals would be affected psychologically by the profits and losses, then none of the computations described above, or to follow, needs necessarily point to the more desirable investment. The possibility of large gain may outweigh in importance to the investor the possibility of a very large loss, or just the opposite.

Illustration of Uncertainty—Introducing a New Product

The introduction of a new product is an interesting example of a business decision involving a large degree of uncertainty. The choice is essentially between:

1. Making large initial outlays, thus opening the possibility of large profits if the expectations are realized, or large losses if expectations are not realized; or,

2. Making relatively small outlays and sampling the market. If the product is successful, the scope of operations can be broadened. If the product is unsuccessful, the maximum amount of losses is not large, since the initial outlays were less than under the first alternative. The maximum possible profits following this procedure are also less, since other companies will be watching the market sampling. If the new product is successful on a small scale, it can be expected that competitors will take action at approximately the same time as the originator takes action. The opportunity to reap the large profits of the innovator has been forsaken in order to reduce the possible loss.

Which of the preceding two alternatives is more desirable? There is no easy answer. The second procedure is the more desirable *if* the maximum profits obtainable are not affected by the speed with which we enter the market. But to assume that the profits will not be affected is naïve. The hoola hoop craze of 1958 is a good example of a new product introduced with competitive market conditions. The retail price of a hoop at the time of introduction was approximately $2.00. In a period of three months the price was successively reduced until one could obtain a fine hoop for $0.69. The innovator of the hoop had an investment decision to make before introducing his product. Should he have built up a large inventory and then released a flood of hoops to take advantage of the initial enthusiasm? With the aid of hindsight it may be concluded that this is what the company should have done. As it turned out, other plastic companies were in nearly as good a position to share in the initial profits as the innovating firm.

Actually, instead of two choices, the business manager has a wide spectrum of alternatives, ranging from incurring a small risk (and a small profit possibility) to a large risk (and a large profit possibility). The initial analysis of probable revenues and costs has indicated that this is a desirable product and, in general, a desirable investment. The exact amount of funds to be invested in the product, i.e., the size of plant, amount of advertising, size of the sales organization, and initial finished goods inventory before beginning sales, are managerial decisions requiring judgment. There is no simple formula or procedure that will give the correct answer. The firm must decide whether it desires a relatively safe position and small profits, or whether it is willing to innovate, with the accompanying risks and possible profits that fall to the innovator.

Allowing for Uncertainty

The rate of discount used to compute the present value of the cash flows is the cost of capital. Should an investment with more uncertainty have a higher rate of discount than an investment with less uncertainty? The answer tentatively suggested is negative.[2] Uncertainty recognized in computing the cash flows is more effective than using a higher discount factor for increased risk.

How should uncertainty be incorporated into the capital-budgeting decision? If one of a pair of mutually exclusive investments has an expected present value of $5,000 and another has $2,000, the first would seem to be the preferred investment. But this analysis ignores the possibility that the expected proceeds may not be realized and that in fact there are other present values which are also possible for the investments. Let us assume that the $2,000 present value is certain of being

[2] For discussion, see Chapter 4.

realized, and that while the $5,000 present value is the most probable present value of the first investment, there is a 40 per cent probability that the present value will be zero or less. Which is the better investment? Although we maximize our profit with the first investment, that investment also results in a large possibility of loss. The choice between the two investments is not obvious.

Recognizing the difficulty of preparing a schedule of possible cash proceeds for all possible contingencies, the following procedure is suggested as one possible practical solution.

1. Determine the present value of the net cash flows for three different assumptions:

   a. Most probable series of events
   b. A reasonably pessimistic series of events
   c. A reasonably optimistic series of events

2. Weigh the three present values, using the best information available or using standard weights such as 50 per cent for the most probable and 25 per cent for the optimistic and pessimistic predictions.

3. The sum of the three weighted present values may be used to represent the present value of the investment, taking uncertainty into consideration (to a limited degree).[3]

Example: Investment A has a present value of cash flows of $10,000. This present value of cash flows is considered certain. Investment B has a most probable net present value of cash

---

[3] A similar procedure, assigning values to outcomes according to their "utility" rather than their present values, has recently been recommended. Unfortunately the author does not specify how he would determine the utility of various outcomes to a corporation. See Robert Schlaifer, *Probability and Statistics for Business Decisions*, McGraw-Hill Book Co., Inc., New York, 1959.

flows of $15,000, but it is also possible for investment B to have a net cash flow of $20,000 or to have net negative cash flows of $5,000. The two investments are mutually exclusive. Which is the more desirable?

As a possible solution let us compute the present value of cash flows, taking into consideration the entire range of possibilities:

				Expected value
Optimistic assumptions......	$20,000	×	25%	$ 5,000
Most probable.............	15,000	×	50%	7,500
Pessimistic assumptions......	(5,000)	×	25%	(1,250)
				$11,250

The weighted present value of cash flows of investment B is $11,250, which is greater than the present value of the cash flows of investment A. Therefore investment B seems more desirable. If there is reason to doubt the assumed probabilities, then other probabilities should be tried to see how changing the probabilities would affect the decision. Another possibility would be to weigh the pessimistic choice more heavily than the optimistic choice. This would be based on the assumption that the amount of grief from a loss exceeds the amount of pleasure from more profit.

The advantage of this method is that it allows us to bring into the investment decision analysis, in a fairly systematic manner, more than one assumption as to the profitability of the investments being considered. The procedure is flexible enough to allow us to include preferences of such goals as a tendency to minimize losses or maximize profits. Note the insertion of the word "tendency." A goal of minimization of losses would result in no investments being made in any project more risky than a government security. Thus a weighting of the pessimistic assumption more heavily than the optimistic assumption tends to minimize the possible losses, since it is a bias against any investment that may show a negative cash flow, although it does not exclude the possibility of such an investment.

Where the several investments being considered have approximately the same present value of cash flows, then we must resort to criteria other than present value in order to make the investment decision. In fact, in all decisions the present-value computation is more of a guide than an "always correct" answer to the investment decision.

Changing the Uncertainty

It is possible for a company to follow courses of action that will decrease to some extent the degree of uncertainty connected with its operations. Increasing the information obtained prior to making a decision is one method of decreasing uncertainty. For example, a thorough job of market research may make the outcome of an investment in a new product much less uncertain than if the product were launched without the market research.

Another method of reducing uncertainty is by increasing the size of operations. A large oil company faces less uncertainty than a small group banded together to drill one well. On the other hand, a decentralized company may not make use of this fact if a division manager cannot take advantage of the "law of large numbers" because his performance is measured by using the operating data of his relatively small operation. In this case he may be in the same position as the manager of a small firm who fears risky investments because of the threat of insolvency.

Product diversification may also decrease the uncertainty, especially if two products compete with each other. Thus a combined gas and electric company servicing a metropolitan city would have less uncertainty than two separate companies, each specializing in either the electric or gas business. If major industrial users switch from electricity to gas, the fortunes of the specialized companies will be drastically affected, whereas if there were only one company there would be less of a change in the company's profits. Product diversification would also decrease uncertainty if the two products were differently affected by changes in business activity. For example, a combined grocery chain and machine equipment company would have less uncertainty than a specialized machine equipment manufacturer.

SUMMARY

Some investments available to a corporation may be more risky than other investments, i.e., there is a higher degree of uncertainty. The introduction of uncertainty opens up the possibility of losses, which in turn forces us to measure the relative importance of the possibility of large profits compared with the possibility of large losses.

It is suggested that management should consciously consider the possibility of not realizing the forecasted results and should incorporate this into the analysis. There remains the question of the psychological impact on business managers and investors of losses and gains. This area of analysis is still in its infancy, and there is little that can presently be brought effectively into the investment decision of a complex corporation.

10

The Cost of Capital—I

The cost of Capital : i.e., [illegible] the rate of discount that is used to compute the present value of the cash flows .

In our discussion up to this point we have stated the rule that investments should be considered desirable (insofar as quantitative estimates of their profitability are the determining factor) if the present value of the cash flows expected from them is positive, using the company's cost of capital as the discount factor. Chapters 2, 3, and 4 demonstrate that this rule has real advantages over alternative methods commonly used in evaluating investment proposals. But we have not explicitly defined the term *cost of capital*. Unless this concept can be defined in a reasonably useful and correct way, the investment criterion we are suggesting cannot be applied in practice.

Funds to finance an investment proposal may be obtained by a firm in a variety of ways: by borrowing from banks, by allowing short-term liabilities to expand, by selling marketable securities such as government bonds, by selling other assets or parts of its business, by issuing additional securities (either bonds, preferred stock, or common stock), or by committing funds generated by operations. These are only some of the more important sources. For certain types of these sources of cash, such as bank loans, there is a generally accepted, although not necessarily correct, definition of the cost of funds obtained. For other sources, such as funds generated by operations, several definitions of the cost of capital have been proposed, including the notion that funds from this source are free.

If an investment proposal is to be financed by borrowing from banks, is the interest rate on the loan the relevant cost of capital for this investment? If this approach were consistently followed, the cost of capital would be an erratic quantity, fluctuating up or down as the firm obtained additional increments of capital from varying sources. Although there are situations in which a particular investment can be related to a specific source of financing,[1] more commonly there exists on the one hand a group of apparently desirable investment proposals, and on the other, a variety of sources of additional capital funds that, taken together, could supply the financing for the increased investment. In such circumstances any procedure for assigning the cost of a particular source of capital funds to a specific investment proposal would be arbitrary and capricious.

Definition of Cost of Capital

Before discussing the complexities of the concept of the cost of capital, we shall state the definition of cost of capital that will be developed in this chapter. This procedure is chosen to give the reader a compass that may assist him in following the necessarily complex explanation that will be discussed.

---

[1] For example, in the railroad industry, acquisitions of additional rolling stock may be financed by issuing equipment trust certificates for which the rolling stock acquired is the collateral. In many firms, inventories are assigned as collateral for bank loans. These examples may be misleading, for lenders may actually examine the firm's earning potential and financial structure before deciding to accept securities based on specific collateral.

The cost of capital of a firm may be defined as a weighted average of the cost of each type of capital. The weight for each type of capital is the ratio of the market value of the securities representing that source of capital to the market value of all securities issued by the company. *The term* security *includes common and preferred stocks and all interest-bearing liabilities, including notes payable.*

Cost of Common Stock Capital

The cost of common stock capital is equal to the return required by common stockholders. This return can be measured by comparing *expected future* dividends to the present market value of the common stock. The rate of discount that equates future dividends for perpetuity to the cost of the stock is the cost of capital for common stock capital.

It is recognized that we cannot be certain as to the amount of future dividends expected by the stockholders. On the other hand it is not unreasonable to assume that the stockholder is in general basing his expectation of the future on the past. It will be shown in Chapter 11 that the cost of capital of common stock equity may be approximated by the formula:

$$r = \frac{D_0}{P_0} + g$$

where r = cost of capital of common stock funds
D_0 = current cash-dividend rate
P_0 = current market price per share
g = expected annual percentage rate of increase in future dividends expressed as a decimal fraction

Suppose that the current dividend is $6.00 per share, the current market price is $150.00 per share, and the dividend per share is expected to increase at about 2 per cent per year. In this case the cost of equity capital could be estimated (as a first approximation) as follows:

$$r = 0.04 + 0.02 = 0.06 \text{ (or 6 per cent)}$$

In estimating the cost of equity capital by using this approach, care must be taken to adjust for expected stock splits and stock dividends, if any. For example, a company may establish a policy of paying a regular dividend of $6.00 per share outstanding and a regular stock dividend of 2 per cent per year. In this case, although the nominal dividend per share is constant, the actual dividends that can be expected by a stockholder holding 100 shares initially (and assuming that he retained all the additional stock dividends issued) would be $600.00 in the first year, $612.00 in the second year, $624.24 in the third year, etc. In other words the dividend actually received would be growing at a steady rate of 2 per cent per year.

Cost of Long-term Debt

The cost of long-term debt capital is the current effective interest rate for long-term securities of the specific firm being studied. It must be recognized that the indicated interest rate of an outstanding debt security may not be the effective rate of interest because the security may be selling at a premium or a discount. The effective rate of interest for an outstanding issue can be determined by comparing the current market price for the security with the remaining payment obligations. For example, the effective rate of interest for a bond outstanding can be found by finding the rate of interest which equates the market price and the present value of the amount due at maturity plus the present value of the series of interest payments.

Cost of Short-term Debt

The cost of short-term debt is analogous to that of long-term debt in that there may be an explicit interest cost (as with a short-term bank loan).

There are several short-term liabilities that do not have explicit interest costs. Among these are taxes payable and wages payable. There are other short-term debts that may or may not have a cost if they are not paid promptly. For example, a trade creditor may offer terms of 2/10, n/30. There is no cost for not paying the bill in the first nine days, since the 2 per cent discount may be taken at any time prior to the lapsing of ten days. If the discount is allowed to lapse, there is a 2 per cent penalty assessed for the use of the funds for a maximum of 20 days. This is equivalent to an annual interest rate of approximately 36 per cent. Some firms may allow the discount to lapse and then pay the bill some time after the 30-day period. Here a cost is added, arising from the loss of credit standing, supplier ill-will, etc.

In the discussions on cash flows (Chapter 7) and income taxes (Chapter 8) it was suggested that any increase in non-interest-bearing liabilities should be subtracted from the increase in current assets required, and only the net amount (increase in current assets minus the increase in current liabilities) should be considered a cash outlay in computing the cash flows. This method of handling the noninterest-bearing liabilities leads to the conclusion that such liabilities should not be treated as a source of capital when computing the cost of capital, since the implicit receipt (and disbursement) of funds is left out of the analysis.

If one prefers to include the noninterest-bearing current liabilities as part of the capital structure when computing the cost of capital, then the total current assets required by the investment should be considered as an outlay made in the period during which the liabilities increase. Any change in the capital structure resulting from an increase in current liabilities would then affect the cost of capital.

The procedure that nets the current liabilities against current assets has been chosen in this book, since it gives sound reasonable answers and simplifies both the computations and explanations of cash flows.

Debt and Income Taxes

When dividends are paid to stockholders, the effective cost of the equity funds can be determined by taking into consideration the amount of the dividend, the price of the stock, and the expected rate of change in the dividends. In computing the effective cost of debt, the interest payments must be adjusted to compensate for the fact that interest is deductible for tax purposes.

Example: Compute the average effective rate of interest, assuming that the yield of the debt outstanding is 6 per cent. the tax rate for the corporation is 52 per cent, and the corporation has taxable income.

Since the interest is deductible for corporate income tax purposes, $1.00 of interest will reduce taxes by $0.52, and effective interest cost will therefore be $0.48 per dollar of interest. The effective interest cost is 0.48 × 6 per cent, or 2.88 per cent, instead of the 6 per cent yield of the debt.

Computing the Average Cost of Capital

Suppose the market value of a company's common stock is estimated at $45 million. The market value of its interest-bearing debt is estimated at $30 million, and the average before-tax yield on these liabilities is 6 per cent per year, which is equivalent on an after-tax basis to 2.88 per cent per year (equal to 6 per cent times 0.48, assuming a 52 per cent tax rate).

Assume that the company described in the preceding paragraph is currently paying a dividend of $8.00 per year and that the stock is selling at a price of $100. The rate of growth of the dividend is projected to be 2 per cent per year. Thus the average cost of the common stock equity is

$$r = \frac{\$8}{\$100} + 0.02 = 0.08 + 0.02 = 0.10, \quad \text{or } 10 \text{ per cent}$$

The average cost of capital for the company as a whole could be estimated as follows:

Estimate of Cost of Capital

Capital source	Proportion of total capital	Cost	
Equity	0.60	0.10	0.06
Debt, interest-bearing ..	0.40	0.0288	0.012
Average cost of capital			0.072, or 7.2%

The Relevance of Cost of Capital

A person who desires neat solutions with one correct answer should avoid the computation of a corporation's cost of capital.

Usually such an answer is impossible. If ten "experts" independently computed the cost of capital of the IBM Corporation, there would be ten answers. Although an exact answer to a corporation's cost of capital is elusive, it is possible to establish a range which, with a high degree of probability, includes the cost of capital. Thus the cost of capital of IBM is probably between 4 per cent (an assumed yield on government securties) and, say, 10 per cent (computed by using the weighted average procedure of Chapter 10). Let us assume that we guess wrong and choose 5 per cent, while the "actual" cost of capital (established through some correct but as yet undiscovered procedure) is 8 per cent. To what extent will this affect the capital-budgeting decision? Investments with positive present values, using 8 per cent (the correct cost of capital), would also generally have a positive present value with a 5 per cent cost of capital (the incorrectly determined but actually used cost of capital). Investments with negative present values, using 8 per cent, would also generally have negative present values with 5 per cent. Different accept or reject decisions would be reached for investments that yielded 5 per cent or greater and less than 8 per cent. The main result will be a failure to attain the theoretical maximum of the economic well-being of the stockholders.

11

The Cost of Capital—II

COST OF COMMON STOCK CAPITAL

The Cost of Capital and the Goals of Organizations

A satisfactory definition of cost of capital is necessary in guiding the internal investment policy of corporate management. The choice of investments represents a strategic decision for the management of a firm, since in large part the choices made now will influence the future course of the firm's development. It is not surprising to find that implicit in any definition of a cost of capital to guide investment policy is a judgment as to the goals toward which the firm is or should be striving. The goals determine the appropriate definition of capital cost. Certainly we cannot assume without proof that seemingly different goals will lead to identical definitions of cost of capital.

The corporate goal that has been conventionally adopted in discussions of this kind is that the corporation seeks to maximize the economic well-being of present stockholders. This requires a balance between maintaining the market value per share [1] of the firm's equities at the highest possible level and paying the highest possible current dividends, assuming that management and the market both correctly assess the firm's future earning and dividend-paying potential.

It is recognized that corporate managements frequently have other goals that are sometimes in conflict with the goal described above: Management may desire to see the corporate organization expand; to ensure that its own tenure and ability to choose its successors is not threatened; to extend or at least maintain the realm in which it is free to make decisions for the organization without reference to outside groups (be they government officials, minority stockholders, bankers, life insurance companies, or labor union officials); to support what it considers to be desirable nonprofit institutions; to undertake activities in the name of the corporation for patriotic motives; or to achieve a high level of material benefits for itself. In attempting to work out a definition of cost of capital based on the goal of maximizing the economic interests of present stockholders, we do not mean to deny the existence or the importance of other goals. If other goals are in competition with the goal of maximizing present stockholders' economic interests, the development of an adequate definition of cost of capital based on stockholders' interests may help us understand the extent to which the various goals are in conflict.

The Cost of Retained Earnings

The costs associated with retaining some part of the current earnings are not always obvious. Frequently corporate officials

---

[1] Adjusted for stock dividends and stock splits.

have taken the position that these funds are without cost. If we stipulate the economic interests of present stockholders as overriding, then these funds are not free, and the cost associated with them must be measured by the opportunities foregone in using them in one way instead of in other possible ways. Essentially there are two kinds of opportunities for the use of corporate earnings. They may be retained within the corporation, or they may be distributed as dividends to stockholders.

If earnings (or some part of earnings) are retained within the corporation, stockholders are deprived of the current dividends that could have been paid with those earnings. This is a cost to the stockholders. On the other hand there are some benefits, the valuation of which will depend upon what the corporation does with the funds. Suppose they are reinvested to increase future earnings of the corporation. If, as a result, the stock of the corporation is worth more, the increase in the value of the stock may more than offset the lower current dividend. If so, stockholders will be better off than if the investment had been rejected and they had received the cash dividends.

The funds that could have been used for dividends need not be reinvested in long-lived assets in order to provide a net benefit to stockholders. They may be used to reduce bank loans or bonded indebtedness, to start a training program for employees, or to add to the financial liquidity of the corporation by increasing the amount of cash on hand. Whatever the use, if it serves to increase the relative market value of the stock, it will serve to offset partially or completely the loss to the stockholder from not receiving a larger immediate dividend.

A simple example will illustrate this point. For the moment we ignore the effects of the personal income tax. Suppose the stock of a company has been selling at a price of $100.00 per share and that normal dividends of $5.00 per share are being paid. The directors are contemplating either declaring a special dividend of $1.00 per share or undertaking an additional investment with the money. According to the criteria we have suggested above, the additional investment would be in the stockholders' interests only if it would result in at least a $1.00 per share increase in the market value of the company's stock. *The cost of using retained earnings is therefore the minimum yield that must be earned on additional investments within the company in order that the additional investment will be as valuable to the stockholder as a corresponding immediate increase in dividends.*

Suppose a corporation whose capital structure consisted entirely of equity was considering an investment that would require an immediate cash outlay of $100,000. The officers of the corporation estimated that if the investment proposal were accepted, the corporation would receive additional cash proceeds of $20,000 (after taxes) per year indefinitely. The officials further estimated that once the stock market had learned about the acceptance of this investment, the common stock of the company would probably be increased in value by $200,000. If the investment proposal were not accepted, the company would be able to pay out an additional $100,000 in dividends. Clearly it would be to the advantage of stockholders to have the company accept the investment proposal.

The information given could also be used to estimate the cost of retained earnings for this company. This estimate is the rate of discount that makes the present value of the expected cash proceeds equal to the change in the price of the common stock. In this example the present value of a perpetuity of $20,000 per year would equal $200,000 at 10 per cent. Investments having a positive net present value at 10 per cent will be advantageous to present stockholders, since they will result in an increase in the market price of the stock.

Whether a particular stockholder will be better or worse off as a result of a somewhat smaller dividend and a somewhat larger rise in the price of the stock (or for that matter a smaller decrease in its value than might otherwise have taken place) will depend upon the income tax rates on ordinary income and on capital gains to which the stockholder is subject.[2] Stockholders differ widely in this regard: Some are subjected to high marginal tax rates, and others, such as foundations and universities, are not subject to income taxes. Thus there is no one minimum yield at which stockholders are better off if the corporation reinvests earnings instead of paying greater dividends; rather there are many groups of stockholders whose personal interests are different.

An investor who is not subject to income taxes (e.g., a university or a nonprofit foundation) may be indifferent to the extra dollar in dividends and/or the extra dollar of capital gains. An investor who has to pay a 50 per cent tax on ordinary income and a 25 per cent tax on capital gains may be willing to sacrifice a dollar in dividends in order to gain less than a dollar in capital gains.

If the stock of corporations were distributed between investors in some random manner, the conflicts of interest between investors would be of great practical importance. Actually, however, most large corporations follow reasonably

[2] The Internal Revenue Code is only one of many factors that create conflicts of interest among stockholders. At the same time some stockholders are attempting to increase their investment portfolios while others are withdrawing a part of their investments. Even if neither group was subject to taxes, the first would tend to prefer capital gains because it would thereby avoid the brokerage fees required to convert dividends into additional stock holdings. The second group would tend to prefer dividends so as to avoid the expenses and inconvenience of selling a part of its holdings periodically.

consistent financial and investment policies. The securities of most listed corporations undoubtedly tend to flow into the portfolios of investors whose personal investment goals are consistent with the known policies of the companies whose stock they hold. Thus conflicts of interest between stockholders of widely held corporations are greatly reduced by the ease with which stock may be sold.

A Theory of Stock Values

For the purpose of understanding the cost of equity capital, a useful theory of stock values is one which assumes that the price of a share of stock tends to be determined by the present value of the dividends which investors as a group expect to be paid by the company. This theory implies that under present institutional arrangements, the stockholder has no real interest in earnings per se except as they affect future dividends or stock prices. As pointed out above, because of personal income tax considerations, some investors prefer situations in which their stock-market gains can be realized in the form of capital gains rather than dividends. But although a stock may for a time show increases in price because some investors come to look upon it as a potential source of capital gains, the stock cannot indefinitely continue to rise in price *only* on the basis of such expectations. If the expectations of capital gains are realized *only* because new groups of investors come to share similar expectations and to act upon them, the situation may be described as a speculative boom, and it will end in a drastic decline in the price of stock as the supply of investors gradually dries up.

If the hopes of capital gains are to be based on a more solid footing, it must be because the stock eventually will become more valuable to some people for a reason other than a desire for capital gains, namely, the expectation of dividend payments.

To illustrate this approach to the theory of stock values, we may start with a very simple case in which a company is assumed to have a financial structure consisting solely of common stock. Suppose that by past behavior, announced policy, and an objective evaluation of the investment opportunities open to it, this company has established a firm expectation that its future dividends will continue to be paid at the constant rate of $6.00 per share per year. When the dividend per share is expected to be constant (and no stock dividends are anticipated), the cost of equity capital can be computed simply as the ratio of the expected dividend to the market price of the shares. In symbolic form, we have

$$r = \frac{D}{P_0}$$

where r = cost of capital

D = (constant) expected future dividend

P_0 = current market price per share

In the example described, if the market price per share is $150, the cost of capital would be estimated as 4 per cent because this is the rate of discount implied by the market price per share and the expectation of the constant $6.00 per year dividend. It is important to note that we are not suggesting that the cost of equity capital is necessarily equal to the dividend price ratio. It turns out to be equal to this ratio only when the current dividend rate is expected to be continued into the indefinite future and when no stock dividends are expected.

More commonly, the market will expect some changes in future dividend rates. It can be shown that if the current dividend is expected to grow at a steady rate, the rate at which the market is discounting future dividends can be roughly approximated from the following expression: [3]

$$r = \frac{D_0}{P_0} + g$$

where r = cost of common stock capital (rate at which future dividends are being discounted) expressed as a decimal fraction

D_0 = current dividend rate

P_0 = current market price per share

g = expected annual percentage rate of increase in future dividends, expressed as a decimal fraction

The formula in the preceding paragraph assumes that the dividends of each period will increase by a constant percentage of the previous period's dividends. This formula does not explicitly consider expected capital gains or relate dividends to

---

[3] To show this, it is convenient mathematically to assume dividends are paid out and discounted continuously. If the initial dividend is D_0, and it is expected to increase at the rate of g per year, then the dividend in year t (i.e., D_t) will be

$$D_t = D_0 e^{gt}$$

By assumption, the current market price will be equal to the present value of this stream of expected dividends. If the (unknown) rate of discount is r, we can write

$$P_0 = \int_0^\infty D_t e^{-rt} dt$$

Substituting and integrating, we have, provided $r > g$:

$$P_0 = \int_0^\infty D_0 e^{t(g-r)} dt = \frac{D_0}{r - g}$$

The expression in the text is found by rearranging terms from the expression

$$P_0 = \frac{D_0}{r - g}$$

See M. J. Gordon and E. Shapiro, "Capital Equipment Analysis: The Required Rate of Profit," *Management Science III*, October 1956, pp. 104–106.

earnings. It is possible to modify the formula to include these elements if this seems desirable. For example, instead of including all future dividends, we could estimate the cost of capital on the basis of the dividends expected during some limited future period, and the expected price of the stock at the end of the period. If we consider only one future period, the basic equation could be written as follows:

$$P_0 = D_0 + \frac{P_1}{1+r}$$

where P_1 is the expected price one period from now, and the remaining symbols are defined as before. Rearranging terms, this reduced to the following expression:

$$r = \frac{D_0 + (P_1 - P_0)}{P_0 - D_0}$$

In this form, the role of capital gains becomes explicit; the estimate of the increase in the price of the stock up to some future date becomes a substitute for the estimate of expected dividends beyond that date.

Since the linkage between dividends and earnings is usually quite close, security analysts and others frequently concentrate their attention on estimates of future earnings. It is also possible to develop formulas for estimating the cost of capital that are expressed in terms of earnings instead of dividends. In so doing, it is important to keep in mind that retained earnings are of value to the ordinary investor only in so far as they constitute an economically profitable use of the company's funds.[4]

The formulas presented in the previous paragraphs should not be thought of as ways of estimating a company's cost of

[4] On this point, see James F. Walter, "Dividend Policies and Common Stock Prices," *Journal of Finance* XI, March, 1956, pp. 29–41.

capital. Rather they are possible frameworks within which such estimates might be made. The framework is useful only to the extent that it facilitates the essential task of assessing the market evaluation of the economic potential of the company's common stock.

Changes in Stock Prices and the Cost of Equity Capital

We all know that stock prices fluctuate quite widely. Does this mean that we are faced with a cost of capital for common stock that changes daily? The answer is a qualified "yes."

Just as bond prices change from day to day as they reflect changes in the interest rate (thus changes in the cost of debt capital), changes in stock prices also will reflect changes in the cost of common stock. There is one prime difference, however, between bonds and stock. The interest payment on bonds is determined by contract and is easily predicted. Common stock dividends are more difficult to predict. They are dependent to some extent on the earnings of the corporation, the cash available, and the decisions of the board of directors. In turn the earnings of the corporation are dependent on numerous factors, such as general business conditions, the actions of competitors, and the desires of consumers. But even if earnings and dividends can be predicted relatively accurately, there are still the whims of the stock market, the waves of optimism and pessimism.

How do the above factors affect the cost of capital? A change in expected dividends and earnings will cause the price of the stock to change, but there may *not* be a change in the cost of common stock capital. For example, if the price of a share of common stock is $10.00 and if future dividends of $1.00 per year are expected, the stock yields 10 per cent. If conditions change and the expected dividends in the future, as seen by the market, are $0.50 per year, the price of the stock may drop to $5.00. The cost of capital remains unchanged at 10 per cent.

It is possible that attitudes toward the company, the industry, or the risks of business in general may change, or there may be a change in the amount of total funds available for investment in industry. In this case the market may still expect the $1.00 dividend to be earned into perpetuity, but the price of the stock may nevertheless change from $10.00 to $8.00. In this case the indicated cost of capital has changed from 10 to 12.5 per cent.

It is, of course, impossible to determine with certainty what factors have caused a change in the price of a stock. Much work remains to be done in the area of isolating the reasons why the price of a share of stock may change.

Cost of Capital and Inflation

Inflation, or the expectation of inflation, may affect the cost of capital of a firm. Let us assume that the market thinks that stock in company X is a good hedge against inflation, i.e., future dividends of company X will increase more as a result of inflation than comparable investments. In this situation it is possible either that the cost of capital is unchanged (but higher future dividends are expected) or that the desirability of the stock has increased relative to other investments, and its cost of capital has decreased.

For the decision maker attempting to determine his company's cost of capital, it will be more difficult to forecast the growth in dividends anticipated by the market, since this growth rate is affected by the prospect of inflation.

Stable Dividend Policy

In the preceding section we discussed the cost of retained earnings as though the alternative to retaining earnings in each year was an increased dividend. Although a discussion in these terms is useful in explaining the ideas underlying the notion of the cost of retained earnings, a too-literal interpretation of the preceding section would result in a financial policy that could have disadvantages in practice. Interpreted literally, the preceding section would suggest that in each year the company would estimate its cost of capital, and with the help of this estimate, would determine what investment opportunities available to it would be profitable. If the investment opportunities accepted did not exhaust all the funds available from current operations, the remainder would be distributed to shareholders as dividends. Such a procedure would almost certainly result in a widely fluctuating annual dividend, since both the quantity of funds that could be profitably reinvested and the quantity of funds available from current operations are likely to fluctuate from year to year.

Financial experts generally believe that a highly unstable dividend is not advantageous to a company.[5] The most common reason stated for this belief is that stockholders prefer a steady income from their investments. There is at least one other important reason for thinking that a highly variable dividend rate may not be in the best interest of a company. We have suggested earlier that, in the long run, the value of a share of stock tends to be determined by the discounted value of the expected dividends. Insofar as this is the case, a widely

[5] There is also a school of thought that believes dividend policy does not affect the value of common stock. Much work remains to be done concerning the effect of dividend policy on stock prices.

fluctuating dividend rate will tend to make it difficult for stock-holders to determine the value of the stock to them, and as a result the stock is likely to sell at a somewhat lower price than comparable stocks paying the same average amount as dividends but making payments at a steady rate.

A recent study suggests that many large corporations tend to pay out a constant fraction of their earnings as dividends. A change in earnings that is expected to be fairly permanent is more or less rapidly reflected in dividend payments, but short-term fluctuations in earnings usually are not allowed to influence dividends. The result is that, although the dividend earnings ratio may vary considerably from year to year, the long-term average tends to be quite constant.[6]

If a policy of this type is adopted, the choice of a long-run pay-out ratio becomes quite important. If the pay-out ratio is set rather high (relative to the quantity of profitable invest-ments available to the company), in many years the company will find that the profitable investments available to it require more funds than are available internally after dividend com-mitments have been met. In such circumstances one of two major alternatives must be chosen if the alternative of changing the dividend policy is not available. The company must either forego some profitable investments or seek additional funds. On the other hand, if the pay-out ratio is set too low relative to the quantity of profitable investments available, the company may either find itself accumulating an unwarranted amount of liquid assets or may be tempted to accept investments that are not truly consistent with the objective of maximizing the eco-nomic well-being of the stockholders.

The disadvantages of too low a dividend pay-out relative to

[6] John Lintner, "Distribution of Incomes of Corporations Among Dividends, Retained Earnings, and Taxes," *American Economic Review*, XLVI, May 1956, pp. 97–113.

the profitable investments available to the company are perhaps the most serious from the point of view of the shareholder.
Also, it is not necessary that a firm keep its dividend pay-out
ratio low enough so that profitable investments can always be
financed out of retained earnings, provided the firm is in a
position to issue new securities when necessary.

Dividend policy must be set in the form of a goal rather than
a rigid rule. On the other hand, having a clear policy has the
advantage of providing the investor or potential investor a
clear basis of choice. The investor, knowing the dividend
policy, can choose the type of company that best fits his individual investment goals. This is desirable, since stockholders
differ in the extent to which they prefer dividends rather than
opportunities for capital appreciation. With the great emphasis
on the tax advantages of capital gains, there is sometimes a
tendency to forget not only that many investors are primarily
interested in income but also that important groups of investors, such as universities, foundations, and private pension
funds, accrue no special advantages from capital gains as
distinct from ordinary income.

The Cost of Raising Equity Capital by Selling Common Stock

A corporation can increase its equity capital by retaining
earnings or by selling new common stock. The basic principles
underlying the costs of capital under either method are the
same. If new common stock could be issued at a price equal
to the market value of shares already outstanding, the costs
would be the same under either method. In practice, the
amount that can be realized per share from a new issue will
be less than the market value of existing stock because of the
need to price the new issue below the market price in order

to attract buyers, and because of the various costs associated with floating a new issue. If the amount realized from a new issue is 20 per cent less than the going market price, the cost of raising equity in this form will be 25 per cent greater than the cost of retained earnings.

THE OPTIMUM CAPITAL STRUCTURE

So far in our discussion in this chapter we have assumed that all capital utilized in the company was obtained as equity capital. Actually this is rarely, if ever, the case. Most corporations will finance at least a part of their operations with funds obtained from creditors. Bank loans are particularly advantageous (apart from considerations of differences in cost) because the funds can be obtained as needed to meet seasonal fluctuations in the demand for funds. Thus the use of bank loans eliminates the necessity of carrying unused funds for a part of the year. It is not uncommon for a business to be regularly in debt to a bank, and to some extent the bank provides a permanent source of funds, although the actual loans may be for a relatively short term. In addition the inclusion of at least some bonded indebtedness is not uncommon, and in some lines of business this source of funds represents a sizeable fraction of the total funds employed in the business.

At the conclusion of the preceding chapter we indicated how a corporation could estimate its average cost of capital for a given capital structure. So far in this book we have assumed that the investments being considered would not result in a change in the capital structure of the firm, i.e., in the relative proportions of each source of capital. If a relatively large investment undertaken is tied to a particular form of financing, a significant change in the capital structure may result. Examples are the purchase of land financed by a mortgage, the acquisition of equipment by a nonrevocable long-term lease, or a corporate merger financed by a stock issue. Although such transactions may temporarily result in a significant change in a company's capital structure, it is useful and appropriate to assume that such changes will be eliminated in a relatively short period of time and that the capital structure will return to normal. If the capital structure is permanently changed, it ought to be as a result of a separate decision that such a change is desirable.

We have also assumed, and it will be normally useful to assume, that the investments contemplated will not significantly change the risks which investors associate with the securities of the company. For example, the purchase of a plant to make glass by General Motors Corporation would not significantly change the public image of that corporation.

There are times when a company will wish to consider a permanent change in its capital structure because management believes that changes in the relative cost of sources of capital, or changes in the business risks faced by the company, would make a different capital structure more desirable. A decision involving a permanent change in capital structure should be considered on its merits independently of any specific decision to acquire assets.

It is advantageous for a company to adopt a capital structure that makes the average cost of capital a minimum for the firm. *The capital structure that results in a minimum average cost of capital will be referred to as the optimum capital structure.* A change in capital structure that reduces a company's average cost of capital will also result in a higher price per share for common stock and therefore is in the best interest of common stockholders.

In discussing the concept of an optimum capital structure, it is convenient to begin by imagining a company financed entirely by equity, and to consider the consequences of substituting increments of debt for the common stock equity.

The suggested procedure is to estimate the effect of a change in the relative proportions of debt and equity on the company's average cost of capital by using the same procedure recommended in Chapter 10 to estimate a company's average cost of capital for a given capital structure. The procedure recommended for estimating a company's average cost of capital is to use a weighted average of the average cost of each source of funds. Thus, if it were estimated that the average cost of equity would be 10 per cent after the issue of the debt and the average cost of debt (after taxes) would be 2 per cent, one could estimate that a structure composed of 90 per cent equity and 10 per cent debt would result in an average cost of capital of 9.2 per cent $(0.9 \times 10\% + 0.1 \times 2\%)$. The change of capital structure would not be desirable if the cost of common stock capital with no debt were less than 9.2 per cent.

Let us assume that with no debt, the cost of capital is 9.0 per cent. It may be tempting to estimate the effect of an increase in the proportion of debt by using the cost of 9.0 per cent for equity, and 2 per cent for debt. The proposed change in capital structure would then be expected to lead to a new average cost of capital of 8.3 per cent $(0.9 \times 9\% + 0.1 \times 2\%)$.

This expectation would be incorrect because it ignores the increase in the cost of raising common stock funds that results because of the increased risk.

At least two kinds of risks to which common stockholders are subject when debt is included in the capital structure of a company need to be distinguished for our purposes. These may be called the risk of bankruptcy [7] and the risk of increased leverage. By using average cost of capital of the firm, all these costs are taken into consideration.

A company financed only with funds obtained from stockholders may eventually have to cease operations because a combination of operating losses and poor investments has exhausted its funds, but shareholders are not exposed to the risk of bankruptcy unless debt in some form is acquired. With debt it is possible equity holders may lose their interest in a company that may again become a profitable operation. With a well-managed and profitable company, the introduction of a small amount of nonequity capital presumably will not increase the risks of bankruptcy appreciably. In practice, the legal possibility of bankruptcy is nearly always present, since a company will always have at least some accounts payable outstanding. However, as the amount of debt rises, the risks of bankruptcy become greater, until the point is reached where the risk is substantial. Just what this point is may be difficult to specify because it varies, depending upon the activities in which a company is engaged. Nevertheless it is well to remember that a very small increase in the chance that a firm may eventually become bankrupt can have a noticeable effect on the price that investors are willing to pay for its common stock, since if bankruptcy occurs, common stockholders are likely to lose their entire investment.

[7] There is a third category of risks or cost associated with the use of debt. This category of costs is the result of limitations on management's freedom of action, which are usually included as a part of the debt agreements. Provisions requiring that sinking funds be accumulated, limiting the conditions under which the corporation can acquire additional debt, and restricting the directors' freedom to declare dividends are examples. These limitations are frequently of great importance, but they will not be discussed here because it is almost always impossible to quantify such costs, and they must be taken into account on a judgment basis. The lack of discussion of this category does not reflect a lack of appreciation of the importance of such costs.

The advantage of debt capital comes from the financial leverage it provides for the remaining equity capital. However, the introduction of debt or increases in the debt ratio generally have two effects on the earnings per share available to common stockholders: It tends to increase the average earnings per share that can be expected; and it tends to increase the year-to-year variability of earnings per share (including negative earnings arising from bankruptcy). The first effect is likely to increase the price per share that investors are willing to pay; the second, by itself, is likely to decrease the price per share that investors are willing to pay.

It is impossible to give any simple rules for determining in advance the optimum capital structure for a particular firm.[8] Theoretically, the optimum structure is reached when an additional debt issue, in substitute for stock equity, will result in a decrease in the price per share of the common stock. The capital structure just prior to the issue of that debt is the optimum capital structure. In determining whether a company's capital structure is optimum, management must to some extent rely on the intuitive judgment of well-informed persons.

THE MANAGEMENT OF SHORT-TERM FUNDS AND THE COST OF CAPITAL

This book is mainly concerned with the problem of making good choices in selecting *long-lived* investments. The problem

---

[8] It has recently been suggested that the average cost of capital of a company is not greatly affected by the company's capital structure because investors can adjust their own portfolios to either increase or decrease the leverage of the equities they own. The validity of this proposition has not yet been effectively tested. See F. Modigliani and M. H. Miller, "The Cost of Capital, Corporation Finance and the Theory of Investment," *American Economic Review*, XLVIII, June 1958, pp. 261–297.

of managing *short-term* funds is closely related and should be solved by methods that are consistent in principle and integrated in practice with those used to make long-run investment decisions. But there are also special problems connected with the management of short-term funds. A thorough analysis and discussion of these problems is beyond the scope of this book. Nevertheless a few brief comments are appropriate.

A firm not subject to capital rationing (the lending and borrowing rates are equal) should not accept investments that have negative present values at the firm's cost of capital. The objection is sometimes raised that such firms often hold assets, either permanently or temporarily, that yield less than the company's cost of capital. Tax anticipation notes, 90-day government notes, and commercial paper are examples. The holding of such assets is not necessarily inconsistent with the principles of analysis suggested in this book.

In discussing this topic, it is useful to distinguish two situations. In the first situation, some quantity of low-yielding liquid assets have a more or less permanent place in the firm's asset structure. In the second case a temporary accumulation of such assets takes place (above amounts regularly held).

The reason for holding highly liquid, low-yielding assets on a regular basis is that usually the possession of such assets has advantages to the firm over and above their cash yield. In the case of highly liquid securities, the advantages are related to the fact that such assets can be converted to cash quickly, at low cost, and at an easily predictable price. The ready supply of cash enables the firm to avoid the costs that could result from unanticipated needs for cash, and to take advantage of unpredictable opportunities requiring a readily accessible supply of funds. Inventories are frequently held in part for similar reasons. Inventories of cash can be held at less expense in the form of short-term marketable notes than in the form of demand deposits. When these advantages are considered, the true yield of such assets should not be less than the cost of capital.

The second situation mentioned above usually occurs when a firm finds that it has an excess of cash over the amounts needed for contingencies, day-to-day operations, or currently available investment opportunities. When this occurs, the firm can either hold the funds in liquid form or make a permanent disposition of them by declaring extra dividends or acquiring "external" investments of a long-term nature. The choice between holding the funds temporarily in liquid form or making a permanent disposition of them will depend in part on when the firm anticipates a profitable application of these funds for internal investments. If a profitable internal use is anticipated in the near future, it is usually less expensive to retain such funds temporarily in the form of short-term liquid investments even though the nominal yield of these investments is less than the cost of capital.

In summary, it is not fruitful to treat low-yielding, liquid short-term securities held as a buffer against contingencies, or in anticipation of a prompt and more profitable use, as though such funds are a violation of the rule that investments should be accepted only when they have a positive present value at the cost of capital.

12

Capital Budgeting under Capital Rationing

The preceding chapters have assumed that each firm had a determinable cost of capital and that this cost of capital was the appropriate rate of discount to use in computing the present value of cash flows. We shall now recognize two distinctly different situations where the cost of capital of the firm is not the appropriate rate of discount. One of these situations arises because of a decision by management to limit investments to a set amount of funds or a set cut-off rate [1] even though other profitable investment opportunities are available. The second type of situation arises because of imperfections in the capital market. Both situations are frequently labeled "capital rationing." To distinguish between them, we shall refer to the former situation as "internal capital rationing" and to the latter situation as "external capital rationing."

Two observations should be noted. First, capital rationing in both the first and the second form is present throughout the economy, but usually to a relatively minor degree, and thus

[1] The term *cut-off rate* is used in this chapter to indicate the evaluation of cash flows by using a rate of discount that is different from the firm's cost of capital.

may frequently not be incorporated into the analysis (although it should not be ignored without trying to estimate its impact). Secondly, where capital rationing is present, there is no simple solution to the internal investment decision. Two possible solutions are offered. The first possibility is to make simplifying assumptions where appropriate and to recognize that the answer obtained is an approximation. The second solution is to use mathematical techniques to develop possible solutions, following different possible investment alternatives (including all possible combinations of investments through the succeeding years). This analytical technique may lead to a sound solution to the capital-budgeting decision under capital rationing, but it is complex and requires detailed knowledge of future investment alternatives that is frequently not available.

External Capital Rationing

In this chapter the term *borrow* is used when a firm obtains capital from the market by issuing any type of security. The term *lend* is used to mean the use of funds to purchase any type of security issued by another firm. We specifically assume that borrowing takes place in such a way that the borrowing firm's capital structure (the relative proportion of the various kinds of securities it has issued) is not changed. Thus *borrowing* would normally involve issuing both debt and equity securities. Similarly we assume that *lending* means acquiring a portfolio of securities issued by other firms and which have approximately the same average risk characteristics as the average of the other assets presently owned by the firm.

If capital markets were such that a firm could lend or borrow as much money as it desired at the going rate of interest, this rate of interest would be the same for both the borrowing and lending transactions. The goal of profit maximization (maximizing the economic well-being of the stockholders) would then require that the firm accept all independent investments whose present values were positive, using this rate of interest. This situation has been assumed in the previous chapters. With such capital markets the choice of investments would not be dependent on the amount of funds available to the firm, since by an appropriate combination of borrowing and lending, each firm could finance investments that had positive present values.

This theoretical situation is an ideal never encountered in practice. There will almost always be some divergence between the rates of interest at which the firm can lend surplus funds and the rates at which it can borrow funds. The size of the gap may vary for many reasons, including the effect of the brokerage costs of raising new money and the fact that there may be hidden costs or risks connected with one or the other of the investments. Another reason is that money lenders may prefer firms having certain characteristics, thus driving up the cost of borrowing by firms that lack these characteristics.

If the borrowing rate and the lending rate are almost equal, then little is lost by neglecting the difference and speaking of a market rate of interest. If the difference is large, it cannot be ignored when determining the investment and financial policies of the firm. This gives rise to the situation we describe as external capital rationing.

An approximate solution to the capital-budgeting process with external capital rationing can be described as follows: Assume that a schedule is prepared, showing the total current outlays required for investments having a positive present value at various rates of discount.[2] Such a schedule will present greater current outlays at lower rates of interest, since some investments whose present values are negative at high discount

[2] Current outlays are the net outlays required in period zero.

rates will have positive present values at low discount rates. The schedules are shown by the curves II in Figures 1*a*, 1*b*, and 1*c*. We let the distance OQ_1 represent the quantity of internally generated funds available for investment during the current period. Three situations are possible. In Figure 1*a* the vertical line drawn up from point Q_1 intersects the curve II at a rate of interest higher than r_2, the borrowing rate. This indicates that some investments which would be profitable at a cost equal to the borrowing rate could not be financed from internally generated funds. It would be profitable for the firm to borrow an amount Q_1Q_2 to enable it to accept all investments that would be profitable at the borrowing rate. It would not be profitable to borrow any more than this amount, since all remaining investments have negative present values at the borrowing rate of discount.

In Figure 1*b* the internally generated funds currently available are more than sufficient to enable the firm to undertake all the investments that would be profitable when evaluated at the lending rate of interest. Only OQ_2 dollars would be invested internally. The remaining funds, Q_1Q_2, would be invested externally by buying the securities of other organizations or by reducing the capitalization of the firm and returning the funds to the original suppliers.

A third possibility is that the firm has sufficient funds to accept all independent investments whose present values are positive when evaluated at the borrowing rate but that the firm does not have enough funds to accept all investments whose present values are positive when evaluated at the lending rate. This is illustrated in Figure 1*c*. Under those circumstances the firm would neither borrow any additional funds nor lend any part of its present funds, and the proper rate of discount for investments would be lower than the borrowing rate but higher than the lending rate.

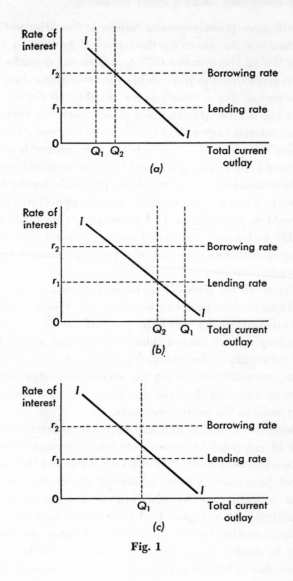

Fig. 1

This analysis assumes a capital market with a significant difference between the borrowing and lending rates. The solution suggested is only approximate, since we have not indicated what assumption is being made as to the probable lending and borrowing rates in the future, and the firm's position relative to them. The appropriate interest rates in future time periods are relevant to decisions made in the present because they affect the profitability of funds reinvested at those times. Cash flows expected in each future time period should be discounted at the rate of interest that will apply in that period. But how is this to be predicted? Generally it will not be difficult to predict future lending and borrowing rates. Given these predictions, it will be safe to assume that the appropriate rate of discount for each future period will lie somewhere between these upper and lower limits. Occasionally a firm will have some basis for predicting whether in a given future year it is more likely to be operating somewhere near its borrowing rate or near its lending rate. If a firm, even in a growing industry, is faced with a temporary excess of capacity, it may feel safe in predicting that, for the next few years, it will have more internally generated funds than it needs for the available profitable investment alternatives. This can be reflected by using a rate of discount for these years that is relatively close to the lending rate. In other cases the firm may anticipate product improvements that are presently in the research and development state but which are expected to be perfected within a few years. If the introduction of these innovations will require large-scale capital investments, the firm may feel confident in predicting that it will be likely to be operating relatively close to its borrowing-rate point during the years these investments are being made.[3]

[3] See Figure 1c and assume that schedule II has shifted upward to the right (meaning there are more profitable investments) until the situation is described by Figure 1a. In this situation the borrowing rate is applicable.

Although such predictions of future cut-off rates under external capital rationing are inevitably rather crude, they serve a useful purpose if the predicted rates are in the right general direction. By using a high rate of discount for a future year in which there is likely to be a shortage of internally generated funds relative to the available investment opportunities in that year, the firm is recognizing that the opportunity cost of funds may be higher in some periods than in others. Investment proposals that release funds for use in periods when the demand is greatest will thus be preferred, all other things being equal, over investments that utilize funds in the periods of high demand. Similarly, if excess funds are likely to be available, the use of a lower discount rate will tend to lead toward the choice of investments that do not generate funds during these periods. The opportunity cost of funds during periods of excess funds is low; thus a low rate of discount is appropriate.

If a company is in a situation of external capital rationing, it may be useful for the top management to predict the appropriate cut-off rate that will apply in future years. By this means the investment planning in various parts of the organization can be coordinated in terms of the best available estimates of future cash needs and requirements for the company as a whole. If fluctuating cut-off rates are expected in the future, the company may wish to prepare and use present-value tables that show the appropriate discount factors to be used for each future period.

Internal Capital Rationing

There are two types of internal capital rationing. In the first, the firm sets a cut-off rate for investments that is higher than the firm's cost of capital (using a higher rate of discount than the cost of capital). In the second type, the firm decides to limit the total amount of funds committed to internal investments in a given year to some fixed sum, even though investments having positive present values at the firm's cost of capital must be rejected as a result of this decision.

Consider the first kind of internal capital rationing. Suppose a firm requires that investments must have a positive present value at 15 per cent, even though the firm's cost of capital is only 10 per cent. In this case, if the same cut-off rate is maintained from year to year, the cut-off rate in future years will be known, and the firm can evaluate all investments *as if* the cost of capital were 15 per cent. This will have some advantages compared to many other measures of investment worth. We have shown in Chapter 2 that whatever rate of discount is used, the present-value measures will avoid some errors in ranking investments that could be committed if the pay-out period or other measures were used.

But although a definite cut-off rate is available, the logic of using that rate to discount cash flows is no longer completely correct. The rate of discount used should measure the alternative uses of funds available to the firm. In the present instance, however, it indicates only that an investment of a dollar now yielding less than 15 per cent will not be undertaken. If next year the company has more internally generated funds than it is willing to invest following the 15 per cent cut-off rule, then an extra dollar of funds that becomes available next year will have an opportunity cost that is less than 15 per cent. How much less will depend on what use the firm makes of the "excess" cash that it will not invest. In extreme cases firms following such rules have been known to invest their excess funds in short-term government securities yielding as low as 1 or 2 per cent.

In the second type of internal capital rationing, the cut-off rate is not specified, but the maximum amount that will be invested is determined. Total internal investments may be arbitrarily limited to an amount equal to depreciation accrued during the period, or they may be limited to "excess cash" or to the sum of depreciation accruals and the increment to retained earnings (less any increase in working capital). The resulting situation is similar to that of external capital rationing, and in fact the two are often difficult to distinguish, particularly if the borrowing rate is very high, as is sometimes the case with very small firms. The approach suggested in connection with external capital rationing may be attempted in this situation, but since there is now no upper limit (the firm may reject internal investments with yields greater than the borrowing rate), the predictions of future cut-off rates will be difficult to make.

Summary—Capital Rationing and Present Value

Capital rationing in one form or another exists to some extent in most corporations. We may distinguish among minor and severe cases of capital rationing. In the minor cases the present-value rules suggested in this book may be used with confidence. In the more severe forms of capital rationing, the present-value method may still be used, but it is no longer correct to use a constant rate of discount for all future years. The rate of discount used for each future year must reflect the cost of obtaining additional funds, the value of external investments available to the firm, or the desires of the owners for present versus future proceeds.

13

A Manual for Investment Decisions

This chapter is written in the form of a manual. Its objective is to explain in detail the computations necessary to evaluate investment proposals when using the present-value method. No attempt is made to explain the theory behind the computations at this point. An attempt is made to give flexible procedures applicable to a wide range of situations. For example, although a corporate income tax rate of 52 per cent is used in the examples, the procedures would be equally applicable if the tax rate were 32 per cent or zero.

The manual is aimed at developing skill in the preparation of forms to be prepared or used by three different groups within the organization. In the first group are the sponsors of the project, the persons who are most familiar with what makes the project desirable and how it will operate. In the second group are the staff men who must summarize the information obtained from the sponsors. The third group is top management who must appraise and make the final investment decisions, using the information prepared for them as well as their experience and intuitive judgment.

This manual focuses attention on the quantitative aspects of the investment decision, but it also allows for the presentation of descriptive material which tells in detail the pros and cons of different investment opportunities. It should be recognized that each computation requires certain assumptions about such things as the future level of general business activity, actions of competitors, costs of factors of production, and sales forecasts. Since there is a large amount of uncertainty connected with each of these factors, it should be appreciated that the resulting computations are, at best, only indications of future operating results.

The authors recognize that it is not possible to devise one set of forms that will be fully satisfactory to every company. The forms presented here are designed to illustrate the main calculations that would be necessary for a thorough analysis of the cash flows that may result from an investment proposal. It is hoped that they will be useful in clarifying the application of the material discussed in earlier chapters and that they will provide a starting point from which a firm unfamiliar with the cash flow method of analyzing investments may proceed in devising administrative practices suitable for its special needs and its particular organizational structure.

The reader will remember that in Chapter 7 we introduced the distinction between absolute and relative cash flows. Absolute cash flows result when cash flows from a given alternative are compared with zero cash flows. Relative cash flows result when we record the difference between the (absolute) cash flows resulting from one alternative and the (absolute) cash flows resulting from a second alternative. The forms presented here can be used directly to compute absolute cash flows or to summarize the results of a relative cash flow comparison. When the figures recorded are relative cash flows, it will ordinarily be necessary to use supplementary work sheets to perform the calculations. Some companies may prefer to have forms that allow space for at least two alternatives and also the difference in cash flows between the two alternatives. The forms suggested here can easily be revised to permit this procedure if it seems desirable.

The Capital Appropriations Request (Form A)

Suggestions from operating personnel on such problems as how to improve processes, replacement of equipment, and possible new products are, of course, desirable. The procedure described here attempts to ensure that all desirable suggestions are properly reviewed by higher levels of management and are given appropriate consideration.

The sponsor of an investment project (outlays of over $5,000 for plant, equipment, or other out-of-the-ordinary items may be classified as investment projects) should prepare form A and the necessary supporting material. Since these forms are the basis of the quantitative analysis, they must be carefully prepared. It is recognized that many of the items on the forms are estimates, but they should be reasonable estimates. If the project is accepted, the estimates made on the forms will be reappraised after several periods of operations to determine whether they set forth objectives possible of attainment.

Technical assistance for filling out the forms should be available for the sponsor of the project. Since a staff man will have to process the data, it is desirable that contact be made with the Capital Budget Department early in the planning. A staff man should be assigned to assist in the preparation of the forms, to ensure that the data are ready for processing and that all alternatives have been considered. At the time the staff man is assigned to the project, a code number should be selected for the investment project so that references and files of information for the numerous investment projects can be easily identified and coordinated.

Form A

CAPITAL APPROPRIATIONS REQUEST FORM

Plant or division: Date:

Proposal: Code No.: _____

A. DESCRIPTION AND JUSTIFICATION SUMMARY:

B. RISK AND INTANGIBLE ANALYSIS SUMMARY:

C. CASH FLOW SUMMARY: Estimated life: _____   Rate of Discount: _____
Outlays are bracketed.

Period	Most probable outcome		Optimistic appraisal		Pessimistic appraisal	
	Dollars	*Present value*	*Dollars*	*Present value*	*Dollars*	*Present value*
Total life						
Year 1						
Year 2						
Year 3						
Year 4						
Year 5						
Years 1–5						
Years 1–10						
Years 1–15						
Years 1–						

Sponsor: _____   Prepared by _____
          (Name)   (Title)   (Name)   (Title)

Routing	Initials	Date	Routing	Initials	Date
Engineering			R & D		
Production			Accounting		
Sales			Div. manager		
Market research					

Space is provided in form A to indicate the routing of the investment proposal from the original sponsor. The particular routing will, of course, vary from one organization to the other. However, one of the main advantages of a systematic capital-budgeting procedure is that, with proper procedures, it provides a framework for the coordination of planning in this area. For example, consider a proposal sponsored by the production manager for acquiring a new machine that he thinks will result in cost saving and also in product improvements. An orderly routing of this proposal to the sales manager concerned will provide a routine mechanism for informing him of the proposed product improvement. To take full advantage of the possibilities provided by systematic capital budgeting, the sales manager should be encouraged to do more than merely note, initial, and forward the appropriation request. He should attach his own memorandum, indicating whether or not he agrees with the estimate of increased sales presented by the sponsor, and include any other pertinent comments. The opportunities for consultation provided by this mechanism will frequently result in further improvements in the character of the investments actually submitted to the final authority. In any case it will provide valuable information for top management in weighing the important intangible factors almost invariably associated with an investment proposal. Later on, it can be used in comparing actual experience and costs with those predicted. This discipline will induce the sponsors to be more honest and precise in their estimates, and there will be less likelihood of bargaining or overoptimism.

Space is provided in form A for recording the cash flows, not only for the most probable outcome of an investment but also for the outcomes of either an optimistic appraisal or a pessimistic appraisal. For reasons discussed in detail in Chapter 9, we do not believe that an estimate of the most probable outcome of an investment contains all the information management may need to know when deciding whether to accept or reject the investment. Because of the costs of preparing the estimates, management may not wish to have the columns "Optimistic Appraisal" and "Pessimistic Appraisal" filled out in the case of every investment. However, space is provided for these estimates so that they can be used when it seems necessary and desirable. If all three estimates are included on form A, then it will be necessary to fill out one copy of form A-1 and of form A-3 for each estimate of cash flows.

Estimating Cash Flows from Operations (Form A-1)

Section A. The sales figure should be the dollar value of sales expected to be recognized during the period under consideration. An adjustment for the timing of the actual collection of the cash receipts resulting from such sales is included by incorporating the change in Accounts Receivable under section C. If the product or products are partly substitutes for other products already produced by the company, an adjustment for the decline in cash proceeds resulting from the new product should be included under section D. The physical volume and price per unit underlying these calculations should also be included in a schedule.

Section B. In section B, the production cost estimates for each period should be those incurred for the *actual* rate of production expected during that period and *not* an estimated rate for the sales of the period. The actual rate of production during a period may be greater or less than the rate of sales, depending upon whether inventories are increasing or decreasing. An adjustment for the cash flows resulting from the tax effect of inventory change is included in section E of form A-1.

Section B should include all costs incurred because of the investment that would have been avoided if the investment had not been undertaken. Any cost that will be incurred, whether or not the investment is undertaken, should be excluded from this section. The value of the alternative uses of any resource for which the cost is unavoidable is discussed in section D.

Section C. In section C, adjustments are made for changes in cash tied up in working capital (other than partly or completely processed inventories). The procedures used in estimating these items are the same as procedures used in preparing cash budgets.

The increase in working cash balances should be the amount estimated as necessary to support the operations resulting from the investment. Excess cash reserves should not be included.

Ordinarily, the items in this section will total to a positive amount (indicating a use of cash) during periods in which the rate of operations is increasing. They will also show negative amounts (indicating a release of cash) during periods when the rate of operations is declining. Similarly, in a period of steady operations, this total will approach zero.

Section D. Most investment proposals will have some effects on the sales, costs, and use of resources in other parts of the organization. Section D is an attempt to allow for such influences. All estimates of cash flows should be on an after-tax basis. Frequently it will be extremely difficult to arrive at a satisfactory basis for estimating the items in this section because they are often difficult to measure and wide differences of opinion may exist as to the importance of individual items. An example would be a new product that could partly substitute for an existing product of the firm. If no agreement can be reached as to the degree of substitution, the item may be listed as an intangible. However, there may be general agree-

Form A-1

Proposal: _____

Code No.: _____

178

SUMMARY OF CASH FLOWS FROM OPERATIONS

	Year 1 19___	Year 2 19___	Year 3 19___	Year 4 19___	Year 5 19___	Year 6 19___	Year 7 19___	Year 8 19___

A. Sales:

B. Costs of production (except depreciation) and other expenses:

  Direct labor
  Raw materials used
  Indirect labor
  Other manufacturing overhead
  Sales and promotion
  Administrative expenses
  Other (include any investment-type outlays that are expended for tax purposes in the period of outlay)

C. Increases (decreases) in current liabilities and nondepreciable assets (except finished inventory or work in process):

Increase in accounts receivable
Increase in inventory of raw materials and supplies (at cost)
Increase in working cash balances
Increase in current payable (subtract an increase)

D. Adjustments for cash flows in other parts of the business resulting from project

Decrease in cash proceeds of other products
Cost of space utilized (cost of foregoing other uses)
Use of executive time
Other

E. Tax adjustments:

Increase in income taxes before allowing for depreciation (see Schedule E)
Tax savings from depreciation (subtract):

Outlays of cash $(B + C + D + E)$

F. After-tax cash flows from operations:
$[A - (B + C + D + E)]$

179

Form A-1

Schedule E:

Computation of income tax (without allowing for depreciation):

	Year 1 19__	Year 2 19__	Year 3 19__	Year 4 19__	Year 5 19__	Year 6 19__	Year 7 19__	Year 8 19__
Sales								
Deductions:								
Beginning inventory *								
Plus: Costs of production incurred †								
Total manufacturing costs								
Less: Ending inventory *								
Cost of goods sold								
Selling and promotion expenses								
Administrative expenses (directly associated with the project)								
Other								
Total deductions								
Amount subject to tax (sales less the total deductions)								
Increase in income taxes before allowing for depreciation (amount subject to tax times tax rate)								

* Includes work in process and finished goods.
† Excludes depreciation of the investment.

180

ment that sales of the old product will decrease, although the amount of the decrease may be in doubt. When some agreement can be reached as to the direction of the effect, if not its size, it is usually wise to include an estimate of the minimal effect and to indicate in the intangible section of form A that only a minimal estimate has been made and that there is disagreement as to the actual amount. In this case the estimate of the minimal decline in after-tax cash proceeds resulting from sales of the old product would be included under "Sales of other products."

Section E. Under section E, the item "increase in income taxes before allowing for depreciation" is computed and obtained from schedule E. The tax rate used in that schedule should be the tax rate expected to apply in that year. The tax rate is applied to the taxable income (excluding the depreciation deduction) expected to result as a result of the revenues and revenue deductions (associated with the investment) allowable for tax purposes. The tax section of the controller's department should be consulted in computing the taxable income to ensure that the assumptions made in preparing schedule E are consistent with the method which will actually be used in preparing the tax returns.

The method of computing the tax saving from depreciation is explained below. The amount is obtained from form A-2.

Section F. Section F gives the after-tax cash flows from operations that result because of the investment. It should be inserted in column 1 of form A-3 for further processing.

Choosing the Most Profitable Depreciation Method

There are actually two problems in connection with depreciation. First, there is the question of choosing the most desirable method of depreciation. Second, if an estimate of the cash flow from the investment in each year of its life is desired for form A, the tax saving resulting from depreciation in each year must be estimated. Once the depreciation method has been chosen, the preparation of such estimates is a routine task.

The method of depreciation accounting that is most desirable for income tax purposes will depend on the firm's cost of capital, the life of the investment, and the salvage expected at the time the investment is scrapped.

If *no salvage value* is expected at the end of the asset's useful life, then the most advantageous depreciation method can be determined quickly by consulting the tables in the Appendix to this book. Table C shows the present value of the depreciation charge resulting from a $1.00 asset depreciated over n years when the rate of discount is r per cent per year, using the sum-of-the-years'-digits method of depreciation. Table D shows a corresponding set of values when the twice straight-line declining balance method of depreciation is used. It automatically allows for switching over to the straight-line method as soon as this becomes advantageous. To determine the most advantageous depreciation method for an asset, look up the values in each table under the column corresponding to the rate of discount being used and in the row corresponding to the life of the asset in years. The highest present value indicates the most advantageous method of depreciation. To determine the present value of the total tax savings, multiply the tabular value by the income tax rate (assuming no change in the rate is expected), and then multiply this product by the original book value of the asset in dollars.

If, in form A, only the total present value of the investment is to be shown, then the steps described above will suffice. If it is desirable to show separately in form A the cash flow in each year, then form A-2 can be used. For this purpose only columns one, two, and three need to be filled in. The entry in column three can then be transferred to section E of form A-1, on which the after-tax cash flows of each year are computed.

If the asset is expected to have positive net salvage value in its final year of life, form A-2 is needed to determine the present value of the tax savings that will result from using the twice straight-line declining balance method of depreciation. All five columns must be filled in for this purpose. The present-value factor necessary for each year should be entered in column four from Table A. The sum of the values in column five give the present value of the tax savings for this method. This value must then be compared with the present value of the tax savings that would result from using the sum-of-the-years'-digits method. The latter can be obtained from Table C just as in the case when the expected salvage value is zero, except that the tabular value is multiplied by the tax rate and by the difference between the original cost and the expected salvage value. Again, the most advantageous depreciation method will be the one giving the highest present value of tax savings.

In discussing the choice of depreciation methods, we have ignored the straight-line method because either one of the alternative methods will *always* be preferable to the straight-line method in the sense that either will always give a higher present value of tax savings for all rates of discount. If the straight-line method is used to reduce the clerical costs involved, the present value of the tax savings from this method can be easily estimated by multiplying the annual depreciation charge by the tax rate and by the present value of an annuity of $1.00 per year for n years, choosing n equal to the expected life of the asset in years.

In case the basic investment proposal is a complex one with more than one type of depreciable asset involved and with possible replacement of one or more assets required during the life of the operation, it is necessary to summarize the basic information relating to the depreciation of each separate asset.

Computing the Annual Depreciation Charges (Form A-2)

Sum-of-the-Years'-Digits Method. The same general procedure is used whether or not the asset is expected to have a positive salvage value. Under the sum-of-the-years'-digits method, the depreciation charge will decrease each year by a constant absolute amount during the asset's life. The depreciation charge in the first year can be determined from the following formula, in which n represents the expected life of the asset, and D is the depreciable base (the original book value minus expected net salvage value).

$$\text{First year's depreciation charge} = \frac{2D}{n+1}$$

To determine the depreciation charge in any later year, subtract from the preceding year's depreciation charge the following amount:

$$\left(\begin{array}{c}\text{Amount to be subtracted to determine} \\ \text{next year's depreciation}\end{array}\right) = \frac{2D}{n(n+1)}$$

Example: Compute the depreciation schedule for an investment with a life of five years and which costs $15,000, using the sum-of-the-years'-digits method.

The sum-of-the-years' digits is

$$1 + 2 + 3 + 4 + 5 = 15$$

The depreciation schedule is

Year			
1	....	$5/15 \times 15{,}000 =$	$ 5,000
2	....	$4/15 \times 15{,}000 =$	4,000
3	....	$3/15 \times 15{,}000 =$	3,000
4	....	$2/15 \times 15{,}000 =$	2,000
5	....	$1/15 \times 15{,}000 =$	1,000
			$15,000

Using the formula, the first year's depreciation charge is found to be

$$\frac{2D}{n+1} = \frac{2 \times 15{,}000}{5+1} = \frac{30{,}000}{6} = \$5{,}000$$

The amount to be substracted to determine the next year's depreciation is

$$\frac{2D}{n(n+1)} = \frac{2 \times 15{,}000}{5 \times 6} = \frac{30{,}000}{30} = \$1{,}000$$

The depreciation for the second year is $5,000 — 1,000, or $4,000; for the third year, $3,000; etc.

Twice Straight-line Declining Balance Method: No Salvage
When the twice straight-line declining balance method is used, the Internal Revenue Code allows the taxpayer to switch from this method to the straight-line method applied to the remaining book value and the remaining depreciable life. The switch should be made when the latter method is advantageous. The first step in computing the annual depreciation charges by this method is to determine in what year it will be advantageous to switch over. This can be done by dividing the expected life in years of the asset by two, and adding one to the quotient. If the resulting number is an integer (whole number), it represents the year in which the switch takes place. If the resulting number is not an integer, the next largest integer is the year in which the switch takes place. For ex-

Form A-2

COMPUTATION OF ANNUAL TAX SAVINGS FROM DEPRECIATION

Proposal:

Code No.: _____

Original cost of asset ° _____   Expected salvage value _____

Expected life of asset _____   Depreciation method _____

Year	(1) Depreciation expense	(2) Tax rate	(3) Tax saving (1) × (2)	(4) Present value factor	(5) Present value of saving (3) × (4)

° If the outlays are to be made over several periods, attach a schedule showing the timing of the outlays.

ample, if the expected life is 20 years, the switch will take place in year 11, i.e., $(20/2) + 1 = 11$. If the expected life is 25 years, the switch will take place in the year 14, i.e., $(25/2) + 1 = 13.5$.

If the expected life is n years, the first year's depreciation charge will be $2/n$ times the cost of the investment. The next year's depreciation charge is the preceding year's charge times $[1 - (2/n)]$, up until the year of the switch. The depreciation charge in the switch year and all subsequent years is simply the book value at the beginning of the switch year divided by the number of years of life remaining.[1]

Twice Straight-line Declining Balance Method: With Salvage. Even though an asset has a positive expected salvage value, the first year's depreciation charge under this method is found by applying twice the straight-line rate to the book value of the asset (not the book value minus the expected salvage as in the straight-line or sum-of-the-year's digits methods). Therefore, for the first few years of life the depreciation charge under this method will be the same whether or not the asset is expected to have any salvage value. The computations proceed either until the book value of the asset is equal to the expected salvage value or until it is advantageous to switch over to the straight-line method. However, if a switch takes place, the annual depreciation charge must then be figured by dividing the number of years of life remaining into the difference between the book value at the time of switch and the expected salvage.

If an asset is expected to have a positive salvage value, there is no simple formula that can be used to determine the year in

[1] The book value at the beginning of any year, up to and including the year in which the switch takes place, can be determined easily from the depreciation charge in the preceding year by multiplying that charge by $[(n/2) - 1]$, where n is the original life of the asset in years.

which it will be advantageous to switch over from twice straight line on the declining balance to straight line. However, a switch, if it is ever advantageous, will occur no sooner with positive salvage of the asset than with a zero expected salvage. To determine whether a switch is advantageous, it is necessary to compute the depreciation charge both ways. But there is no need to try this comparison until the year $[(n/2) + 1]$ at least. If the book value of the asset has been reduced to salvage value, no further depreciation will be allowable.

Summarizing the Cash Flow Information and Computing Present Values (Form A-3)

Form A-3 is provided for the purpose of summarizing all the information on cash flows, and also to allow space for computing the present value of these cash flows by years.

If the sum of the present values of the net cash flows (total of column 5 of form A-3) is positive, this means that the investment has passed the test of the present value of cash flows. It promises to return a yield greater than the company's cost of capital, thus warranting further consideration, and therefore would ordinarily be recommended to top management. Important exceptions to this rule may arise in the case of mutually exclusive investments (Is there another way of accomplishing the same objective that will be even more profitable?) or in cases where the investment has important intangible disadvantages. Similarly, investments with negative present values would not ordinarily be recommended to top management, but exceptions may occur in cases where the investment had important intangible advantages.

Form A-3

SUMMARY OF CASH FLOWS AND COMPUTATION
OF PRESENT VALUES

Proposal:

Code No.: _____

Year	(1) Cash flows from operations	(2) Outlays for assets	(3) Net cash flows (1) + (2)	(4) Present-value factor	(5) Present-value of cash flows (3) × (4)

Instructions for Using Form A-3

General: Indicate outflows of cash (cash outlays) by bracketing the corresponding figures.

Column (1): This column is filled in from line F of form A-1.

Column (2): Information for this column is obtained from form A-2. Check to be sure that outlays charged to expense have been included in the appropriate line of form A-1. Also include outlays for assets which are non-depreciable.

Column (3): This is the algebraic sum of columns (1) and (2). Enter this column in the appropriate column of form A.

Column (4): Copy present-value factors from the appropriate column of Table A. The present value factor for immediate outlays is always 1.000.

Column (5): This column is computed as the product of columns (3) and (4). If the entry in column (3) is bracketed, the entry on the same row in column (5) should also be bracketed to indicate net cash outlays. This column should also be entered into the appropriate column of form A.

Avoiding Errors Due to Improper Comparisons

Frequently the gains from making investments will be so large that no formal analysis is required to justify them. For example, a railroad must either replace a broken rail or abandon the line in which the broken rail occurs. The main danger to be avoided in analyzing such investments is the too-ready assumption that if only the present *necessary* investment is made, future cash flows will proceed indefinitely. If the investment is at all a borderline case, then what is required is a projection, not only of the present investment but also of the necessary additional investments that will be required in the future, thus making it possible to decide whether the whole series of these investments will be profitable. Otherwise, one may find oneself rebuilding an unprofitable road, rail by rail and tie by tie, with each small expenditure defended as absolutely necessary.

The sales and expenses estimates must always be on a comparative basis. That is, the estimates should attempt to measure the difference between what would occur if the investment under question were undertaken and if it were not undertaken. If the investment will reduce operating costs but not increase sales, then the appropriate entry for sales is zero. Similarly, if the investment will increase both sales and expenses, the amounts of increase of each should be estimated.

Since every estimate of cash flows involves an implied comparison, it is extremely important that a realistic situation be projected as the one likely to occur if the investment is not undertaken. The weakest professional football team would look good in a contest with an Ivy League college team, but no one would use the score of such a contest to judge the professional team's chances of winning the title in its own league. In the same way, an investment may look good if the cash flow analysis is made by comparing its performance against an absurd and unprofitable alternative. Thus, in deciding whether to replace a five-year-old truck now with a new truck, we should not make the comparison as though a decision against replacement meant that the old truck would be operated for another ten years. Similarly, if operating the old truck is unprofitable from the viewpoint that using a common carrier would be less expensive, a decision to replace the old truck with a new model should probably be supplemented by comparing the costs of the new model with the costs of using a common carrier as well as with the costs of continuing to operate the old truck.

Since it is frequently difficult to decide in advance what alternative to the present investment is "realistic," it is important in such situations to try to analyze simultaneously all the significant available alternatives. If all available alternatives are considered, the choice of an unrealistic alternative as the common standard will not bias the results. Thus, if both replacing the old truck with a new model and using a common carrier are compared with the alternative of continuing to operate the old truck, it may become clear that, although buying a new truck may be preferable to continuing to operate the old one (that is, the present value of the cash outlays of the new truck will be less than those of the old truck), using a common carrier is better than buying the new truck (the present value of the cash outlays from using a common carrier is less than from buying a new truck).

Mutual exclusive investments are investments directly and adversely affecting the earning possibilities of each other (e.g., ten different models of furnaces being considered when only one furnace is needed). With investments of this type the appropriate forms should be prepared for each investment. The net cash flow for each investment should be obtained and listed. Form A-3 can be used for this purpose. The investment with the highest present value is the most desirable investment from the point of view of this one criterion. The best investment should be listed on form A, but the fact that it is one of a set of mutually exclusive investments should be indicated. If top management wants to review the other possibilities, then the entire file of schedules should be presented with this form as a cover sheet.

A Selected Bibliography on Capital Budgeting

Alchian, Armen A., *Economic Replacement Policy*, The RAND Corporation, Santa Monica, 1952.

————, "The Rate of Interest, Fisher's Rate of Return over Costs, and Keynes' Internal Rate of Return," *Am. Econ. Rev.*, vol. XLV, December, 1955, pp. 938–943.

Bierman, Harold Jr., and Seymour Smidt, "Capital Budgeting and the Problem of Reinvesting Cash Proceeds," *J. Business*, vol. XXX, October, 1957, pp. 276–279.

Bodenhorn, Diran, "On the Problem of Capital Budgeting," *J. Finance*, vol. XIV, December, 1959, pp. 473–492.

Christenson, Charles, "Construction of Present Value Tables for Use in Evaluating Capital Investment Opportunities," *Accounting Rev.*, vol. XXX, October, 1955, pp. 666–672.

Dean, Joel, *Capital Budgeting*, Columbia University Press, New York, 1951.

————, "Measuring the Productivity of Capital," *Harvard Business Rev.*, vol. XXXII, January–February, 1954, pp. 120–130.

Durand, David, "Costs of Debt and Equity Funds for Business: Trends and Problems of Measurement," in *Conference on Research in Business Finance*, Natl Bur Econ Research, New York, 1952.

————, "Growth Stocks and the St. Petersburg Paradox," *J. Finance*, vol. XII, September, 1957, pp. 348–363.

————, "The Cost of Capital in an Imperfect Market: A Reply to

Modigliani and Miller," *Am. Econ. Rev.*, vol. XLIX, September, 1959, pp. 639–654.

Eiteman, Wilford J., "Contemporary Problems: Finance and Investment," in *Segments of the Economy*, Howard Allen, Inc., for the Case Institute of Technology, Cleveland, 1957, pp. 156–189.

Fisher, Irving, *The Theory of Interest*, The Macmillan Company, New York, 1930.

Gordon, Myron, J., "The Payoff Period and the Rate of Profit," *J. Business*, vol. XXVIII, October, 1955, pp. 253–261.

Gordon, Myron J. and Eli Shapiro, "Capital Equipment Analysis: The Required Rate of Profit," *Management Science*, vol. III, October, 1956, pp. 102–110.

Hirshleifer, Jack, "On the Theory of Optimal Investment Decision," *J. Political Economy*, vol. LXVI, August, 1958, pp. 329–352.

Lintner, John, "Distribution of Incomes of Corporations Among Dividends, Retained Earnings, and Taxes," *Am. Econ. Rev.*, vol. XLVI, May, 1956, pp. 97–113.

Lorie, James H., and Leonard J. Savage, "Three Problems in Rationing Capital," *J. Business*, vol. XXVIII, October, 1955, pp. 229–239.

Lutz, Friedrich, and Vera Lutz, *The Theory of Investment of the Firm*, Princeton University Press, Princeton, 1951.

McKean, Roland N., *Efficiency in Government Through Systems Analysis*, John Wiley & Sons, New York, 1958.

Martin, A. D., "Mathematical Programming of Portfolio Selection," *Management Science*, vol. I, January, 1955, pp. 152–166.

Modigliani, Franco, and Merton H. Miller, "The Cost of Capital, Corporation Finance and the Theory of Investment," *Am. Econ. Rev.*, vol. XLVIII, June, 1958, pp. 261–297.

Norton, Frank E., "Administrative Organization in Capital Budgeting," *J. Business*, vol. XXVIII, October, 1955, pp. 291–295.

Preinreich, Gabriel A. D., "The Economic Life of Industrial Equipment," *Econometrica*, vol. VIII, January, 1940, pp. 12–44.

Schlaifer, Robert, *Probability and Statistics for Business Decisions*, McGraw-Hill Book Company, New York, 1959.

Shillinglaw, Gordon, "Guides to Internal Profit Measurement," *Harvard Business Rev.*, vol. XXXV, March–April, 1957.

————, "Residual Values in Investment Analysis," *J. Business,* vol. XXVIII, October, 1955, pp. 275–284.

Smidt, Seymour, "Evaluating Measures of Investment Worth," *Federal Accountant,* vol. VII, June, 1958, pp. 38–54.

Solomon, Ezra, "Measuring a Company's Cost of Capital," *J. Business,* vol. XXVIII, October, 1955, pp. 240–252.

————, "The Arithmetic of Capital Budgeting Decisions," *J. Business,* vol. XXIX, April, 1956, pp. 124–129.

————, *The Management of Corporate Capital,* The Free Press, Glencoe, Illinois, 1959.

Soule, Roland P., "Trends in the Cost of Capital," *Harvard Business Rev.,* vol. XXXI, March–April, 1953, pp. 33–47.

Terborgh, George, *Business Investment Policy,* Machinery and Allied Products Institute, Washington, 1958.

Walter, James F., "Dividend Policies and Common Stock Prices," *J. Finance,* vol. XI, March, 1956, pp. 29–41.

————, "Liquidity and Corporate Spending," *J. Finance,* vol. VIII, December, 1953, pp. 369–387.

Weaver, James B., "False and Multiple Solutions by the Discounted Cash Flow Method for Determining Interest Rate of Return," *Eng. Econ.,* vol. III, Spring, 1958, pp. 1–31.

Appendix A
Problems and Cases[1]

2–1. For each of the following cash flows, compute the net present value. Assume a cost of capital of 10 per cent.

	Period				
	0	1	2	3	4	5
A	($1,000)	$100	$100	$100	$100	$1,100
B	(1,000)	264	264	264	264	264
C	(1,000)	...	...	...	...	1,611

2–2. For each of the cash flows in problem 1, compute the yield.

2–3. For each of the cash flows in problem 1, compute the payback. Assuming a required payback period of four years, which (if any) of the cash flows would be accepted as a desirable investment?

2–4. Assuming a cost of capital of 5 per cent, compute the net present value of the cash flows of problem 1.

2–5. Assuming a cost of capital of 15 per cent, compute the net present value of the cash flows of problem 1. Compare with the results obtained from problems 1 and 4.

2–6. The Arrow Company is considering the purchase of equipment that will return cash proceeds as follows:

[1] Applicable to chapters indicated by digits preceding dashed line.

197

End of Period

$$
\begin{array}{ll}
1 \ldots\ldots\ldots\ldots\ldots & \$5,000 \\
2 \ldots\ldots\ldots\ldots\ldots & 3,000 \\
3 \ldots\ldots\ldots\ldots\ldots & 2,000 \\
4 \ldots\ldots\ldots\ldots\ldots & 1,000 \\
5 \ldots\ldots\ldots\ldots\ldots & 500 \\
\end{array}
$$

Assuming a cost of capital of 10 per cent, what is the maximum amount the Company could pay for the machine and still be financially no worse off than if it did not buy the machine?

2–7. The Ithaca Machine Company has a maximum two-year payback period for equipment and a nine-year requirement for buildings. The cost of capital for the firm is considered to be 10 per cent. Equipment commonly lasts between 10 and 20 years. Buildings are expected to last in excess of 20 years.

Do you consider their criteria to be useful? Explain.

3–1. Accept or reject the following independent investment proposals, using yield and present-value procedures. Assume a cost of capital of 10 per cent.

	Period		
	0	1	2
A	($10,000)	$ 2,000	$12,000
B	(10,000)	10,500	
C	10,000	(12,000)	

3–2. (a) Assume that there are three mutually exclusive investments. Which of the three investments should be chosen? Assume a cost of capital of 10 per cent.

	Period				
	0	1	2	3	Yield (%)
A	($1,000)	$ 505	$ 505	$ 505	24
B	(10,000)	2,000	2,000	12,000	20
C	(11,000)	5,304	5,304	5,304	21

(b) Considering only investments B and C in problem 3–2 (a), compute the corresponding incremental cash flow. Compute the yield or yields of this incremental cash flow. Is investment B or C more desirable?

3–3. The Apple Company is attempting to choose between two different machines that accomplish essentially the same task (the machines are mutually exclusive). A comparison of the cash flows of the two machines shows that if the less expensive of the two machines is chosen, there will be a saving of $1,000 at the time of purchase, but there will be additional outlays of $333 per year over the five-year life of the machines. The cost of capital of the Apple Company is 10 per cent.

Required: Compute the yield of the incremental cash flows and determine whether or not the cheaper of the two machines should be purchased. Make the same decision, using the present-value procedure.

3–4. There are two mutually exclusive investments. Assume a cost of capital of 10 per cent. Choose the better of the two investments.

	Period			
	0	1	2	Yield (%)
A	($16,050)	$10,000	$10,000	16
B	(100,000)	60,000	60,000	13

4–1. Assuming a cost of capital of 10 per cent, how much could you afford to pay per year for $1,000 (payable at the end of each year, beginning a year from now) for:

(a) Five years
(b) Ten years
(c) Twenty years
(d) Thirty years
(e) Perpetuity

4–2. It costs $20,000 to make a new machine that promises to return cash flows of $10,000 per year for five years. Assume a cost of capital of 10 per cent. How much could you pay the owner for the patent rights to this machine and still be no worse off than if the new machine were not made?

4–3. If the patent rights for the machine described in problem 4–2 could be purchased for $10,000, what is the largest extra dividend the company could declare immediately on the basis of the net cash flows expected from these transactions?

4–4. Assuming the transactions described in problem 4–3 were financed by a "loan" costing 10 per cent, how large a loan would be required? Set up a repayment schedule for this loan so that the machine is self-financing.

4–5. If the "loan" described in problem 4–4 were to be repaid in a single payment (including "interest") due in five years, what financial arrangements would be required?

5–1. The Roger Company has the choice between two different types of dies. One type costs less but also has a shorter life expectancy. The expected cash flows after taxes for the two different dies are as follows:

	Period				
	0	1	2	3	4
A	($10,000)	$8,000	$8,000		
B	(12,000)	5,000	5,000	$5,000	$5,000

The cost of capital of the firm is 10 per cent.

Required: Choose the more desirable die. Explain.

5–2. Assume that there are two mutually exclusive investments which have the following cash flows:

	Period		Yield (%)
	0	1	
A	($10,000)	$12,000	20
B	(5,000)	6,100	22

Assume that either investment will require modification to the basic building structure, which will cost $1,000, and that this amount is not included in the above computations. The cost of capital is 10 per cent.

Required: a. Compute the actual yields of the investments.

           b. Does the additional $1,000 change the ranking of the two investments? Explain.

7–1. The Bright Machine Tool Shop is considering replacement of the equipment in a section of its shop. The equipment performs a function that could be completely eliminated. A comparison of the present equipment being used and the new equipment indicates the following relative cash flows would result if the new machine were purchased instead of continuing with the old:

Period	
0	1
($10,000)	$12,000

The yield of the investment is 20 per cent and the cost of capital is 15 per cent. The net present value of the investment is $435. Based on the positive net present value, the decision was made to replace the present equipment.

In the period of operation, the machine performed exactly as predicted, and all costs were as predicted. The absolute cash flows were as follows:

Period	
0	1
($10,000)	$11,000

Required: Comment on the investment decision made by the Bright Machine Tool Shop.

7–2. The Dotted Airline Company is considering replacement of its fleet of ten two-engine planes with five new model jets. The airplane company has prepared an analysis showing that each new plane will cost $343,000 and will earn cash proceeds of $100,000 per year for five years. Assume that after five years the salvage value will be zero for both the new and old planes. The analysis was based on the load and operating characteristics of the new plane and the past experience of the airline, as well as number of passengers and the routes traveled, adjusted in a reasonable manner for additional passengers who will be attracted by the new planes.

The planes currently being used are considered to be safe work horses but are not so glamorous as the new planes. In competition with jets, they are expected to earn net cash proceeds of only $10,000 per year per plane. There is no discernible trend of earnings.

The cost of capital of the Dotted Airline is 10 per cent. Assume the company has access to the necessary funds.

Required: Should the Dotted Airline purchase the new jets? Explain.

8-1. Manufacturers of heavy electric generating equipment have been arguing for years the value of placing orders well in advance. The following analysis was presented by one manufacturer in order to persuade utilities to order in advance under a "buy and store" plan.

It is "estimated" that for each $1,000,000 investment in a boiler purchased a year early and stored by the utility, there would be a net saving of $57,000, as follows: Obviously, advance buying and manufacturing entails financing for an extra year. Since 10 per cent of the $1,000,000 would be withheld until completion of the contract, the actual amount to be borrowed would be $900,000. Assuming a short-term bank loan at 4 per cent, and half the interest charges recoverable in the form of a reduction in income tax, the net interest charges would amount to $18,000.

"Erection savings are estimated at . . . $15,000. . . . Storage costs have been estimated at $10,000. ('When the equipment is finished, it is shipped to the plant site and stored there until the power plant builders need it.') An additional source of 'savings for the utilities stems from an average increase in cost of 7 per cent per year in the boiler industry, largely the result of higher prices paid for finished steel and shop labor.' "

"Summing up, a utility that orders a year ahead of time will save $70,000 in escalation charges, plus $15,000 in erection costs, against which $28,000 must be debited for interest and storage charges."

Consider erection costs to be built into the original invoice cost; thus 90 per cent of an additional erection cost must be paid at the commencement of construction. Also, assume that the boilers take a year to complete and that the storage payments are made at the end of a year of storage. Assume that the boiler is to be placed into use at the beginning of the third year from now. Income is taxed at a 52 per cent rate. Assume public utilities have a cost of capital of 7 per cent.

Prepare an estimate of the incremental after-tax cash flows resulting from ordering a boiler one year earlier. The estimated cash flows should be suitable for determining the value of advance ordering, using a discounted cash flow approach. Assume the boiler would be depreciated on a straight-line basis over a 20-year period from the date it is installed and ready to use. (Quoted material is reproduced by permission from the *New York Times*, May 16, 1959.)

9–1. The Rocky Boat Company is considering the purchase of a Maniac Business Machine. The alternative is to rent it. The purchase price of the machine is $100,000. The rental per year of the same machine is $30,000. The $30,000 includes all repairs and service. If the machine is purchased, a comparable service contract can be obtained for $1,000 a year.

The salesman of the Maniac Corporation has cited evidence indicating that the expected useful service life of this machine is five years.

The cost of capital of the firm is 10 per cent.

Required: Prepare a comprehensive analysis for the controller of the Rocky Boat Company, indicating whether purchase or rent is more desirable. Assume a tax rate of zero.

9–2. The Rocky Boat Company (see problem 9–1) has purchased the machine on January 1, 1959. How should the machine be depreciated for tax purposes? Assume a life of five years is acceptable to the Internal Revenue Service and that the tax rate is 52 per cent. The net salvage value of the machinery is zero since the removal costs will be equal to the salvage proceeds.

    a. Prepare an analysis backing up your answer.
    b. Recompute the investment decision of problem 9–1, taking income taxes into consideration and assuming that a five-year life is valid.

13–1. The Allen Company is faced with the decision whether to buy or rent data processing equipment. The initial outlay for the equipment is $380,000, if purchased. The rentals are $100,000 per year. Similar service contracts may be obtained if the equipment is purchased or rented.

The cost of capital is 10 per cent. The income tax rate is zero.

The best estimate of service life is five years, but an analysis of the life of equipment of a similar nature indicates that the life may be as follows:

Year	Probability (%)
1............................	0
2............................	1
3............................	2
4............................	25
5............................	40
6............................	30
7............................	2
8............................	0

Required: Should the equipment be purchased or rented?

✓ **13-2.** High Voltage Electric Company has $10,000,000 of debt outstanding which pays 7 per cent interest annually. The maturity date of the securities is 15 years from the present. There are $100,000 of bond issue costs and $200,000 of bond discount currently on the books.

Assume a 15-year debt security could be issued which would yield 6 per cent annually. The issue costs on the new issue would be $300,000, and the call premium on the old issue would be $500,000.

 a. The company has a 10 per cent cost of capital. Assuming a zero tax rate, should the old bonds be replaced with new securities?

 b. Assuming a cost of capital of 7 per cent, what would be your answer?

13-3. Referring to problem 13-2, assume that the tax rate is 52 per cent. Assume that the remaining issue costs and the bond discount of the old issue can be written off at time of retirement of the issue for tax purposes. Should the company refund?

13-4. Referring to problem 13-2, how would your answer be affected by the possibility of interest rates decreasing in the future and the new bonds being issued for a 30-year period?

13–5. The Giant Motor Car Company is considering the size of plant which would be most desirable for its next assembly plant. We shall assume that there are the following two alternatives:

	Large Plant	Small Plant
Initial costs	$20,000,000	$4,000,000
Out-of-pocket cost savings per year, assuming the assembly of different numbers of cars per year:		
100,000 cars		1,000,000
200,000 cars	...	...
300,000 cars	2,000,000	
400,000 cars	4,000,000	

A forecast of car sales indicates the following demand for automobiles assembled in this plant:

First year after completion of the plant............100,000 cars
Second year after completion of the plant...........200,000
Third year after completion of the plant............200,000
Fourth year after completion of the plant...........300,000
Fifth year and thereafter for the expected
  life of the plant of 20 years...................400,000

The company has a cost of capital of 10 per cent. For purposes of this problem assume an income tax rate of zero.

Required: Which of the two plants is the more desirable? If more than two plants were being considered, how would you solve the problem of choosing the optimum size of plant?

13–6. The National Money Company, in deciding on to make or to buy decisions, considers only direct labor and direct material as being relevant costs. The sum of these two cost factors is compared with the cost of purchasing the items, and a decision is made on this basis.

Required: Appraise the make or buy procedure of the National Money Company.

13–7. The Ithaca Manufacturing Company currently has excess capacity and is considering manufacturing a component part that is currently being purchased. The estimate of the cost of producing one unit of product is:

Direct labor	$2.00
Material	3.00
Variable overhead	1.00
Fixed overhead (based on accounting procedures of a generally accepted nature)	2.50
	$8.50

The average increase in net working capital which will be required if the item is produced internally is $50,000.

The firm uses 100,000 of the parts per year. The unit cost of purchasing the parts is $6.05. Assume a zero tax rate.

Required: Should the company make or buy?

Appendix B
Tables

Table A

Present Value of $1

(cash flow is different for each period)
$$(1 + r)^{-n}$$

n	1%	2%	3%	4%	5%	6%	7%	8%
1	0.9901	0.9804	0.9709	0.9615	0.9524	0.9434	0.9346	0.9259
2	0.9803	0.9612	0.9426	0.9246	0.9070	0.8900	0.8734	0.8573
3	0.9706	0.9423	0.9151	0.8890	0.8638	0.8396	0.8163	0.7938
4	0.9610	0.9238	0.8885	0.8548	0.8227	0.7921	0.7629	0.7350
5	0.9515	0.9057	0.8626	0.8219	0.7835	0.7473	0.7130	0.6806
6	0.9420	0.8880	0.8375	0.7903	0.7462	0.7050	0.6663	0.6302
7	0.9327	0.8706	0.8131	0.7599	0.7107	0.6651	0.6227	0.5835
8	0.9235	0.8535	0.7894	0.7307	0.6768	0.6274	0.5820	0.5403
9	0.9143	0.8368	0.7664	0.7026	0.6446	0.5919	0.5439	0.5002
10	0.9053	0.8203	0.7441	0.6756	0.6139	0.5584	0.5083	0.4632
11	0.8963	0.8043	0.7224	0.6496	0.5847	0.5268	0.4751	0.4289
12	0.8874	0.7885	0.7014	0.6246	0.5568	0.4970	0.4440	0.3971
13	0.8787	0.7730	0.6810	0.6006	0.5303	0.4688	0.4150	0.3677
14	0.8700	0.7579	0.6611	0.5775	0.5051	0.4423	0.3878	0.3405
15	0.8613	0.7430	0.6419	0.5553	0.4810	0.4173	0.3624	0.3152
16	0.8528	0.7284	0.6232	0.5339	0.4581	0.3936	0.3387	0.2919
17	0.8444	0.7142	0.6050	0.5134	0.4363	0.3714	0.3166	0.2703
18	0.8360	0.7002	0.5874	0.4936	0.4155	0.3503	0.2959	0.2502
19	0.8277	0.6864	0.5703	0.4746	0.3957	0.3305	0.2765	0.2317
20	0.8195	0.6730	0.5537	0.4564	0.3769	0.3118	0.2584	0.2145
21	0.8114	0.6598	0.5375	0.4388	0.3589	0.2942	0.2415	0.1987
22	0.8034	0.6468	0.5219	0.4220	0.3418	0.2775	0.2257	0.1839
23	0.7954	0.6342	0.5067	0.4057	0.3256	0.2618	0.2109	0.1703
24	0.7876	0.6217	0.4919	0.3901	0.3101	0.2470	0.1971	0.1577
25	0.7798	0.6095	0.4776	0.3751	0.2953	0.2330	0.1842	0.1460
26	0.7720	0.5976	0.4637	0.3607	0.2812	0.2198	0.1722	0.1352
27	0.7644	0.5859	0.4502	0.3468	0.2678	0.2074	0.1609	0.1252
28	0.7568	0.5744	0.4371	0.3335	0.2551	0.1956	0.1504	0.1159
29	0.7493	0.5631	0.4243	0.3207	0.2429	0.1846	0.1406	0.1073
30	0.7419	0.5521	0.4120	0.3083	0.2314	0.1741	0.1314	0.0994
35	0.7059	0.5000	0.3554	0.2534	0.1813	0.1301	0.0937	0.0676
40	0.6717	0.4529	0.3066	0.2083	0.1420	0.0972	0.0668	0.0460
45	0.6391	0.4102	0.2644	0.1712	0.1113	0.0727	0.0476	0.0313
50	0.6080	0.3715	0.2281	0.1407	0.0872	0.0543	0.0339	0.0213

Table A. Present Value of $1 (cont'd)

n	9%	10%	11%	12%	13%	14%	15%	16%
1	0.9174	0.9091	0.9009	0.8929	0.8850	0.8772	0.8696	0.8621
2	0.8417	0.8264	0.8116	0.7972	0.7831	0.7695	0.7561	0.7432
3	0.7722	0.7513	0.7312	0.7118	0.6931	0.6750	0.6575	0.6407
4	0.7084	0.6830	0.6587	0.6355	0.6133	0.5921	0.5718	0.5523
5	0.6499	0.6209	0.5935	0.5674	0.5428	0.5194	0.4972	0.4761
6	0.5963	0.5645	0.5346	0.5066	0.4803	0.4556	0.4323	0.4104
7	0.5470	0.5132	0.4817	0.4523	0.4251	0.3996	0.3759	0.3538
8	0.5019	0.4665	0.4339	0.4039	0.3762	0.3506	0.3269	0.3050
9	0.4604	0.4241	0.3909	0.3606	0.3329	0.3075	0.2843	0.2630
10	0.4224	0.3855	0.3522	0.3220	0.2946	0.2697	0.2472	0.2267
11	0.3875	0.3505	0.3173	0.2875	0.2607	0.2366	0.2149	0.1954
12	0.3555	0.3186	0.2858	0.2567	0.2307	0.2076	0.1869	0.1685
13	0.3262	0.2897	0.2575	0.2292	0.2042	0.1821	0.1625	0.1452
14	0.2992	0.2633	0.2320	0.2046	0.1807	0.1597	0.1413	0.1252
15	0.2745	0.2394	0.2090	0.1827	0.1599	0.1401	0.1229	0.1079
16	0.2519	0.2176	0.1883	0.1631	0.1415	0.1229	0.1069	0.0930
17	0.2311	0.1978	0.1696	0.1456	0.1252	0.1078	0.0929	0.0802
18	0.2120	0.1799	0.1528	0.1300	0.1108	0.0946	0.0808	0.0691
19	0.1945	0.1635	0.1377	0.1161	0.0981	0.0829	0.0703	0.0596
20	0.1784	0.1486	0.1240	0.1037	0.0868	0.0728	0.0611	0.0514
21	0.1637	0.1351	0.1117	0.0926	0.0768	0.0638	0.0531	0.0443
22	0.1502	0.1228	0.1007	0.0826	0.0680	0.0560	0.0462	0.0382
23	0.1378	0.1117	0.0907	0.0738	0.0601	0.0491	0.0402	0.0329
24	0.1264	0.1015	0.0817	0.0659	0.0532	0.0431	0.0349	0.0284
25	0.1160	0.0923	0.0736	0.0588	0.0471	0.0378	0.0304	0.0245
26	0.1064	0.0839	0.0663	0.0525	0.0417	0.0331	0.0264	0.0211
27	0.0976	0.0763	0.0597	0.0469	0.0369	0.0291	0.0230	0.0182
28	0.0895	0.0693	0.0538	0.0419	0.0326	0.0255	0.0200	0.0157
29	0.0822	0.0630	0.0485	0.0374	0.0289	0.0224	0.0174	0.0135
30	0.0754	0.0573	0.0437	0.0334	0.0256	0.0196	0.0151	0.0116
35	0.0490	0.0356	0.0259	0.0189	0.0139	0.0102	0.0075	0.0055
40	0.0318	0.0221	0.0154	0.0107	0.0075	0.0053	0.0037	0.0026
45	0.0207	0.0137	0.0091	0.0061	0.0041	0.0027	0.0019	0.0013
50	0.0134	0.0085	0.0054	0.0035	0.0022	0.0014	0.0009	0.0006

Table A. Present Value of $1 (cont'd)

n	17%	18%	19%	20%	21%	22%	23%	24%
1	0.8547	0.8475	0.8403	0.8333	0.8264	0.8197	0.8130	0.8065
2	0.7305	0.7182	0.7062	0.6944	0.6830	0.6719	0.6610	0.6504
3	0.6244	0.6086	0.5934	0.5787	0.5645	0.5507	0.5374	0.5245
4	0.5337	0.5158	0.4987	0.4823	0.4665	0.4514	0.4369	0.4230
5	0.4561	0.4371	0.4190	0.4019	0.3855	0.3700	0.3552	0.3411
6	0.3898	0.3704	0.3521	0.3349	0.3186	0.3033	0.2888	0.2751
7	0.3332	0.3139	0.2959	0.2791	0.2633	0.2486	0.2348	0.2218
8	0.2848	0.2660	0.2487	0.2326	0.2176	0.2038	0.1909	0.1789
9	0.2434	0.2255	0.2090	0.1938	0.1799	0.1670	0.1552	0.1443
10	0.2080	0.1911	0.1756	0.1615	0.1486	0.1369	0.1262	0.1164
11	0.1778	0.1619	0.1476	0.1346	0.1228	0.1122	0.1026	0.0938
12	0.1520	0.1372	0.1240	0.1122	0.1015	0.0920	0.0834	0.0757
13	0.1299	0.1163	0.1042	0.0935	0.0839	0.0754	0.0678	0.0610
14	0.1110	0.0985	0.0876	0.0779	0.0693	0.0618	0.0551	0.0492
15	0.0949	0.0835	0.0736	0.0649	0.0573	0.0507	0.0448	0.0397
16	0.0811	0.0708	0.0618	0.0541	0.0474	0.0415	0.0364	0.0320
17	0.0693	0.0600	0.0520	0.0451	0.0391	0.0340	0.0296	0.0258
18	0.0592	0.0508	0.0437	0.0376	0.0323	0.0279	0.0241	0.0208
19	0.0506	0.0431	0.0367	0.0313	0.0267	0.0229	0.0196	0.0168
20	0.0433	0.0365	0.0308	0.0261	0.0221	0.0187	0.0159	0.0135
21	0.0370	0.0309	0.0259	0.0217	0.0183	0.0154	0.0129	0.0109
22	0.0316	0.0262	0.0218	0.0181	0.0151	0.0126	0.0105	0.0088
23	0.0270	0.0222	0.0183	0.0151	0.0125	0.0103	0.0086	0.0071
24	0.0231	0.0188	0.0154	0.0126	0.0103	0.0085	0.0070	0.0057
25	0.0197	0.0160	0.0129	0.0105	0.0085	0.0069	0.0057	0.0046
26	0.0169	0.0135	0.0109	0.0087	0.0070	0.0057	0.0046	0.0037
27	0.0144	0.0115	0.0091	0.0073	0.0058	0.0047	0.0037	0.0030
28	0.0123	0.0097	0.0077	0.0061	0.0048	0.0038	0.0030	0.0024
29	0.0105	0.0082	0.0064	0.0051	0.0040	0.0031	0.0025	0.0020
30	0.0090	0.0070	0.0054	0.0042	0.0033	0.0026	0.0020	0.0016
35	0.0041	0.0030	0.0023	0.0017	0.0013	0.0009	0.0007	0.0005
40	0.0019	0.0013	0.0010	0.0007	0.0005	0.0004	0.0002	0.0002
45	0.0009	0.0006	0.0004	0.0003	0.0002	0.0001	0.0001	0.0001
50	0.0004	0.0003	0.0002	0.0001	0.0001	0.0000	0.0000	0.0000

Table A. Present Value of $1 (cont'd)

n	25%	26%	27%	28%	29%	30%	31%	32%
1	0.8000	0.7937	0.7874	0.7813	0.7752	0.7692	0.7634	0.7576
2	0.6400	0.6299	0.6200	0.6104	0.6009	0.5917	0.5827	0.5739
3	0.5120	0.4999	0.4882	0.4768	0.4658	0.4552	0.4448	0.4348
4	0.4096	0.3968	0.3844	0.3725	0.3611	0.3501	0.3396	0.3294
5	0.3277	0.3149	0.3027	0.2910	0.2799	0.2693	0.2592	0.2495
6	0.2621	0.2499	0.2383	0.2274	0.2170	0.2072	0.1979	0.1890
7	0.2097	0.1983	0.1877	0.1776	0.1682	0.1594	0.1510	0.1432
8	0.1678	0.1574	0.1478	0.1388	0.1304	0.1226	0.1153	0.1085
9	0.1342	0.1249	0.1164	0.1084	0.1011	0.0943	0.0880	0.0822
10	0.1074	0.0992	0.0916	0.0847	0.0784	0.0725	0.0672	0.0623
11	0.0859	0.0787	0.0721	0.0662	0.0607	0.0558	0.0513	0.0472
12	0.0687	0.0625	0.0568	0.0517	0.0471	0.0429	0.0392	0.0357
13	0.0550	0.0496	0.0447	0.0404	0.0365	0.0330	0.0299	0.0271
14	0.0440	0.0393	0.0352	0.0316	0.0283	0.0253	0.0228	0.0205
15	0.0352	0.0312	0.0277	0.0247	0.0219	0.0195	0.0174	0.0155
16	0.0281	0.0248	0.0218	0.0193	0.0170	0.0150	0.0133	0.0118
17	0.0225	0.0197	0.0172	0.0150	0.0132	0.0116	0.0101	0.0089
18	0.0180	0.0156	0.0135	0.0118	0.0102	0.0089	0.0077	0.0068
19	0.0144	0.0124	0.0107	0.0092	0.0079	0.0068	0.0059	0.0051
20	0.0115	0.0098	0.0084	0.0072	0.0061	0.0053	0.0045	0.0039
21	0.0092	0.0078	0.0066	0.0056	0.0048	0.0040	0.0034	0.0029
22	0.0074	0.0062	0.0052	0.0044	0.0037	0.0031	0.0026	0.0022
23	0.0059	0.0049	0.0041	0.0034	0.0029	0.0024	0.0020	0.0017
24	0.0047	0.0039	0.0032	0.0027	0.0022	0.0018	0.0015	0.0013
25	0.0038	0.0031	0.0025	0.0021	0.0017	0.0014	0.0012	0.0010
26	0.0030	0.0025	0.0020	0.0016	0.0013	0.0011	0.0009	0.0007
27	0.0024	0.0019	0.0016	0.0013	0.0010	0.0008	0.0007	0.0006
28	0.0019	0.0015	0.0012	0.0010	0.0008	0.0006	0.0005	0.0004
29	0.0015	0.0012	0.0010	0.0008	0.0006	0.0005	0.0004	0.0003
30	0.0012	0.0010	0.0008	0.0006	0.0005	0.0004	0.0003	0.0002
35	0.0004	0.0003	0.0002	0.0002	0.0001	0.0001	0.0001	0.0001
40	0.0001	0.0001	0.0001	0.0001	0.0000	0.0000	0.0000	0.0000
45	0.0000	0.0000	0.0000	0.0000				
50								

Table A. Present Value of $1 (cont'd)

n	33%	34%	35%	36%	37%	38%	39%	40%
1	0.7519	0.7463	0.7407	0.7353	0.7299	0.7246	0.7194	0.7143
2	0.5653	0.5569	0.5487	0.5407	0.5328	0.5251	0.5176	0.5102
3	0.4251	0.4156	0.4064	0.3975	0.3889	0.3805	0.3724	0.3644
4	0.3196	0.3102	0.3011	0.2923	0.2839	0.2757	0.2679	0.2603
5	0.2403	0.2315	0.2230	0.2149	0.2072	0.1998	0.1927	0.1859
6	0.1807	0.1727	0.1652	0.1580	0.1512	0.1448	0.1386	0.1328
7	0.1358	0.1289	0.1224	0.1162	0.1104	0.1049	0.0997	0.0949
8	0.1021	0.0962	0.0906	0.0854	0.0806	0.0760	0.0718	0.0678
9	0.0768	0.0718	0.0671	0.0628	0.0588	0.0551	0.0516	0.0484
10	0.0577	0.0536	0.0497	0.0462	0.0429	0.0399	0.0371	0.0346
11	0.0434	0.0400	0.0368	0.0340	0.0313	0.0289	0.0267	0.0247
12	0.0326	0.0298	0.0273	0.0250	0.0229	0.0210	0.0192	0.0176
13	0.0245	0.0223	0.0202	0.0184	0.0167	0.0152	0.0138	0.0126
14	0.0185	0.0166	0.0150	0.0135	0.0122	0.0110	0.0099	0.0090
15	0.0139	0.0124	0.0111	0.0099	0.0089	0.0080	0.0072	0.0064
16	0.0104	0.0093	0.0082	0.0073	0.0065	0.0058	0.0051	0.0046
17	0.0078	0.0069	0.0061	0.0054	0.0047	0.0042	0.0037	0.0033
18	0.0059	0.0052	0.0045	0.0039	0.0035	0.0030	0.0027	0.0023
19	0.0044	0.0038	0.0033	0.0029	0.0025	0.0022	0.0019	0.0017
20	0.0033	0.0029	0.0025	0.0021	0.0018	0.0016	0.0014	0.0012
21	0.0025	0.0021	0.0018	0.0016	0.0013	0.0012	0.0010	0.0009
22	0.0019	0.0016	0.0014	0.0012	0.0010	0.0008	0.0007	0.0006
23	0.0014	0.0012	0.0010	0.0008	0.0007	0.0006	0.0005	0.0004
24	0.0011	0.0009	0.0007	0.0006	0.0005	0.0004	0.0004	0.0003
25	0.0008	0.0007	0.0006	0.0005	0.0004	0.0003	0.0003	0.0002
26	0.0006	0.0005	0.0004	0.0003	0.0003	0.0002	0.0002	0.0002
27	0.0005	0.0004	0.0003	0.0002	0.0002	0.0002	0.0001	0.0001
28	0.0003	0.0003	0.0002	0.0002	0.0001	0.0001	0.0001	0.0001
29	0.0003	0.0002	0.0002	0.0001	0.0001	0.0001	0.0001	0.0001
30	0.0002	0.0002	0.0001	0.0001	0.0001	0.0001	0.0001	0.0000
35	0.0000	0.0000	0.0000	0.0000	0.0000	0.0000	0.0000	
40								
45								
50								

Table A. Present Value of $1 (cont'd)

n	41%	42%	43%	44%	45%	46%	47%	48%
1	0.7092	0.7042	0.6993	0.6944	0.6897	0.6849	0.6803	0.6757
2	0.5030	0.4959	0.4890	0.4823	0.4756	0.4691	0.4628	0.4565
3	0.3567	0.3492	0.3420	0.3349	0.3280	0.3213	0.3148	0.3085
4	0.2530	0.2459	0.2391	0.2326	0.2262	0.2201	0.2142	0.2084
5	0.1794	0.1732	0.1672	0.1615	0.1560	0.1507	0.1457	0.1408
6	0.1273	0.1220	0.1169	0.1122	0.1076	0.1032	0.0991	0.0952
7	0.0903	0.0859	0.0818	0.0779	0.0742	0.0707	0.0674	0.0643
8	0.0640	0.0605	0.0572	0.0541	0.0512	0.0484	0.0459	0.0434
9	0.0454	0.0426	0.0400	0.0376	0.0353	0.0332	0.0312	0.0294
10	0.0322	0.0300	0.0280	0.0261	0.0243	0.0227	0.0212	0.0198
11	0.0228	0.0211	0.0196	0.0181	0.0168	0.0156	0.0144	0.0134
12	0.0162	0.0149	0.0137	0.0126	0.0116	0.0107	0.0098	0.0091
13	0.0115	0.0105	0.0096	0.0087	0.0080	0.0073	0.0067	0.0061
14	0.0081	0.0074	0.0067	0.0061	0.0055	0.0050	0.0045	0.0041
15	0.0058	0.0052	0.0047	0.0042	0.0038	0.0034	0.0031	0.0028
16	0.0041	0.0037	0.0033	0.0029	0.0026	0.0023	0.0021	0.0019
17	0.0029	0.0026	0.0023	0.0020	0.0018	0.0016	0.0014	0.0013
18	0.0021	0.0018	0.0016	0.0014	0.0012	0.0011	0.0010	0.0009
19	0.0015	0.0013	0.0011	0.0010	0.0009	0.0008	0.0007	0.0006
20	0.0010	0.0009	0.0008	0.0007	0.0006	0.0005	0.0005	0.0004
21	0.0007	0.0006	0.0005	0.0005	0.0004	0.0004	0.0003	0.0003
22	0.0005	0.0004	0.0004	0.0003	0.0003	0.0002	0.0002	0.0002
23	0.0004	0.0003	0.0003	0.0002	0.0002	0.0002	0.0001	0.0001
24	0.0003	0.0002	0.0002	0.0002	0.0001	0.0001	0.0001	0.0001
25	0.0002	0.0002	0.0001	0.0001	0.0001	0.0001	0.0001	0.0001
26	0.0001	0.0001	0.0001	0.0001	0.0001	0.0001	0.0000	0.0000
27	0.0001	0.0001	0.0001	0.0001	0.0000	0.0000		
28	0.0001	0.0001	0.0000	0.0000				
29	0.0000	0.0000						
30								
35								
40								
45								
50								

Table B

Present Value of $1 Received per Period

$$\frac{1 - (1+r)^{-n}}{r}$$

n	1%	2%	3%	4%	5%	6%	7%
1	0.9901	0.9804	0.9709	0.9615	0.9524	0.9434	0.9346
2	1.9704	1.9416	1.9135	1.8861	1.8594	1.8334	1.8080
3	2.9410	2.8839	2.8286	2.7751	2.7232	2.6730	2.6243
4	3.9020	3.8077	3.7171	3.6299	3.5460	3.4651	3.3872
5	4.8534	4.7135	4.5797	4.4518	4.3295	4.2124	4.1002
6	5.7955	5.6014	5.4172	5.2421	5.0757	4.9173	4.7665
7	6.7282	6.4720	6.2303	6.0021	5.7864	5.5824	5.3893
8	7.6517	7.3255	7.0197	6.7327	6.4632	6.2098	5.9713
9	8.5660	8.1622	7.7861	7.4353	7.1078	6.8017	6.5152
10	9.4713	8.9826	8.5302	8.1109	7.7217	7.3601	7.0236
11	10.3676	9.7868	9.2526	8.7605	8.3064	7.8869	7.4987
12	11.2551	10.5753	9.9540	9.3851	8.8633	8.3838	7.9427
13	12.1337	11.3484	10.6350	9.9856	9.3936	8.8527	8.3577
14	13.0037	12.1062	11.2961	10.5631	9.8986	9.2950	8.7455
15	13.8651	12.8493	11.9379	11.1184	10.3797	9.7122	9.1079
16	14.7179	13.5777	12.5611	11.6523	10.8378	10.1059	9.4466
17	15.5623	14.2919	13.1661	12.1657	11.2741	10.4773	9.7632
18	16.3983	14.9920	13.7535	12.6593	11.6896	10.8276	10.0591
19	17.2260	15.6785	14.3238	13.1339	12.0853	11.1581	10.3356
20	18.0456	16.3514	14.8775	13.5903	12.4622	11.4699	10.5940
21	18.8570	17.0112	15.4150	14.0292	12.8212	11.7641	10.8355
22	19.6604	17.6580	15.9369	14.4511	13.1630	12.0416	11.0612
23	20.4558	18.2922	16.4436	14.8568	13.4886	12.3034	11.2722
24	21.2434	18.9139	16.9355	15.2470	13.7986	12.5504	11.4693
25	22.0232	19.5235	17.4131	15.6221	14.0939	12.7834	11.6536
26	22.7952	20.1210	17.8768	15.9828	14.3752	13.0032	11.8258
27	23.5596	20.7069	18.3270	16.3296	14.6430	13.2105	11.9867
28	24.3164	21.2813	18.7641	16.6631	14.8981	13.4062	12.1371
29	25.0658	21.8444	19.1885	16.9837	15.1411	13.5907	12.2777
30	25.8077	22.3965	19.6004	17.2920	15.3725	13.7648	12.4090
31	26.5423	22.9377	20.0004	17.5885	15.5928	13.9291	12.5318
32	27.2696	23.4683	20.3888	17.8736	15.8027	14.0840	12.6466
33	27.9897	23.9886	20.7658	18.1476	16.0025	14.2302	12.7538
34	28.7027	24.4986	21.1318	18.4112	16.1929	14.3681	12.8540
35	29.4086	24.9986	21.4872	18.6646	16.3742	14.4982	12.9477
40	32.8347	27.3555	23.1148	19.7928	17.1591	15.0463	13.3317
45	36.0945	29.4902	24.5187	20.7200	17.7741	15.4558	13.6055
50	39.1961	31.4236	25.7298	21.4822	18.2559	15.7619	13.8007

215

Table B. Present Value of $1 Received per Period (cont'd)

n	8%	9%	10%	11%	12%	13%	14%
1	0.9259	0.9174	0.9091	0.9009	0.8929	0.8850	0.8772
2	1.7833	1.7591	1.7355	1.7125	1.6901	1.6681	1.6467
3	2.5771	2.5313	2.4869	2.4437	2.4018	2.3612	2.3216
4	3.3121	3.2397	3.1699	3.1024	3.0373	2.9745	2.9137
5	3.9927	3.8897	3.7908	3.6959	3.6048	3.5172	3.4331
6	4.6229	4.4859	4.3553	4.2305	4.1114	3.9975	3.8887
7	5.2064	5.0330	4.8684	4.7122	4.5638	4.4226	4.2883
8	5.7466	5.5348	5.3349	5.1461	4.9676	4.7988	4.6389
9	6.2469	5.9952	5.7590	5.5370	5.3282	5.1317	4.9464
10	6.7101	6.4177	6.1446	5.8892	5.6502	5.4262	5.2161
11	7.1390	6.8051	6.4951	6.2065	5.9377	5.6869	5.4527
12	7.5361	7.1607	6.8137	6.4924	6.1944	5.9176	5.6603
13	7.9038	7.4869	7.1034	6.7499	6.4235	6.1218	5.8424
14	8.2442	7.7862	7.3667	6.9819	6.6282	6.3025	6.0021
15	8.5595	8.0607	7.6061	7.1909	6.8109	6.4624	6.1422
16	8.8514	8.3126	7.8237	7.3792	6.9740	6.6039	6.2651
17	9.1216	8.5436	8.0216	7.5488	7.1196	6.7291	6.3729
18	9.3719	8.7556	8.2014	7.7016	7.2497	6.8399	6.4674
19	9.6036	8.9501	8.3649	7.8393	7.3658	6.9380	6.5504
20	9.8181	9.1285	8.5136	7.9633	7.4694	7.0248	6.6231
21	10.0168	9.2922	8.6487	8.0751	7.5620	7.1015	6.6870
22	10.2007	9.4424	8.7715	8.1757	7.6446	7.1695	6.7429
23	10.3711	9.5802	8.8832	8.2664	7.7184	7.2297	6.7921
24	10.5288	9.7066	8.9847	8.3481	7.7843	7.2829	6.8351
25	10.6748	9.8226	9.0770	8.4217	7.8431	7.3300	6.8729
26	10.8100	9.9290	9.1609	8.4881	7.8957	7.3717	6.9061
27	10.9352	10.0266	9.2372	8.5478	7.9426	7.4086	6.9352
28	11.0511	10.1161	9.3066	8.6016	7.9844	7.4412	6.9607
29	11.1584	10.1983	9.3696	8.6501	8.0218	7.4701	6.9830
30	11.2578	10.2737	9.4269	8.6938	8.0552	7.4957	7.0027
31	11.3498	10.3428	9.4790	8.7331	8.0850	7.5183	7.0199
32	11.4350	10.4062	9.5264	8.7686	8.1116	7.5383	7.0350
33	11.5139	10.4644	9.5694	8.8005	8.1354	7.5560	7.0482
34	11.5869	10.5178	9.6086	8.8293	8.1566	7.5717	7.0599
35	11.6546	10.5668	9.6442	8.8552	8.1755	7.5856	7.0700
40	11.9246	10.7574	9.7791	8.9511	8.2438	7.6344	7.1050
45	12.1084	10.8812	9.8628	9.0079	8.2825	7.6609	7.1232
50	12.2335	10.9617	9.9148	9.0417	8.3045	7.6752	7.1327

Table B. Present Value of $1 Received per Period (cont'd)

n	15%	16%	17%	18%	19%	20%	21%
1	0.8696	0.8621	0.8547	0.8475	0.8403	0.8333	0.8264
2	1.6257	1.6052	1.5852	1.5656	1.5465	1.5278	1.5095
3	2.2832	2.2459	2.2096	2.1743	2.1399	2.1065	2.0739
4	2.8550	2.7982	2.7432	2.6901	2.6386	2.5887	2.5404
5	3.3522	3.2743	3.1993	3.1272	3.0576	2.9906	2.9260
6	3.7845	3.6847	3.5892	3.4976	3.4098	3.3255	3.2446
7	4.1604	4.0386	3.9224	3.8115	3.7057	3.6046	3.5079
8	4.4873	4.3436	4.2072	4.0776	3.9544	3.8372	3.7256
9	4.7716	4.6065	4.4506	4.3030	4.1633	4.0310	3.9054
10	5.0188	4.8332	4.6586	4.4941	4.3389	4.1925	4.0541
11	5.2337	5.0286	4.8364	4.6560	4.4865	4.3271	4.1769
12	5.4206	5.1971	4.9884	4.7932	4.6105	4.4392	4.2784
13	5.5831	5.3423	5.1183	4.9095	4.7147	4.5327	4.3624
14	5.7245	5.4675	5.2293	5.0081	4.8023	4.6106	4.4317
15	5.8474	5.5755	5.3242	5.0916	4.8759	4.6755	4.4890
16	5.9542	5.6685	5.4053	5.1624	4.9377	4.7296	4.5364
17	6.0472	5.7487	5.4746	5.2223	4.9897	4.7746	4.5755
18	6.1280	5.8178	5.5339	5.2732	5.0333	4.8122	4.6079
19	6.1982	5.8775	5.5845	5.3162	5.0700	4.8435	4.6346
20	6.2593	5.9288	5.6278	5.3527	5.1009	4.8696	4.6567
21	6.3125	5.9731	5.6648	5.3837	5.1268	4.8913	4.6750
22	6.3587	6.0113	5.6964	5.4099	5.1486	4.9094	4.6900
23	6.3988	6.0442	5.7234	5.4321	5.1668	4.9245	4.7025
24	6.4338	6.0726	5.7465	5.4509	5.1822	4.9371	4.7128
25	6.4641	6.0971	5.7662	5.4669	5.1951	4.9476	4.7213
26	6.4906	6.1182	5.7831	5.4804	5.2060	4.9563	4.7284
27	6.5135	6.1364	5.7975	5.4919	5.2151	4.9636	4.7342
28	6.5335	6.1520	5.8099	5.5016	5.2228	4.9697	4.7390
29	6.5509	6.1656	5.8204	5.5098	5.2292	4.9747	4.7430
30	6.5660	6.1772	5.8294	5.5168	5.2347	4.9789	4.7463
31	6.5791	6.1872	5.8371	5.5227	5.2392	4.9824	4.7490
32	6.5905	6.1959	5.8437	5.5277	5.2430	4.9854	4.7512
33	6.6005	6.2034	5.8493	5.5320	5.2462	4.9878	4.7531
34	6.6091	6.2098	5.8541	5.5356	5.2489	4.9898	4.7546
35	6.6166	6.2153	5.8582	5.5386	5.2512	4.9915	4.7559
40	6.6418	6.2335	5.8713	5.5482	5.2582	4.9966	4.7596
45	6.6543	6.2421	5.8773	5.5523	5.2611	4.9986	4.7610
50	6.6605	6.2463	5.8801	5.5541	5.2623	4.9995	4.7616

Table B. Present Value of $1 Received per Period (cont'd)

n	22%	23%	24%	25%	26%	27%	28%
1	0.8197	0.8130	0.8065	0.8000	0.7937	0.7874	0.7813
2	1.4915	1.4740	1.4568	1.4400	1.4235	1.4074	1.3916
3	2.0422	2.0114	1.9813	1.9520	1.9234	1.8956	1.8684
4	2.4936	2.4483	2.4043	2.3616	2.3202	2.2800	2.2410
5	2.8636	2.8035	2.7454	2.6893	2.6351	2.5827	2.5320
6	3.1669	3.0923	3.0205	2.9514	2.8850	2.8210	2.7594
7	3.4155	3.3270	3.2423	3.1611	3.0833	3.0087	2.9370
8	3.6193	3.5179	3.4212	3.3289	3.2407	3.1564	3.0758
9	3.7863	3.6731	3.5655	3.4631	3.3657	3.2728	3.1842
10	3.9232	3.7993	3.6819	3.5705	3.4648	3.3644	3.2689
11	4.0354	3.9018	3.7757	3.6564	3.5435	3.4365	3.3351
12	4.1274	3.9852	3.8514	3.7251	3.6059	3.4933	3.3868
13	4.2028	4.0530	3.9124	3.7801	3.6555	3.5381	3.4272
14	4.2646	4.1082	3.9616	3.8241	3.6949	3.5733	3.4587
15	4.3152	4.1530	4.0013	3.8593	3.7261	3.6010	3.4834
16	4.3567	4.1894	4.0333	3.8874	3.7509	3.6228	3.5026
17	4.3908	4.2190	4.0591	3.9099	3.7705	3.6400	3.5177
18	4.4187	4.2431	4.0799	3.9279	3.7861	3.6536	3.5294
19	4.4415	4.2627	4.0967	3.9424	3.7985	3.6642	3.5386
20	4.4603	4.2786	4.1103	3.9539	3.8083	3.6726	3.5458
21	4.4756	4.2916	4.1212	3.9631	3.8161	3.6792	3.5514
22	4.4882	4.3021	4.1300	3.9705	3.8223	3.6844	3.5558
23	4.4985	4.3106	4.1371	3.9764	3.8273	3.6885	3.5592
24	4.5070	4.3176	4.1428	3.9811	3.8312	3.6918	3.5619
25	4.5139	4.3232	4.1474	3.9849	3.8342	3.6943	3.5640
26	4.5196	4.3278	4.1511	3.9879	3.8367	3.6963	3.5656
27	4.5243	4.3316	4.1542	3.9903	3.8387	3.6979	3.5669
28	4.5281	4.3346	4.1566	3.9923	3.8402	3.6991	3.5679
29	4.5312	4.3371	4.1585	3.9938	3.8414	3.7001	3.5687
30	4.5338	4.3391	4.1601	3.9950	3.8424	3.7009	3.5693
31	4.5359	4.3407	4.1614	3.9960	3.8432	3.7015	3.5697
32	4.5376	4.3421	4.1624	3.9968	3.8438	3.7019	3.5701
33	4.5390	4.3431	4.1632	3.9975	3.8443	3.7023	3.5704
34	4.5402	4.3440	4.1639	3.9980	3.8447	3.7026	3.5706
35	4.5411	4.3447	4.1644	3.9984	3.8450	3.7028	3.5708
40	4.5439	4.3467	4.1659	3.9995	3.8458	3.7034	3.5712
45	4.5449	4.3474	4.1664	3.9998	3.8460	3.7036	3.5714
50	4.5452	4.3477	4.1666	3.9999	3.8461	3.7037	3.5714

Table B. Present Value of $1 Received per Period (cont'd)

n	29%	30%	31%	32%	33%	34%	35%
1	0.7752	0.7692	0.7634	0.7576	0.7519	0.7463	0.7407
2	1.3761	1.3609	1.3461	1.3315	1.3172	1.3032	1.2894
3	1.8420	1.8161	1.7909	1.7663	1.7423	1.7188	1.6959
4	2.2031	2.1662	2.1305	2.0957	2.0618	2.0290	1.9969
5	2.4830	2.4356	2.3897	2.3452	2.3021	2.2604	2.2200
6	2.7000	2.6427	2.5875	2.5342	2.4828	2.4331	2.3852
7	2.8682	2.8021	2.7386	2.6775	2.6187	2.5620	2.5075
8	2.9986	2.9247	2.8539	2.7860	2.7208	2.6582	2.5982
9	3.0997	3.0190	2.9419	2.8681	2.7976	2.7300	2.6653
10	3.1781	3.0915	3.0091	2.9304	2.8553	2.7836	2.7150
11	3.2388	3.1473	3.0604	2.9776	2.8987	2.8236	2.7519
12	2.2859	3.1903	3.0995	3.0133	2.9314	2.8534	2.7792
13	3.3224	3.2233	3.1294	3.0404	2.9559	2.8757	2.7994
14	3.3507	3.2487	3.1522	3.0609	2.9744	2.8923	2.8144
15	3.3726	3.2682	3.1696	3.0764	2.9883	2.9047	2.8255
16	3.3896	3.2832	3.1829	3.0882	2.9987	2.9140	2.8337
17	3.4028	3.2948	3.1931	3.0971	3.0065	2.9209	2.8398
18	3.4130	3.3037	3.2008	3.1039	3.0124	2.9260	2.8443
19	3.4210	3.3105	3.2067	3.1090	3.0169	2.9299	2.8476
20	3.4271	3.3158	3.2112	3.1129	3.0202	2.9327	2.8501
21	3.4319	3.3198	3.2147	3.1158	3.0227	2.9349	2.8520
22	3.4356	3.3230	3.2173	3.1180	3.0246	2.9365	2.8533
23	3.4384	3.3253	3.2193	3.1197	3.0260	2.9377	2.8543
24	3.4406	3.3272	3.2209	3.1210	3.0271	2.9386	2.8550
25	3.4423	3.3286	3.2220	3.1220	3.0279	2.9392	2.8556
26	3.4437	3.3297	3.2229	3.1227	3.0285	2.9397	2.8560
27	3.4447	3.3305	3.2236	3.1233	3.0289	2.9401	2.8563
28	3.4455	3.3312	3.2241	3.1237	3.0293	2.9404	2.8565
29	3.4461	3.3316	3.2245	3.1240	3.0295	2.9406	2.8567
30	3.4466	3.3321	3.2248	3.1242	3.0297	2.9407	2.8568
31	3.4470	3.3324	3.2251	3.1244	3.0299	2.9408	2.8569
32	3.4473	3.3326	3.2252	3.1246	3.0300	2.9409	2.8569
33	3.4475	3.3328	3.2254	3.1247	3.0301	2.9410	2.8570
34	3.4477	3.3329	3.2255	3.1248	3.0301	2.9410	2.8570
35	3.4478	3.3330	3.2256	3.1248	3.0302	2.9411	2.8571
40	3.4481	3.3332	3.2257	3.1250	3.0303	2.9412	2.8571
45	3.4482	3.3333	3.2258	3.1250	3.0303	2.9412	2.8571
50	3.4483	3.3333	3.2258	3.1250	3.0303	2.9412	2.8571

Table B. Present Value of $1 Received per Period (cont'd)

n	36%	37%	38%	39%	40%	41%	42%
1	0.7353	0.7299	0.7246	0.7194	0.7143	0.7092	0.7042
2	1.2760	1.2627	1.2497	1.2370	1.2245	1.2122	1.2002
3	1.6735	1.6516	1.6302	1.6093	1.5889	1.5689	1.5494
4	1.9658	1.9355	1.9060	1.8772	1.8492	1.8219	1.7954
5	2.1807	2.1427	2.1058	2.0699	2.0352	2.0014	1.9686
6	2.3388	2.2939	2.2506	2.2086	2.1680	2.1286	2.0905
7	2.4550	2.4043	2.3555	2.3083	2.2628	2.2189	2.1764
8	2.5404	2.4849	2.4315	2.3801	2.3306	2.2829	2.2369
9	2.6033	2.5437	2.4866	2.4317	2.3790	2.3283	2.2795
10	2.6495	2.5867	2.5265	2.4689	2.4136	2.3605	2.3095
11	2.6834	2.6180	2.5555	2.4956	2.4383	2.3833	2.3307
12	2.7084	2.6409	2.5764	2.5148	2.4559	2.3995	2.3455
13	2.7268	2.6576	2.5916	2.5286	2.4685	2.4110	2.3560
14	2.7403	2.6698	2.6026	2.5386	2.4775	2.4192	2.3634
15	2.7502	2.6787	2.6106	2.5457	2.4839	2.4249	2.3686
16	2.7575	2.6852	2.6164	2.5509	2.4885	2.4290	2.3722
17	2.7629	2.6899	2.6206	2.5546	2.4918	2.4319	2.3748
18	2.7668	2.6934	2.6236	2.5573	2.4941	2.4340	2.3766
19	2.7697	2.6959	2.6258	2.5592	2.4958	2.4355	2.3779
20	2.7718	2.6977	2.6274	2.5606	2.4970	2.4365	2.3788
21	2.7734	2.6991	2.6285	2.5616	2.4979	2.4372	2.3794
22	2.7746	2.7000	2.6294	2.5623	2.4985	2.4378	2.3799
23	2.7754	2.7008	2.6300	2.5628	2.4989	2.4381	2.3802
24	2.7760	2.7013	2.6304	2.5632	2.4992	2.4384	2.3804
25	2.7765	2.7017	2.6307	2.5634	2.4994	2.4386	2.3806
26	2.7768	2.7019	2.6310	2.5636	2.4996	2.4387	2.3807
27	2.7771	2.7022	2.6311	2.5637	2.4997	2.4388	2.3808
28	2.7773	2.7023	2.6313	2.5638	2.4998	2.4389	2.3808
29	2.7774	2.7024	2.6313	2.5639	2.4999	2.4389	2.3809
30	2.7775	2.7025	2.6314	2.5640	2.4999	2.4389	2.3809
31	2.7776	2.7025	2.6315	2.5640	2.4999	2.4390	2.3809
32	2.7776	2.7026	2.6315	2.5640	2.4999	2.4390	2.3809
33	2.7777	2.7026	2.6315	2.5641	2.5000	2.4390	2.3809
34	2.7777	2.7026	2.6315	2.5641	2.5000	2.4390	2.3809
35	2.7777	2.7027	2.6315	2.5641	2.5000	2.4390	2.3809
40	2.7778	2.7027	2.6316	2.5641	2.5000	2.4390	2.3810
45	2.7778	2.7027	2.6316	2.5641	2.5000	2.4390	2.3810
50	2.7778	2.7027	2.6316	2.5641	2.5000	2.4390	2.3810

Table B. Present Value of $1 Received per Period (cont'd)

n	43%	44%	45%	46%	47%	48%	49%
1	0.6993	0.6944	0.6897	0.6849	0.6803	0.6757	0.6711
2	1.1883	1.1767	1.1653	1.1541	1.1430	1.1322	1.0216
3	1.5303	1.5116	1.4933	1.4754	1.4579	1.4407	1.4239
4	1.7694	1.7442	1.7195	1.6955	1.6720	1.6491	1.6268
5	1.9367	1.9057	1.8755	1.8462	1.8177	1.7899	1.7629
6	2.0536	2.0178	1.9831	1.9495	1.9168	1.8851	1.8543
7	2.1354	2.0957	2.0573	2.0202	1.9842	1.9494	1.9156
8	2.1926	2.1498	2.1085	2.0686	2.0301	1.9928	1.9568
9	2.2326	2.1874	2.1438	2.1018	2.0613	2.0222	1.9844
10	2.2605	2.2134	2.1681	2.1245	2.0825	2.0420	2.0030
11	2.2801	2.2316	2.1849	2.1401	2.0969	2.0554	2.0154
12	2.2938	2.2441	2.1965	2.1507	2.1068	2.0645	2.0238
13	2.3033	2.2529	2.2045	2.1580	2.1134	2.0706	2.0294
14	2.3100	2.2589	2.2100	2.1630	2.1180	2.0747	2.0331
15	2.3147	2.2632	2.2138	2.1665	2.1211	2.0775	2.0357
16	2.3180	2.2661	2.2164	2.1688	2.1232	2.0794	2.0374
17	2.3203	2.2681	2.2182	2.1704	2.1246	2.0807	2.0385
18	2.3219	2.2695	2.2195	2.1715	2.1256	2.0815	2.0393
19	2.3230	2.2705	2.2203	2.1723	2.1263	2.0821	2.0398
20	2.3238	2.2712	2.2209	2.1728	2.1267	2.0825	2.0401
21	2.3243	2.2717	2.2213	2.1731	2.1270	2.0828	2.0403
22	2.3247	2.2720	2.2216	2.1734	2.1272	2.0830	2.0405
23	2.3250	2.2722	2.2218	2.1736	2.1274	2.0831	2.0406
24	2.3251	2.2724	2.2219	2.1737	2.1275	2.0832	2.0407
25	2.3253	2.2725	2.2220	2.1737	2.1275	2.0832	2.0407
26	2.3254	2.2726	2.2221	2.1738	2.1276	2.0833	2.0408
27	2.3254	2.2726	2.2221	2.1738	2.1276	2.0833	2.0408
28	2.3255	2.2726	2.2222	2.1739	2.1276	2.0833	2.0408
29	2.3255	2.2727	2.2222	2.1739	2.1276	2.0833	2.0408
30	2.3255	2.2727	2.2222	2.1739	2.1276	2.0833	2.0408
31	2.3255	2.2727	2.2222	2.1739	2.1276	2.0833	2.0408
32	2.3256	2.2727	2.2222	2.1739	2.1277	2.0833	2.0408
33	2.3256	2.2727	2.2222	2.1739	2.1277	2.0833	2.0408
34	2.3256	2.2727	2.2222	2.1739	2.1277	2.0833	2.0408
35	2.3256	2.2727	2.2222	2.1739	2.1277	2.0833	2.0408
40	2.3256	2.2727	2.2222	2.1739	2.1277	2.0833	2.0408
45	2.3256	2.2727	2.2222	2.1739	2.1277	2.0833	2.0408
50	2.3256	2.2727	2.2222	2.1739	2.1277	2.0833	2.0408

Table C

Present Value of Depreciation Charges from $1.00 of Assets Depreciated over *n* Years, Using the Sum-of-the-Year's-Digits Depreciation Method, Discounting at *r* Per Cent per Year, Assuming No Salvage Value.*

n	1%	2%	3%	4%	5%	6%	7%	8%	9%	10%
3	0.983580	0.967639	0.952159	0.937121	0.922507	0.908300	0.894486	0.881048	0.867973	0.855247
4	0.980344	0.961356	0.943005	0.925262	0.908099	0.891491	0.875412	0.859841	0.844756	0.830135
5	0.977125	0.955135	0.933984	0.913629	0.894031	0.875151	0.856955	0.839408	0.822481	0.806142
6	0.973922	0.948974	0.925093	0.902218	0.880293	0.859266	0.839089	0.819715	0.801101	0.783209
7	0.970734	0.942873	0.916330	0.891023	0.866876	0.843821	0.821791	0.800728	0.780574	0.761279
8	0.967562	0.936831	0.907692	0.880038	0.853771	0.828799	0.805040	0.782417	0.760858	0.740298
9	0.964405	0.930848	0.899179	0.869260	0.840968	0.814188	0.788815	0.764753	0.741914	0.720217
10	0.961264	0.924923	0.890786	0.858684	0.828460	0.799974	0.773096	0.747709	0.723706	0.700988
11	0.958139	0.919054	0.882513	0.848304	0.816238	0.786143	0.757863	0.731257	0.706197	0.682566
12	0.955029	0.913243	0.874357	0.838117	0.804294	0.772683	0.743098	0.715372	0.689355	0.664911
13	0.951934	0.907487	0.866317	0.828119	0.792621	0.759582	0.728783	0.700031	0.673150	0.647983
14	0.948854	0.901786	0.858390	0.818304	0.781211	0.746828	0.714902	0.685210	0.657550	0.631744
15	0.945790	0.896140	0.850574	0.808669	0.770057	0.734410	0.701439	0.670888	0.642529	0.616160
16	0.942740	0.890548	0.842867	0.799210	0.759152	0.722317	0.688377	0.657043	0.628059	0.601198
17	0.939705	0.885009	0.835268	0.789923	0.748488	0.710538	0.675703	0.643657	0.614115	0.586827
18	0.936685	0.879523	0.827775	0.780805	0.738060	0.699064	0.663401	0.630710	0.600674	0.573017
19	0.933680	0.874089	0.820386	0.771850	0.727861	0.687885	0.651459	0.618184	0.587713	0.559741
20	0.930689	0.868706	0.813099	0.763056	0.717885	0.676799	0.639863	0.606063	0.575209	0.546973
21	0.927713	0.863375	0.805913	0.754420	0.708125	0.666373	0.628601	0.594329	0.563144	0.534688
22	0.924751	0.858093	0.798825	0.745937	0.698577	0.656022	0.617660	0.582967	0.551496	0.522864
23	0.921804	0.852862	0.791835	0.737605	0.689234	0.645931	0.607030	0.571963	0.540249	0.511478
24	0.918871	0.847679	0.784940	0.729420	0.680091	0.636091	0.596698	0.561302	0.529385	0.500508
25	0.915952	0.842545	0.778139	0.721379	0.671142	0.626495	0.586656	0.550970	0.518886	0.489937

Table C. Sum-of-the-Years'-Digits (cont'd)

n	1%	2%	3%	4%	5%	6%	7%	8%	9%	10%
26	0.913047	0.837459	0.771430	0.713478	0.662383	0.617134	0.576891	0.540955	0.508738	0.479745
27	0.910157	0.832421	0.764812	0.705715	0.653808	0.608001	0.567396	0.531244	0.498925	0.469915
28	0.907280	0.827430	0.758283	0.698087	0.645412	0.599090	0.558159	0.521826	0.489433	0.460429
29	0.904417	0.822485	0.751843	0.690591	0.637192	0.590394	0.549173	0.512689	0.480248	0.451273
30	0.901568	0.817586	0.745488	0.683224	0.629142	0.581906	0.540429	0.503823	0.471358	0.442432
31	0.898733	0.812732	0.739219	0.675983	0.621258	0.573619	0.531918	0.495217	0.462751	0.433891
32	0.895911	0.807923	0.733033	0.668866	0.613535	0.565529	0.523632	0.486861	0.454414	0.425637
33	0.893102	0.803158	0.726929	0.661870	0.605970	0.557628	0.515564	0.478746	0.446337	0.417657
34	0.890308	0.798438	0.720906	0.654992	0.598558	0.549912	0.507707	0.470863	0.438509	0.409940
35	0.887527	0.793760	0.714962	0.648230	0.591295	0.542374	0.500053	0.463203	0.430920	0.402474
36	0.884759	0.789126	0.709097	0.641581	0.584179	0.535010	0.492595	0.455758	0.423561	0.395247
37	0.882004	0.784534	0.703308	0.635043	0.577204	0.527815	0.485328	0.448521	0.416422	0.388251
38	0.879263	0.779984	0.697595	0.628615	0.570367	0.520782	0.478244	0.441483	0.409494	0.381476
39	0.876534	0.775475	0.691957	0.622292	0.563666	0.513909	0.471338	0.434638	0.402770	0.374911
40	0.873819	0.771007	0.686391	0.616074	0.557095	0.507189	0.464604	0.427978	0.396242	0.368548
41	0.871116	0.766580	0.680898	0.609958	0.550653	0.500619	0.458037	0.421498	0.389901	0.362379
42	0.868427	0.762193	0.675476	0.603942	0.544336	0.494194	0.451630	0.415189	0.383741	0.356396
43	0.865750	0.757846	0.670123	0.598023	0.538141	0.487911	0.445379	0.409048	0.377755	0.350592
44	0.863086	0.753537	0.664839	0.592201	0.532065	0.481764	0.439280	0.403067	0.371936	0.344958
45	0.860434	0.749268	0.659623	0.586472	0.526105	0.475751	0.433326	0.397241	0.366278	0.339490
46	0.857795	0.745036	0.654473	0.580836	0.520258	0.469868	0.427514	0.391565	0.360775	0.334179
47	0.855169	0.740843	0.649388	0.575290	0.514521	0.464110	0.421839	0.386034	0.355421	0.329019
48	0.852555	0.736687	0.644368	0.569831	0.508892	0.458475	0.416296	0.380643	0.350212	0.324006
49	0.849953	0.732568	0.639411	0.564460	0.503368	0.452958	0.410883	0.375386	0.345141	0.319132
50	0.847364	0.728486	0.634516	0.559173	0.497946	0.447557	0.405594	0.370260	0.340203	0.314393

* Values tabled are

$$C(n,r) = \sum_{i=1}^{n} \frac{2(n-i+1)}{n(n+1)(1+r)^i}$$

223

Table C. Sum-of-the-Years'-Digits (cont'd)

n	11%	12%	13%	14%	15%	16%	17%	18%	19%	20%
3	0.842856	0.830790	0.819035	0.807581	0.796417	0.785532	0.774917	0.764562	0.754459	0.744599
4	0.815958	0.802209	0.788868	0.775920	0.763348	0.751137	0.739274	0.727743	0.716534	0.705633
5	0.790365	0.775124	0.760394	0.746152	0.732375	0.719044	0.706139	0.693640	0.681532	0.669796
6	0.766001	0.749442	0.733498	0.718140	0.703339	0.689067	0.675298	0.662010	0.649179	0.636783
7	0.742793	0.725072	0.708074	0.691759	0.676091	0.661035	0.646559	0.632633	0.619230	0.606323
8	0.720676	0.701935	0.684023	0.666892	0.650496	0.634793	0.619745	0.605314	0.591467	0.578172
9	0.699586	0.679954	0.661256	0.643433	0.626432	0.610202	0.594697	0.579874	0.565692	0.552115
10	0.679466	0.659057	0.639686	0.621284	0.603786	0.587133	0.571272	0.556153	0.541729	0.527957
11	0.660260	0.639179	0.619238	0.600354	0.582453	0.565469	0.549339	0.534006	0.519418	0.505526
12	0.641917	0.620259	0.599837	0.580559	0.562340	0.545104	0.528779	0.513303	0.498616	0.484666
13	0.624389	0.602239	0.581419	0.561824	0.543359	0.525939	0.509484	0.493925	0.479195	0.465237
14	0.607631	0.585066	0.563920	0.544077	0.525430	0.507885	0.491356	0.475764	0.461039	0.447116
15	0.591601	0.568690	0.547283	0.527252	0.508479	0.490862	0.474305	0.458723	0.444041	0.430189
16	0.576259	0.553065	0.531455	0.511289	0.492439	0.474793	0.458249	0.442714	0.428108	0.414354
17	0.561569	0.538146	0.516385	0.496132	0.477248	0.459612	0.443114	0.427657	0.413152	0.399522
18	0.547495	0.523895	0.502028	0.481728	0.462847	0.445254	0.428832	0.413477	0.399097	0.385608
19	0.534005	0.510273	0.488341	0.468031	0.449185	0.431663	0.415341	0.400110	0.385872	0.372540
20	0.521068	0.497244	0.475284	0.454995	0.436212	0.418784	0.402583	0.387493	0.373412	0.360248
21	0.508655	0.484776	0.462819	0.442580	0.423883	0.406571	0.390508	0.375573	0.361659	0.348673
22	0.496739	0.472838	0.450912	0.430747	0.412156	0.394977	0.379066	0.364297	0.350561	0.337758
23	0.485295	0.461400	0.439530	0.419460	0.400994	0.383962	0.368214	0.353621	0.340068	0.327454
24	0.474299	0.450436	0.428644	0.408687	0.390361	0.373487	0.357912	0.343501	0.330136	0.317715
25	0.463727	0.439919	0.418225	0.398397	0.380222	0.363517	0.348122	0.333899	0.320726	0.308499

Table C. Sum-of-the-Years'-Digits (cont'd)

n	11%	12%	13%	14%	15%	16%	17%	18%	19%	20%
26	0.453560	0.429828	0.408247	0.388562	0.370549	0.354021	0.338812	0.324779	0.311801	0.299767
27	0.443776	0.420138	0.398686	0.379154	0.361313	0.344967	0.329948	0.316110	0.303326	0.291487
28	0.434357	0.410829	0.389519	0.370150	0.352487	0.336329	0.321503	0.307860	0.295271	0.283625
29	0.425285	0.401881	0.380723	0.361526	0.344043	0.328081	0.313450	0.300002	0.287607	0.276152
30	0.416544	0.393276	0.372280	0.353262	0.335971	0.320199	0.305763	0.292511	0.280309	0.269044
31	0.408117	0.384997	0.364171	0.345336	0.328238	0.312661	0.298422	0.285364	0.273353	0.262274
32	0.399990	0.377026	0.356377	0.337730	0.320826	0.305446	0.291403	0.278538	0.266716	0.255820
33	0.392148	0.369350	0.348882	0.330427	0.313720	0.298536	0.284688	0.272014	0.260378	0.249663
34	0.384579	0.361953	0.341672	0.323411	0.306901	0.291914	0.278259	0.265774	0.254321	0.243783
35	0.377269	0.354821	0.334730	0.316666	0.300353	0.285562	0.272099	0.259800	0.248528	0.238162
36	0.370207	0.347943	0.328045	0.310178	0.294063	0.279466	0.266192	0.254077	0.242981	0.232786
37	0.363382	0.341305	0.321603	0.303934	0.288015	0.273611	0.260524	0.248590	0.237668	0.227638
38	0.356783	0.334897	0.315391	0.297921	0.282197	0.267984	0.255082	0.243325	0.232573	0.222705
39	0.350400	0.328707	0.309400	0.292127	0.276598	0.262573	0.249853	0.238270	0.227684	0.217975
40	0.344223	0.322726	0.303617	0.286541	0.271205	0.257366	0.244825	0.233413	0.222990	0.213435
41	0.338244	0.316944	0.298034	0.281154	0.266008	0.252353	0.239988	0.228744	0.218479	0.209076
42	0.332453	0.311351	0.292640	0.275955	0.260998	0.247524	0.235331	0.224251	0.214142	0.204886
43	0.326844	0.305941	0.287427	0.270935	0.256164	0.242868	0.230845	0.219926	0.209969	0.200856
44	0.321407	0.300703	0.282387	0.266086	0.251499	0.238378	0.226521	0.215759	0.205951	0.196978
45	0.316136	0.295632	0.277511	0.261399	0.246993	0.234045	0.222351	0.211743	0.202079	0.193243
46	0.311024	0.290719	0.272792	0.256868	0.242640	0.229861	0.218327	0.207869	0.198347	0.189644
47	0.306064	0.285957	0.268223	0.252484	0.238432	0.225819	0.214441	0.204131	0.194747	0.186174
48	0.301250	0.281341	0.263798	0.248241	0.234362	0.221912	0.210688	0.200521	0.191273	0.182826
49	0.296577	0.276863	0.259510	0.244133	0.230424	0.218134	0.207060	0.197034	0.187918	0.179594
50	0.292038	0.272519	0.255353	0.240153	0.226611	0.214479	0.203552	0.193664	0.184676	0.176473

Table C. Sum-of-the-Years'-Digits (cont'd)

n	21%	22%	23%	24%	25%	26%	27%	28%	29%	30%
3	0.734973	0.725575	0.716395	0.707428	0.698667	0.690104	0.681733	0.673548	0.665544	0.657715
4	0.695028	0.684709	0.674664	0.664885	0.655360	0.646081	0.637039	0.628226	0.619633	0.611253
5	0.658418	0.647382	0.636675	0.626282	0.616192	0.606392	0.596871	0.587618	0.578622	0.569873
6	0.624804	0.613221	0.602018	0.591176	0.580681	0.570517	0.560670	0.551126	0.541872	0.532897
7	0.593887	0.581898	0.570336	0.559179	0.548409	0.538006	0.527955	0.518238	0.508841	0.499749
8	0.565400	0.553123	0.541315	0.529951	0.519010	0.508469	0.498310	0.488513	0.479060	0.469935
9	0.539107	0.526638	0.514676	0.503194	0.492166	0.481568	0.471376	0.461570	0.452130	0.443037
10	0.514798	0.502216	0.490176	0.478647	0.467600	0.457007	0.446842	0.437083	0.427708	0.418695
11	0.492285	0.479656	0.467599	0.456080	0.445066	0.434528	0.424437	0.414768	0.405496	0.396599
12	0.471401	0.458778	0.446754	0.435290	0.424353	0.413908	0.403925	0.394378	0.385239	0.376485
13	0.451996	0.439422	0.427471	0.416099	0.405270	0.394949	0.385101	0.375699	0.366715	0.358122
14	0.433937	0.421447	0.409600	0.398349	0.387654	0.377478	0.367786	0.358546	0.349731	0.341312
15	0.417103	0.404727	0.393008	0.381899	0.371358	0.361344	0.351821	0.342756	0.334120	0.325883
16	0.401388	0.389147	0.377576	0.366627	0.356253	0.346412	0.337069	0.328187	0.319735	0.311685
17	0.386694	0.374606	0.363199	0.352421	0.342224	0.332566	0.323408	0.314713	0.306450	0.298588
18	0.372936	0.361014	0.349781	0.339183	0.329171	0.319700	0.310731	0.302225	0.294151	0.286478
19	0.360035	0.348289	0.337238	0.326826	0.317003	0.307722	0.298943	0.290627	0.282741	0.275254
20	0.347921	0.336358	0.325494	0.315273	0.305640	0.296550	0.287961	0.279833	0.272133	0.264829
21	0.336529	0.325155	0.314482	0.304452	0.295011	0.286111	0.277710	0.269768	0.262250	0.255125
22	0.325804	0.314620	0.304140	0.294302	0.285052	0.276340	0.268124	0.260364	0.253025	0.246074
23	0.315692	0.304701	0.294413	0.284766	0.275704	0.267179	0.259145	0.251563	0.244398	0.237616
24	0.306146	0.295348	0.285252	0.275794	0.266918	0.258575	0.250719	0.243311	0.236315	0.229698
25	0.297123	0.286518	0.276612	0.267341	0.258647	0.250482	0.242800	0.235561	0.228728	0.222271

Table C. Sum-of-the-Years'-Digits (cont'd)

n	21%	22%	23%	24%	25%	26%	27%	28%	29%	30%
26	0.288585	0.278171	0.268452	0.259364	0.250850	0.242859	0.235346	0.228270	0.221596	0.215292
27	0.280496	0.270271	0.260736	0.251828	0.243489	0.235667	0.228318	0.221401	0.214881	0.208725
28	0.272824	0.262784	0.253431	0.244698	0.236529	0.228873	0.221683	0.214920	0.208548	0.202535
29	0.265539	0.255682	0.246506	0.237945	0.229942	0.222445	0.215410	0.208796	0.202567	0.196692
30	0.258615	0.248936	0.239934	0.231540	0.223698	0.216357	0.209471	0.203001	0.196910	0.191168
31	0.252026	0.242523	0.233689	0.225459	0.217774	0.210583	0.203842	0.197510	0.191553	0.185938
32	0.245750	0.236418	0.227750	0.219678	0.212145	0.205100	0.198499	0.192302	0.186473	0.180981
33	0.239767	0.230602	0.222094	0.214177	0.206792	0.199888	0.193422	0.187354	0.181649	0.176276
34	0.234057	0.225056	0.216704	0.208936	0.201694	0.194928	0.188592	0.182649	0.177063	0.171804
35	0.228602	0.219761	0.211561	0.203939	0.196836	0.190201	0.183993	0.178170	0.172699	0.167550
36	0.223388	0.214701	0.206650	0.199169	0.192200	0.185694	0.179607	0.173901	0.168541	0.163498
37	0.218399	0.209863	0.201956	0.194611	0.187772	0.181391	0.175422	0.169828	0.164575	0.159634
38	0.213620	0.205232	0.197464	0.190252	0.183540	0.177278	0.171423	0.165938	0.160789	0.155946
39	0.209041	0.200795	0.193163	0.186080	0.179490	0.173345	0.167600	0.162220	0.157170	0.152422
40	0.204648	0.196542	0.189042	0.182084	0.175612	0.169579	0.163941	0.158662	0.153708	0.149052
41	0.200431	0.192460	0.185088	0.178252	0.171895	0.165970	0.160436	0.155254	0.150394	0.145825
42	0.196381	0.188541	0.181294	0.174574	0.168329	0.162510	0.157075	0.151988	0.147217	0.142734
43	0.192486	0.184775	0.177648	0.171043	0.164906	0.159188	0.153850	0.148855	0.144170	0.139770
44	0.188740	0.181153	0.174144	0.167650	0.161617	0.155998	0.150753	0.145846	0.141246	0.136925
45	0.185134	0.177668	0.170773	0.164386	0.158455	0.152932	0.147777	0.142956	0.138436	0.134192
46	0.181661	0.174312	0.167528	0.161245	0.155412	0.149982	0.144915	0.140176	0.135735	0.131565
47	0.178312	0.171079	0.164402	0.158220	0.152482	0.147142	0.142160	0.137502	0.133137	0.129038
48	0.175083	0.167961	0.161388	0.155305	0.149660	0.144407	0.139507	0.134926	0.130635	0.126606
49	0.171967	0.164953	0.158482	0.152494	0.146939	0.141770	0.136950	0.132445	0.128224	0.124263
50	0.168958	0.162049	0.155677	0.149782	0.144314	0.139227	0.134484	0.130052	0.125900	0.122004

Table C. Sum-of-the-Years'-Digits (cont'd)

n	31%	32%	33%	34%	35%	36%	37%	38%	39%	40%
3	0.650055	0.642560	0.635223	0.628042	0.621010	0.614123	0.607378	0.600770	0.594295	0.587949
4	0.603079	0.595103	0.587319	0.579720	0.572301	0.565054	0.557976	0.551059	0.544300	0.537693
5	0.561363	0.553082	0.545022	0.537174	0.529531	0.522085	0.514830	0.507758	0.500863	0.494139
6	0.524189	0.515737	0.507531	0.499560	0.491815	0.484289	0.476971	0.469854	0.462931	0.456194
7	0.490948	0.482426	0.474171	0.466172	0.458416	0.450894	0.443597	0.436515	0.429639	0.422961
8	0.461123	0.452608	0.444378	0.436418	0.428717	0.421263	0.414045	0.407053	0.400278	0.393708
9	0.434273	0.425823	0.417671	0.409802	0.402203	0.394861	0.387764	0.380901	0.374260	0.367833
10	0.410025	0.401681	0.393646	0.385903	0.378439	0.371240	0.364292	0.357583	0.351102	0.344838
11	0.388057	0.379849	0.371958	0.364368	0.357061	0.350024	0.343243	0.336704	0.330397	0.324308
12	0.368093	0.360043	0.352316	0.344893	0.337759	0.330897	0.324294	0.317935	0.311808	0.305900
13	0.349897	0.342019	0.334468	0.327224	0.320270	0.313591	0.307170	0.300995	0.295051	0.289327
14	0.333265	0.325568	0.318200	0.311140	0.304371	0.297876	0.291641	0.285649	0.279888	0.274345
15	0.318021	0.310509	0.303327	0.296453	0.289870	0.283560	0.277508	0.271698	0.266116	0.260751
16	0.304010	0.296686	0.289690	0.283003	0.276604	0.270476	0.264603	0.258971	0.253565	0.248373
17	0.291101	0.283964	0.277153	0.270648	0.264430	0.258481	0.252784	0.247324	0.242088	0.237062
18	0.279177	0.272224	0.265596	0.259270	0.253229	0.247453	0.241926	0.236633	0.231560	0.226694
19	0.268137	0.261365	0.254914	0.248764	0.242893	0.237285	0.231922	0.226790	0.221873	0.217160
20	0.257892	0.251296	0.245019	0.239037	0.233332	0.227885	0.222680	0.217702	0.212936	0.208369
21	0.248363	0.241940	0.235830	0.230012	0.224466	0.219175	0.214121	0.209290	0.204667	0.200239
22	0.239483	0.233226	0.227278	0.221617	0.216225	0.211083	0.206174	0.201483	0.196997	0.192703
23	0.231191	0.225094	0.219301	0.213793	0.208548	0.203548	0.198778	0.194222	0.189866	0.185698
24	0.223431	0.217489	0.211848	0.206485	0.201381	0.196518	0.191880	0.187452	0.183221	0.179173
25	0.216158	0.210365	0.204868	0.199645	0.194676	0.189944	0.185433	0.181127	0.177014	0.173081

Table C. Sum-of-the-Years'-Digits (cont'd)

n	31%	32%	33%	34%	35%	36%	37%	38%	39%	40%
26	0.209329	0.203679	0.198321	0.193232	0.188392	0.183786	0.179395	0.175206	0.171206	0.167382
27	0.202905	0.197394	0.192168	0.187207	0.182492	0.178005	0.173730	0.169652	0.165759	0.162039
28	0.196853	0.191474	0.186376	0.181539	0.176942	0.172569	0.168404	0.164433	0.160642	0.157021
29	0.191142	0.185891	0.180916	0.176196	0.171713	0.167449	0.163390	0.159520	0.155827	0.152300
30	0.185745	0.180616	0.175759	0.171153	0.166778	0.162619	0.158660	0.154887	0.151288	0.147850
31	0.180638	0.175627	0.170883	0.166385	0.162115	0.158056	0.154193	0.150512	0.147001	0.143649
32	0.175799	0.170901	0.166265	0.161871	0.157700	0.153737	0.149966	0.146374	0.142948	0.139678
33	0.171207	0.166418	0.161886	0.157591	0.153517	0.149645	0.145962	0.142455	0.139110	0.135918
34	0.166845	0.162160	0.157728	0.153529	0.149546	0.145762	0.142164	0.138737	0.135470	0.132353
35	0.162695	0.158111	0.153775	0.149668	0.145773	0.142073	0.138556	0.135206	0.132014	0.128968
36	0.158744	0.154256	0.150013	0.145994	0.142183	0.138565	0.135124	0.131849	0.128728	0.125751
37	0.154978	0.150583	0.146428	0.142494	0.138764	0.135223	0.131857	0.128653	0.125600	0.122688
38	0.151383	0.147078	0.143008	0.139155	0.135504	0.132037	0.128742	0.125607	0.122620	0.119770
39	0.147950	0.143730	0.139742	0.135968	0.132391	0.128996	0.125770	0.122700	0.119776	0.116987
40	0.144666	0.140530	0.136621	0.132923	0.129418	0.126091	0.122931	0.119924	0.117060	0.114329
41	0.141524	0.137467	0.133635	0.130009	0.126573	0.123313	0.120216	0.117270	0.114464	0.111788
42	0.138514	0.134534	0.130775	0.127219	0.123850	0.120654	0.117618	0.114730	0.111980	0.109358
43	0.135628	0.131722	0.128034	0.124545	0.121241	0.118106	0.115128	0.112297	0.109600	0.107029
44	0.132858	0.129024	0.125404	0.121981	0.118738	0.115663	0.112742	0.109964	0.107319	0.104798
45	0.130198	0.126434	0.122880	0.119519	0.116336	0.113318	0.110451	0.107725	0.105130	0.102657
46	0.127642	0.123945	0.120454	0.117154	0.114029	0.111065	0.108251	0.105576	0.103029	0.100601
47	0.125183	0.121551	0.118122	0.114880	0.111810	0.108900	0.106137	0.103510	0.101009	0.098626
48	0.122817	0.119247	0.115877	0.112692	0.109676	0.106817	0.104103	0.101522	0.099067	0.096726
49	0.120538	0.117028	0.113716	0.110585	0.107622	0.104812	0.102145	0.099610	0.097197	0.094898
50	0.118341	0.114889	0.111633	0.108555	0.105642	0.102880	0.100259	0.097768	0.095396	0.093137

Table C. Sum-of-the-Years'-Digits (cont'd)

n	41%	42%	43%	44%	45%	46%	47%	48%	49%	50%
3	0.581730	0.575632	0.569653	0.563790	0.558038	0.552397	0.546861	0.541429	0.536098	0.530864
4	0.531232	0.524915	0.518736	0.512690	0.506775	0.500985	0.495317	0.489768	0.484335	0.479012
5	0.487580	0.481181	0.474935	0.468838	0.462885	0.457071	0.451391	0.445842	0.440418	0.435117
6	0.449635	0.443250	0.437030	0.430971	0.425066	0.419311	0.413698	0.408225	0.402885	0.397675
7	0.416473	0.410167	0.404037	0.398075	0.392276	0.386632	0.381139	0.375790	0.370580	0.365504
8	0.387337	0.381156	0.375156	0.369331	0.363673	0.358175	0.352832	0.347637	0.342584	0.337669
9	0.361610	0.355581	0.349738	0.344073	0.338578	0.333247	0.328072	0.323047	0.318166	0.313423
10	0.338781	0.332921	0.327250	0.321758	0.316439	0.311284	0.306286	0.301439	0.296736	0.292170
11	0.318428	0.312747	0.307255	0.301943	0.296804	0.291829	0.287010	0.282342	0.277816	0.273428
12	0.300202	0.294703	0.289392	0.284262	0.279302	0.274506	0.269865	0.265372	0.261021	0.256805
13	0.283811	0.278493	0.273362	0.268410	0.263627	0.259005	0.254537	0.250215	0.246033	0.241984
14	0.269009	0.263869	0.258914	0.254135	0.249524	0.245072	0.240770	0.236613	0.232592	0.228702
15	0.255591	0.250623	0.245839	0.241228	0.236782	0.232492	0.228350	0.224349	0.220482	0.216743
16	0.243382	0.238581	0.233961	0.229511	0.225222	0.221087	0.217097	0.213244	0.209523	0.205927
17	0.232234	0.227594	0.223130	0.218834	0.214696	0.210707	0.206861	0.203150	0.199566	0.196105
18	0.222023	0.217535	0.213221	0.209071	0.204075	0.201226	0.197517	0.193938	0.190485	0.187150
19	0.212638	0.208297	0.204125	0.200114	0.196254	0.192537	0.188956	0.185503	0.182172	0.178957
20	0.203990	0.199787	0.195750	0.191870	0.188139	0.184547	0.181087	0.177753	0.174537	0.171434
21	0.195996	0.191925	0.188017	0.184261	0.180651	0.177177	0.173832	0.170610	0.167503	0.164506
22	0.188588	0.184642	0.180856	0.177219	0.173723	0.170361	0.167124	0.164007	0.161003	0.158105
23	0.181706	0.177879	0.174208	0.170683	0.167296	0.164039	0.160905	0.157887	0.154979	0.152175
24	0.175298	0.171584	0.168022	0.164603	0.161319	0.158162	0.155124	0.152200	0.149383	0.146667
25	0.169316	0.165710	0.162252	0.158934	0.155747	0.152684	0.149738	0.146902	0.144171	0.141539

Table C. Sum-of-the-Years'-Digits (cont'd)

n	41%	42%	43%	44%	45%	46%	47%	48%	49%	50%
26	0.163722	0.160218	0.156858	0.153635	0.150541	0.147567	0.144708	0.141956	0.139306	0.136752
27	0.158480	0.155072	0.151806	0.148673	0.145666	0.142777	0.140000	0.137327	0.134754	0.132275
28	0.153557	0.150241	0.147064	0.144018	0.141094	0.138285	0.135585	0.132988	0.130488	0.128079
29	0.148927	0.145698	0.142606	0.139641	0.136796	0.134063	0.131437	0.128911	0.126480	0.124138
30	0.144564	0.141419	0.138407	0.135519	0.132749	0.130089	0.127533	0.125075	0.122709	0.120430
31	0.140446	0.137380	0.134445	0.131632	0.128933	0.126341	0.123852	0.121458	0.119154	0.116935
32	0.136553	0.133564	0.130701	0.127958	0.125327	0.122802	0.120375	0.118042	0.115798	0.113636
33	0.132868	0.129951	0.127158	0.124482	0.121916	0.119453	0.117087	0.114812	0.112624	0.110517
34	0.129375	0.126527	0.123801	0.121189	0.118684	0.116281	0.113972	0.111753	0.109618	0.107563
35	0.126059	0.123277	0.120614	0.118064	0.115618	0.113271	0.111018	0.108851	0.106768	0.104762
36	0.122907	0.120188	0.117586	0.115094	0.112705	0.110413	0.108211	0.106096	0.104061	0.102102
37	0.119908	0.117249	0.114706	0.112270	0.109934	0.107694	0.105543	0.103475	0.101487	0.099573
38	0.117050	0.114450	0.111962	0.109579	0.107296	0.105105	0.103001	0.100980	0.099037	0.097166
39	0.114324	0.111780	0.109345	0.107014	0.104780	0.102637	0.100579	0.098602	0.096701	0.094872
40	0.111722	0.109231	0.106847	0.104565	0.102379	0.100281	0.098268	0.096333	0.094473	0.092683
41	0.109235	0.106794	0.104460	0.102226	0.100084	0.098031	0.096059	0.094165	0.092344	0.090592
42	0.106855	0.104464	0.102177	0.099988	0.097890	0.095879	0.093948	0.092093	0.090309	0.088594
43	0.104576	0.102232	0.099991	0.097846	0.095790	0.093819	0.091926	0.090109	0.088362	0.086681
44	0.102392	0.100094	0.097896	0.095793	0.093777	0.091845	0.089990	0.088208	0.086496	0.084848
45	0.100297	0.098042	0.095887	0.093824	0.091847	0.089952	0.088133	0.086386	0.084707	0.083092
46	0.098285	0.096073	0.093958	0.091934	0.089994	0.088135	0.086351	0.084637	0.082990	0.081406
47	0.096352	0.094181	0.092105	0.090118	0.088215	0.086390	0.084639	0.082958	0.081342	0.079787
48	0.094493	0.092361	0.090323	0.088372	0.086504	0.084713	0.082994	0.081343	0.079757	0.078231
49	0.092705	0.090610	0.088608	0.086693	0.084858	0.083099	0.081411	0.079790	0.078233	0.076735
50	0.090982	0.088924	0.086957	0.085075	0.083273	0.081545	0.079887	0.078295	0.076765	0.075294

Table D

Present Value of Depreciation Charges from $1.00 of Assets Depreciated over n Years, Using the Twice Straight-Line Declining Balance Depreciation Method, Discounting at r Per cent per Year, Assuming No Salvage Value.*

n	1%	2%	3%	4%	5%	6%	7%	8%	9%	10%
3	0.985753	0.971890	0.958397	0.945260	0.932465	0.919999	0.907850	0.896007	0.884459	0.873195
4	0.981570	0.963759	0.946539	0.929883	0.913765	0.898161	0.883049	0.868405	0.854212	0.840448
5	0.977620	0.956126	0.935471	0.915611	0.896505	0.878113	0.860399	0.843330	0.826873	0.810998
6	0.973593	0.948394	0.924329	0.901332	0.879339	0.858291	0.838135	0.818819	0.800297	0.782525
7	0.969722	0.941004	0.913741	0.887838	0.863204	0.839757	0.817424	0.796133	0.775819	0.756424
8	0.965781	0.933528	0.903095	0.874349	0.847170	0.821445	0.797073	0.773962	0.752024	0.731181
9	0.961962	0.926326	0.892896	0.861498	0.831973	0.804178	0.777979	0.753259	0.729907	0.707825
10	0.958088	0.919063	0.882674	0.848693	0.816918	0.787165	0.759267	0.733076	0.708455	0.685282
11	0.949229	0.907285	0.868399	0.832287	0.798700	0.767411	0.738218	0.710941	0.685416	0.661497
12	0.950500	0.904965	0.862998	0.824248	0.788403	0.755187	0.724354	0.695684	0.668981	0.644070
13	0.943096	0.898100	0.850355	0.809631	0.772158	0.737607	0.705689	0.676145	0.648749	0.623298
14	0.943010	0.891213	0.844023	0.800930	0.761488	0.725308	0.692046	0.661403	0.633114	0.606944
15	0.936555	0.881971	0.832525	0.789745	0.748676	0.711188	0.675237	0.643907	0.615104	0.588564
16	0.935615	0.877793	0.825713	0.778670	0.736058	0.697352	0.662101	0.629912	0.600443	0.573398
17	0.884065	0.829269	0.780009	0.716847	0.695406	0.644390	0.625781	0.595514	0.567821	0.542415
18	0.928312	0.864694	0.808038	0.757408	0.712010	0.671167	0.634304	0.600927	0.570615	0.543003
19	0.924714	0.858296	0.799475	0.747187	0.700533	0.658756	0.621213	0.587360	0.556731	0.528930
20	0.921098	0.851904	0.790970	0.737088	0.689251	0.646613	0.608464	0.574262	0.543320	0.515386
21	0.917543	0.845654	0.782695	0.727311	0.678378	0.634960	0.596275	0.561668	0.530588	0.502568
22	0.913974	0.839417	0.774483	0.717659	0.667697	0.623565	0.584409	0.549515	0.518288	0.490228
23	0.910460	0.833309	0.766484	0.708303	0.657388	0.612613	0.573046	0.537917	0.506587	0.478522
24	0.906935	0.827220	0.758552	0.699072	0.647267	0.601908	0.561985	0.526671	0.495281	0.467249
25	0.903462	0.821253	0.750819	0.690114	0.637488	0.591605	0.551378	0.515921	0.484505	0.456531

Table D. Twice Sample $D(n, r)$ Values*

n	1%	2%	3%	4%	5%	6%	7%	8%	9%	10%
26	0.899982	0.815307	0.743155	0.681282	0.627890	0.581536	0.541054	0.505496	0.474090	0.446205
27	0.896551	0.809476	0.735677	0.672703	0.618607	0.571835	0.531140	0.495515	0.464146	0.436369
28	0.893113	0.803669	0.728269	0.664247	0.609498	0.562356	0.521489	0.485834	0.454531	0.426886
29	0.889722	0.797971	0.721036	0.656027	0.600680	0.553212	0.512211	0.476552	0.445336	0.417837
30	0.886326	0.792298	0.713874	0.647928	0.592029	0.544278	0.503178	0.467547	0.436441	0.409106
31	0.882975	0.786730	0.706877	0.640049	0.583647	0.535651	0.494483	0.458900	0.427921	0.400760
32	0.879620	0.781188	0.699949	0.632287	0.575425	0.527222	0.486017	0.450509	0.419674	0.392703
33	0.876309	0.775745	0.693179	0.624732	0.567452	0.519076	0.477859	0.442442	0.411764	0.384988
34	0.872996	0.770330	0.686477	0.617289	0.559631	0.511116	0.469914	0.434610	0.404104	0.377534
35	0.869723	0.765010	0.679923	0.610041	0.552043	0.503416	0.462249	0.427071	0.396746	0.370386
36	0.866450	0.759718	0.673439	0.602902	0.544599	0.495891	0.454783	0.419749	0.389616	0.363474
37	0.863215	0.754516	0.667094	0.595946	0.537371	0.488606	0.447573	0.412693	0.382758	0.356836
38	0.859981	0.749345	0.660817	0.589095	0.530281	0.481486	0.440548	0.405836	0.376109	0.350413
39	0.856785	0.744259	0.654672	0.582415	0.523391	0.474586	0.433757	0.399221	0.369706	0.344236
40	0.853589	0.739204	0.648595	0.575837	0.516633	0.467841	0.427138	0.392790	0.363493	0.338254
41	0.850431	0.734231	0.642644	0.569420	0.510063	0.461302	0.420735	0.386580	0.357504	0.332493
42	0.847273	0.729289	0.636758	0.563101	0.503617	0.454907	0.414491	0.380540	0.351689	0.326910
43	0.844151	0.724426	0.630991	0.556934	0.497346	0.448702	0.408445	0.374701	0.346076	0.321526
44	0.841032	0.719594	0.625290	0.550862	0.491193	0.442633	0.402549	0.369018	0.340624	0.316306
45	0.837946	0.714838	0.619702	0.544933	0.485204	0.436740	0.396834	0.363520	0.335354	0.311265
46	0.834864	0.710113	0.614177	0.539095	0.479328	0.430976	0.391258	0.358166	0.330233	0.306373
47	0.831814	0.705461	0.608760	0.533392	0.473605	0.425375	0.385850	0.352981	0.325279	0.301644
48	0.828768	0.700840	0.603405	0.527776	0.467988	0.419894	0.380571	0.347930	0.320460	0.297051
49	0.825753	0.696289	0.598153	0.522287	0.462514	0.414564	0.375446	0.343034	0.315794	0.292607
50	0.822743	0.691769	0.592961	0.516883	0.457142	0.409349	0.370443	0.338262	0.311253	0.288288

* Values tabled are

$$D(n,r) = \sum_{i=1}^{n} \frac{d_i}{(1+r)^i}$$

where $d_i = \begin{cases} \dfrac{(2/n)(1-2/n)^{i-1}}{} & \text{for } i < k \\[2ex] \dfrac{(1-2/n)^{k-1}}{n+1-k} & \text{for } i \geqq k \end{cases}$ and k is the smallest integer greater than or equal to $(n/2 + 1)$

Table D. Twice Straight-Line Declining Balance (cont'd)

n	11%	12%	13%	14%	15%	16%	17%	18%	19%	20%
3	0.862205	0.851479	0.841009	0.830785	0.820799	0.811044	0.801512	0.792194	0.783085	0.774177
4	0.827096	0.814139	0.801561	0.789345	0.777477	0.765944	0.754731	0.743827	0.733220	0.722897
5	0.795677	0.780884	0.766593	0.752782	0.739427	0.726509	0.714007	0.701903	0.690179	0.678819
6	0.765462	0.749069	0.733311	0.718155	0.703569	0.689524	0.675993	0.662949	0.650369	0.638231
7	0.737892	0.720171	0.703213	0.686975	0.671415	0.656496	0.642180	0.628435	0.615231	0.602537
8	0.711362	0.692499	0.674530	0.657399	0.641054	0.625447	0.610531	0.596266	0.582613	0.569537
9	0.686922	0.667114	0.648326	0.630487	0.613533	0.597406	0.582052	0.567419	0.553463	0.540141
10	0.663444	0.642841	0.623381	0.604978	0.587558	0.571048	0.555386	0.540513	0.526374	0.512921
11	0.641678	0.617959	0.598114	0.579417	0.561780	0.545123	0.529371	0.514460	0.500327	0.486918
12	0.620795	0.599014	0.578601	0.559443	0.541436	0.524488	0.508516	0.493443	0.479202	0.465728
13	0.601340	0.579138	0.556910	0.537623	0.519553	0.502599	0.486668	0.471675	0.458535	0.444211
14	0.582687	0.560159	0.539199	0.519662	0.501419	0.484356	0.468368	0.453365	0.439263	0.425989
15	0.564055	0.542468	0.520342	0.500799	0.482603	0.465631	0.450508	0.434923	0.420999	0.407921
16	0.548517	0.525574	0.504368	0.484726	0.466494	0.449534	0.433726	0.418964	0.405154	0.392209
17	0.519047	0.497501	0.477587	0.459138	0.442008	0.421545	0.411209	0.397326	0.384330	0.369197
18	0.517778	0.494669	0.473441	0.453890	0.435837	0.419128	0.403626	0.389212	0.375779	0.363235
19	0.503616	0.480496	0.459318	0.439865	0.421946	0.405398	0.390077	0.375859	0.362632	0.350301
20	0.490034	0.466948	0.445860	0.426537	0.408781	0.392417	0.377297	0.363290	0.350281	0.338171
21	0.477215	0.454194	0.433219	0.414046	0.396465	0.380295	0.365382	0.351588	0.338798	0.326907
22	0.464915	0.441993	0.421160	0.402160	0.384774	0.368814	0.354118	0.340548	0.327982	0.316315
23	0.453276	0.430474	0.409799	0.390984	0.373799	0.358052	0.343575	0.330225	0.317880	0.306431
24	0.442102	0.419446	0.398950	0.380335	0.363365	0.347840	0.333588	0.320464	0.308341	0.297111
25	0.431503	0.409007	0.388700	0.370291	0.353538	0.338234	0.324205	0.311301	0.299395	0.288377

Table D. Twice Straight-Line Declining Balance (cont'd)

n	11%	12%	13%	14%	15%	16%	17%	18%	19%	20%
26	0.421320	0.399004	0.378899	0.360707	0.344178	0.329101	0.315298	0.302616	0.290926	0.280118
27	0.411640	0.389513	0.369616	0.351643	0.335337	0.320483	0.306900	0.294434	0.282954	0.272349
28	0.402333	0.380407	0.360728	0.342981	0.326903	0.312275	0.298913	0.286662	0.275390	0.264984
29	0.393467	0.371748	0.352289	0.334766	0.318913	0.304506	0.291359	0.279316	0.268244	0.258030
30	0.384935	0.363433	0.344200	0.326906	0.311278	0.297092	0.284160	0.272322	0.261448	0.251423
31	0.376792	0.355509	0.336501	0.319432	0.304026	0.290056	0.277331	0.265693	0.255008	0.245164
32	0.368948	0.347891	0.329112	0.312270	0.297086	0.283330	0.270810	0.259368	0.248870	0.239203
33	0.361449	0.340617	0.322065	0.305446	0.290478	0.276930	0.264609	0.253355	0.243036	0.233540
34	0.354219	0.333616	0.315293	0.298897	0.284144	0.270801	0.258676	0.247608	0.237465	0.228134
35	0.347294	0.326919	0.308820	0.292643	0.278099	0.264956	0.253020	0.242131	0.232157	0.222986
36	0.340612	0.320467	0.302593	0.286633	0.272297	0.259350	0.247600	0.236886	0.227077	0.218062
37	0.334201	0.314283	0.296630	0.280882	0.266747	0.253991	0.242420	0.231876	0.222226	0.213360
38	0.328010	0.308319	0.290886	0.275348	0.261412	0.248844	0.237449	0.227070	0.217575	0.208855
39	0.322060	0.302594	0.285377	0.270043	0.256300	0.243913	0.232688	0.222469	0.213124	0.204544
40	0.316309	0.297067	0.280063	0.264931	0.251379	0.239170	0.228112	0.218049	0.208850	0.200406
41	0.310775	0.291752	0.274957	0.260023	0.246655	0.234618	0.223721	0.213809	0.204750	0.196439
42	0.305420	0.286616	0.270028	0.255287	0.242101	0.230233	0.219494	0.209729	0.200807	0.192624
43	0.300261	0.281670	0.265284	0.250732	0.237722	0.226018	0.215432	0.205808	0.197019	0.188960
44	0.295264	0.276886	0.260699	0.246333	0.233496	0.221952	0.211515	0.202030	0.193371	0.185432
45	0.290443	0.272273	0.256280	0.242095	0.229425	0.218037	0.207745	0.198394	0.189859	0.182037
46	0.285770	0.267806	0.252005	0.237997	0.225492	0.214257	0.204105	0.194885	0.186473	0.178764
47	0.281255	0.263492	0.247878	0.234044	0.221698	0.210611	0.200596	0.191503	0.183208	0.175610
48	0.276876	0.259312	0.243882	0.230218	0.218029	0.207086	0.197204	0.188235	0.180056	0.172564
49	0.272641	0.255271	0.240020	0.226521	0.214484	0.203682	0.193930	0.185081	0.177013	0.169625
50	0.268529	0.251351	0.236277	0.222940	0.211052	0.200387	0.190762	0.182030	0.174071	0.166784

Table D. Twice Straight-Line Declining Balance (cont'd)

n	21%	22%	23%	24%	25%	26%	27%	28%	29%	30%
3	0.765464	0.756941	0.748600	0.740436	0.732445	0.724619	0.716956	0.709449	0.702094	0.694887
4	0.712849	0.703065	0.693535	0.684249	0.675200	0.666378	0.657775	0.649384	0.641196	0.633206
5	0.667807	0.657129	0.646769	0.636715	0.626954	0.617475	0.608265	0.599314	0.590612	0.582149
6	0.626511	0.615192	0.604254	0.593678	0.583449	0.573551	0.563968	0.554687	0.545694	0.536977
7	0.590327	0.578576	0.567259	0.556356	0.545844	0.535704	0.525919	0.516470	0.507342	0.498520
8	0.557004	0.544983	0.533445	0.522365	0.511716	0.501475	0.491622	0.482135	0.472995	0.464185
9	0.527414	0.515245	0.503600	0.492449	0.481763	0.471514	0.461679	0.452233	0.443156	0.434426
10	0.500109	0.487895	0.476241	0.465112	0.454474	0.444299	0.434558	0.425224	0.416275	0.407688
11	0.474182	0.463428	0.450546	0.440776	0.429094	0.420181	0.409550	0.400419	0.391681	0.384180
12	0.452966	0.440865	0.429376	0.418457	0.408068	0.398175	0.388742	0.379741	0.371143	0.362923
13	0.431611	0.420501	0.409156	0.397683	0.387511	0.377839	0.368635	0.359866	0.351502	0.343517
14	0.413476	0.401663	0.390496	0.379925	0.369906	0.360399	0.351366	0.342773	0.334591	0.326791
15	0.396162	0.384023	0.373083	0.362744	0.352960	0.343689	0.334893	0.326865	0.318588	0.311020
16	0.380056	0.368626	0.357860	0.347702	0.338105	0.329025	0.320421	0.312258	0.304504	0.297128
17	0.360695	0.349922	0.339769	0.330184	0.321122	0.312543	0.304410	0.296689	0.289350	0.282366
18	0.351499	0.340496	0.330162	0.320440	0.311277	0.302628	0.294451	0.286709	0.279369	0.272399
19	0.338780	0.327994	0.317878	0.308321	0.299421	0.290981	0.283009	0.275468	0.268324	0.261546
20	0.326873	0.316310	0.306413	0.297123	0.288385	0.280153	0.272384	0.265040	0.258088	0.251496
21	0.315828	0.305481	0.295797	0.286715	0.278181	0.270148	0.262572	0.255415	0.248645	0.242229
22	0.305456	0.295326	0.285854	0.276979	0.268646	0.260807	0.253419	0.246445	0.239851	0.233606
23	0.295787	0.285866	0.276598	0.267920	0.259779	0.252126	0.244917	0.238116	0.231688	0.225604
24	0.286680	0.276966	0.267899	0.259416	0.251462	0.243989	0.236954	0.230320	0.224053	0.218123
25	0.278152	0.268637	0.259762	0.251464	0.243689	0.236387	0.229517	0.223042	0.216927	0.211144

Table D. Twice Straight-Line Declining Balance (cont'd)

n	21%	22%	23%	24%	25%	26%	27%	28%	29%	30%
26	0.270096	0.260778	0.252091	0.243974	0.236372	0.229236	0.222526	0.216204	0.210236	0.204593
27	0.262522	0.253391	0.244885	0.236940	0.229503	0.222526	0.215967	0.209790	0.203961	0.198451
28	0.255349	0.246401	0.238070	0.230293	0.223016	0.216192	0.209779	0.203742	0.198047	0.192665
29	0.248579	0.239807	0.231643	0.224026	0.216902	0.210224	0.203950	0.198045	0.192477	0.187218
30	0.242151	0.233550	0.225549	0.218087	0.211111	0.204573	0.198434	0.192657	0.187211	0.182068
31	0.236064	0.227627	0.219783	0.212469	0.205633	0.199230	0.193218	0.187564	0.182234	0.177202
32	0.230271	0.221994	0.214300	0.207130	0.200430	0.194157	0.188269	0.182731	0.177514	0.172589
33	0.224769	0.216645	0.209096	0.202063	0.195494	0.189344	0.183574	0.178149	0.173038	0.168215
34	0.219521	0.211545	0.204136	0.197236	0.190794	0.184763	0.179107	0.173790	0.168782	0.164058
35	0.214523	0.206689	0.199415	0.192643	0.186321	0.180405	0.174857	0.169644	0.164735	0.160104
36	0.209746	0.202050	0.194907	0.188258	0.182052	0.176247	0.170805	0.165691	0.160877	0.156337
37	0.205185	0.197622	0.190604	0.184074	0.177980	0.172282	0.166940	0.161922	0.157199	0.152745
38	0.200817	0.193383	0.186487	0.180071	0.174086	0.168490	0.163245	0.158320	0.153685	0.149315
39	0.196638	0.189328	0.182549	0.176243	0.170363	0.164865	0.159714	0.154877	0.150327	0.146037
40	0.192629	0.185439	0.178773	0.172574	0.166795	0.161393	0.156332	0.151581	0.147112	0.142900
41	0.188785	0.181711	0.175154	0.169059	0.163376	0.158066	0.153093	0.148425	0.144034	0.139897
42	0.185090	0.178130	0.171679	0.165683	0.160095	0.154874	0.149985	0.145396	0.141082	0.137017
43	0.181542	0.174690	0.168342	0.162442	0.156945	0.151810	0.147002	0.142491	0.138249	0.134254
44	0.178127	0.171381	0.165132	0.159326	0.153917	0.148865	0.144136	0.139699	0.135529	0.131601
45	0.174841	0.168197	0.162044	0.156328	0.151004	0.146033	0.141380	0.137016	0.132914	0.129051
46	0.171674	0.165130	0.159070	0.153442	0.148201	0.143307	0.138728	0.134433	0.130398	0.126598
47	0.168622	0.162174	0.156205	0.150661	0.145500	0.140682	0.136174	0.131947	0.127976	0.124237
48	0.165677	0.159322	0.153441	0.147980	0.142896	0.138152	0.133713	0.129552	0.125642	0.121962
49	0.162835	0.156571	0.150774	0.145393	0.140385	0.135711	0.131340	0.127242	0.123393	0.119770
50	0.160088	0.153913	0.148198	0.142895	0.137960	0.133355	0.129049	0.125013	0.121222	0.117655

Table D. Twice Straight-Line Declining Balance (cont'd)

n	31%	32%	33%	34%	35%	36%	37%	38%	39%	40%
3	0.687823	0.680898	0.674109	0.667451	0.660920	0.654514	0.648228	0.642059	0.636005	0.630062
4	0.625406	0.617790	0.610351	0.603084	0.595983	0.589043	0.582258	0.575623	0.569134	0.562786
5	0.573916	0.565904	0.558105	0.550510	0.543112	0.535904	0.528879	0.522030	0.515351	0.508836
6	0.528525	0.520324	0.512366	0.504640	0.497137	0.489846	0.482761	0.475872	0.469172	0.462654
7	0.489989	0.481735	0.473747	0.466012	0.458518	0.451255	0.444214	0.437383	0.430756	0.424322
8	0.455688	0.447489	0.439572	0.431924	0.424532	0.417385	0.410469	0.403776	0.397294	0.391014
9	0.426027	0.417939	0.410146	0.402634	0.395388	0.388395	0.381642	0.375117	0.368809	0.362708
10	0.399442	0.391519	0.383899	0.376568	0.369508	0.362707	0.356150	0.349825	0.343720	0.337824
11	0.376111	0.367590	0.360200	0.353100	0.346273	0.339705	0.333381	0.327861	0.321415	0.315749
12	0.355058	0.347525	0.340304	0.333377	0.326727	0.320337	0.314194	0.308283	0.302591	0.297107
13	0.335887	0.328589	0.321601	0.314906	0.308486	0.302323	0.296404	0.291016	0.285239	0.279969
14	0.319347	0.312237	0.305438	0.298932	0.292699	0.286722	0.280988	0.275481	0.270187	0.265096
15	0.303805	0.296920	0.290343	0.284054	0.278034	0.272267	0.266738	0.261431	0.256490	0.251433
16	0.290105	0.283409	0.277020	0.270915	0.265077	0.259488	0.254134	0.248998	0.244069	0.239335
17	0.274717	0.269365	0.262478	0.257513	0.251280	0.246664	0.240997	0.236695	0.232009	0.227505
18	0.265774	0.259467	0.253458	0.247724	0.242247	0.237011	0.232000	0.227199	0.222596	0.218178
19	0.255107	0.248982	0.243148	0.237586	0.232276	0.227201	0.222347	0.217699	0.213244	0.208970
20	0.245238	0.239288	0.233625	0.228227	0.223077	0.218157	0.213453	0.208950	0.204636	0.200498
21	0.236141	0.230357	0.224853	0.219610	0.214609	0.209835	0.205271	0.200903	0.196721	0.192710
22	0.227682	0.222056	0.216706	0.211611	0.206753	0.202117	0.197686	0.193448	0.189390	0.185501
23	0.219835	0.214359	0.209153	0.204197	0.199474	0.194967	0.190661	0.186544	0.182603	0.178826
24	0.212504	0.207171	0.202103	0.197280	0.192685	0.188302	0.184115	0.180113	0.176283	0.172614
25	0.205666	0.200468	0.195530	0.190832	0.186358	0.182091	0.178017	0.174123	0.170397	0.166828

Table D. Twice Straight-Line Declining Balance (cont'd)

n	31%	32%	33%	34%	35%	36%	37%	38%	39%	40%
26	0.199250	0.194182	0.189368	0.184790	0.180431	0.176275	0.172308	0.168516	0.164890	0.161417
27	0.193236	0.188290	0.183595	0.179130	0.174880	0.170828	0.166962	0.163268	0.159735	0.156353
28	0.187572	0.182744	0.178162	0.173805	0.169659	0.165707	0.161937	0.158336	0.154892	0.151596
29	0.182241	0.177525	0.173049	0.168795	0.164747	0.160890	0.157211	0.153698	0.150339	0.147125
30	0.177203	0.172594	0.168221	0.164065	0.160112	0.156345	0.152753	0.149324	0.146046	0.142909
31	0.172444	0.167936	0.163660	0.159598	0.155734	0.152054	0.148545	0.145195	0.141994	0.138931
32	0.167933	0.163523	0.159340	0.155368	0.151590	0.147992	0.144562	0.141289	0.138160	0.135168
33	0.163656	0.159340	0.155246	0.151359	0.147663	0.144144	0.140790	0.137589	0.134531	0.131606
34	0.159592	0.155365	0.151357	0.147552	0.143935	0.140492	0.137210	0.134078	0.131087	0.128226
35	0.155728	0.151587	0.147661	0.143935	0.140392	0.137021	0.133808	0.130743	0.127816	0.125017
36	0.152047	0.147988	0.144141	0.140490	0.137020	0.133718	0.130572	0.127571	0.124705	0.121965
37	0.148538	0.144558	0.140787	0.137208	0.133807	0.130572	0.127489	0.124549	0.121742	0.119059
38	0.145188	0.141284	0.137585	0.134076	0.130742	0.127570	0.124549	0.121667	0.118917	0.116288
39	0.141987	0.138156	0.134527	0.131085	0.127814	0.124704	0.121741	0.118917	0.116220	0.113644
40	0.138924	0.135163	0.131602	0.128224	0.125015	0.121964	0.119058	0.116288	0.113643	0.111117
41	0.135991	0.132299	0.128802	0.125486	0.122337	0.119342	0.116491	0.113773	0.111179	0.108700
42	0.133180	0.129553	0.126119	0.122863	0.119771	0.116831	0.114032	0.111364	0.108818	0.106387
43	0.130484	0.126920	0.123546	0.120348	0.117311	0.114423	0.111675	0.109056	0.106557	0.104170
44	0.127894	0.124392	0.121076	0.117933	0.114950	0.112113	0.109414	0.106841	0.104387	0.102043
45	0.125406	0.121963	0.118704	0.115614	0.112682	0.109895	0.107242	0.104715	0.102304	0.100002
46	0.123013	0.119627	0.116422	0.113385	0.110502	0.107762	0.105155	0.102672	0.100303	0.098041
47	0.120710	0.117379	0.114227	0.111240	0.108405	0.105711	0.103148	0.100707	0.098378	0.096155
48	0.118492	0.115214	0.112113	0.109174	0.106386	0.103737	0.101217	0.098816	0.096526	0.094341
49	0.116354	0.113128	0.110076	0.107185	0.104441	0.101835	0.099356	0.096995	0.094743	0.092593
50	0.114292	0.111116	0.108112	0.105266	0.102566	0.100002	0.097562	0.095239	0.093024	0.090910

Table D. Twice Straight-Line Declining Balance (cont'd)

n	41%	42%	43%	44%	45%	46%	47%	48%	49%	50%
3	0.624226	0.618496	0.612869	0.607341	0.601911	0.596575	0.591331	0.586178	0.581112	0.576132
4	0.556575	0.550496	0.544545	0.538719	0.533013	0.527424	0.521949	0.516584	0.511327	0.506173
5	0.502479	0.496275	0.490218	0.484304	0.478527	0.472884	0.467369	0.461979	0.456709	0.451556
6	0.456310	0.450135	0.444120	0.438261	0.432552	0.426987	0.421562	0.416270	0.411107	0.406070
7	0.418074	0.412004	0.406105	0.400370	0.394793	0.389367	0.384086	0.378945	0.373938	0.369061
8	0.384928	0.379026	0.373300	0.367744	0.362349	0.357109	0.352018	0.347070	0.342258	0.337577
9	0.356805	0.351090	0.345554	0.340189	0.334988	0.329943	0.325048	0.320297	0.315682	0.311198
10	0.332126	0.326618	0.321289	0.316132	0.311139	0.306301	0.301612	0.297065	0.292654	0.288373
11	0.310280	0.304998	0.299894	0.294958	0.290589	0.285563	0.281087	0.276751	0.272548	0.268791
12	0.291820	0.286719	0.281795	0.277038	0.272441	0.267996	0.263695	0.259531	0.255498	0.251590
13	0.274893	0.270239	0.265277	0.260720	0.256319	0.252065	0.248135	0.243972	0.240120	0.236389
14	0.260195	0.255475	0.250924	0.246535	0.242299	0.238208	0.234254	0.230431	0.226733	0.223153
15	0.246720	0.242182	0.237810	0.233595	0.229636	0.225603	0.221906	0.218147	0.214603	0.211252
16	0.234782	0.230402	0.226185	0.222121	0.218203	0.214422	0.210772	0.207246	0.203837	0.200540
17	0.222763	0.219005	0.214643	0.211121	0.207388	0.203787	0.200308	0.196715	0.193697	0.190553
18	0.213935	0.209855	0.205931	0.202152	0.198511	0.195000	0.191613	0.188343	0.185184	0.182130
19	0.204866	0.200922	0.197130	0.193479	0.189963	0.186573	0.183304	0.180148	0.177101	0.174156
20	0.196527	0.192712	0.189044	0.185514	0.182115	0.178840	0.175681	0.172634	0.169691	0.166847
21	0.188862	0.185167	0.181615	0.178197	0.174908	0.171738	0.168683	0.165735	0.162889	0.160140
22	0.181770	0.178187	0.174745	0.171434	0.168247	0.165178	0.162219	0.159365	0.156611	0.153951
23	0.175205	0.171728	0.168388	0.165176	0.162086	0.159110	0.156242	0.153476	0.150807	0.148230
24	0.169096	0.165719	0.162476	0.159359	0.156359	0.153471	0.150689	0.148006	0.145417	0.142918
25	0.163408	0.160126	0.156974	0.153944	0.151030	0.148225	0.145522	0.142917	0.140404	0.137979

Table D. Twice Straight-Line Declining Balance (cont'd)

n	41%	42%	43%	44%	45%	46%	47%	48%	49%	50%
26	0.158089	0.154897	0.151831	0.148885	0.146052	0.143325	0.140699	0.138167	0.135726	0.133369
27	0.153112	0.150004	0.147020	0.144152	0.141396	0.138743	0.136188	0.133726	0.131351	0.129060
28	0.148438	0.145410	0.142503	0.139711	0.137027	0.134444	0.131957	0.129561	0.127250	0.125021
29	0.144045	0.141093	0.138260	0.135538	0.132923	0.130406	0.127984	0.125650	0.123399	0.121229
30	0.139905	0.137025	0.134261	0.131608	0.129057	0.126604	0.124242	0.121968	0.119775	0.117659
31	0.135998	0.133187	0.130490	0.127900	0.125412	0.123018	0.120715	0.118496	0.116358	0.114295
32	0.132304	0.129558	0.126924	0.124396	0.121967	0.119630	0.117382	0.115217	0.113131	0.111118
33	0.128806	0.126123	0.123550	0.121080	0.118707	0.116425	0.114229	0.112215	0.110078	0.108114
34	0.125489	0.122865	0.120350	0.117936	0.115616	0.113387	0.111242	0.109176	0.107186	0.105267
35	0.122339	0.119773	0.117313	0.114951	0.112684	0.110504	0.108407	0.106388	0.104443	0.102567
36	0.119343	0.116832	0.114425	0.112115	0.109896	0.107764	0.105712	0.103738	0.101836	0.100003
37	0.116492	0.114033	0.111676	0.109415	0.107243	0.105156	0.103149	0.101217	0.099357	0.097563
38	0.113773	0.111365	0.109056	0.106842	0.104716	0.102672	0.100707	0.098816	0.096995	0.095240
39	0.111179	0.108819	0.106557	0.104388	0.102305	0.100303	0.098379	0.096527	0.094743	0.093025
40	0.108700	0.106387	0.104170	0.102043	0.100002	0.098041	0.096155	0.094341	0.092594	0.090910
41	0.106330	0.104061	0.101887	0.099803	0.097801	0.095879	0.094030	0.092252	0.090540	0.088890
42	0.104061	0.101835	0.099703	0.097658	0.095695	0.093810	0.091997	0.090254	0.088575	0.086957
43	0.101887	0.099703	0.097610	0.095604	0.093678	0.091828	0.090050	0.088340	0.086693	0.085107
44	0.099802	0.097658	0.095604	0.093634	0.091744	0.089929	0.088184	0.086506	0.084890	0.083334
45	0.097801	0.095695	0.093678	0.091744	0.089888	0.088106	0.086394	0.084746	0.083160	0.081633
46	0.095879	0.093810	0.091828	0.089929	0.088106	0.086356	0.084674	0.083057	0.081500	0.080000
47	0.094030	0.091997	0.090050	0.088184	0.086394	0.084674	0.083022	0.081433	0.079904	0.078432
48	0.092252	0.090253	0.088340	0.086506	0.084746	0.083057	0.081433	0.079872	0.078370	0.076923
49	0.090539	0.088575	0.086693	0.084890	0.083160	0.081500	0.079904	0.078370	0.076894	0.075472
50	0.088889	0.086957	0.085107	0.083334	0.081633	0.080000	0.078432	0.076923	0.075472	0.074074

Index